Also by Nigel West

Spy! (with Richard Deacon)
MI5: British Security Service Operations 1909-45
MI6: Secret Intelligence Service Operations 1909-45
A Matter of Trust: MI5 1945-72
Unreliable Witness: Espionage Myths of World War II
The Branch: A History of the Metropolitan Police Special Branch
GARBO (with Juan Pujol)
GCHQ: The Secret Wireless War
The Friends: Britain's Postwar Secret Intelligence Operations
Molehunt
Games of Intelligence
Seven Spies Who Changed the World
Secret War: The Story of SOE
The Faber Book of Espionage
The Illegals
The Faber Book of Treachery
The Secret War for the Falklands
Counterfeit Spies
Crown Jewels (with Oleg Tsarev)
VENONA: The Greatest Secret of the Cold War
The Third Secret

Fiction

Blue List
Cuban Bluff
Murder in the Commons
Murder in the Lords

It seems to me Bohr ought to be confined, or at any rate made to see that he is very near the edge of mortal crimes.

Winston Churchill to Lord Cherwell, about Niels Bohr

I believe a scientist is all the more use in the world if, like Benjamin Franklin, he takes an active part in politics and does not always behave like a perfect gentleman.

J. B. S. Haldane

The internationalist cooperation of scientists has been made even more difficult and uncertain by the pervasive problem of secrecy.

Philip Morrison

CONTENTS

Acknowledgments

My thanks are due to the many intelligence professionals who made this book possible. I owe particular gratitude to those that assisted my research, among them Robert Louis Benson of the National Security Agency; Rex Tomb, Linda Colten and Ernie Porter of the FBI; Special Agent John Walsh; Colonel Hayden Peake of the U.S. Joint Defense Intelligence School; Dan Mulvenna of the RCMP Security Service; and the legendary Vladimir Barkovsky, whom I first met in Moscow in 1996. He served at the London *rezidentura* between 1941 and 1946, and at Washington from 1956–1963 as the scientific-technical *rezident.*

I am also grateful to Lady Sainsbury for help regarding her parents, George and Dolly Eltenton; Herbert Romerstein; H. Keith Melton; Sam Halpern; and Arnold Kramish.

Abbreviations

AEC	U.S. Atomic Energy Commission
AFSA	Armed Forces Security Agency
ASDIC	Anti-Submarine Devices Investigation Committee
CAScW	Canadian Association of Scientific Workers
CIA	Central Intelligence Agency
CIC	Counter-Intelligence Corps
CNRC	Canadian National Research Council
CPGB	Communist Party of Great Britain
CPUSA	Communist Party of the United States of America
DCI	Director of Central Intelligence
DSM	Development of Substitute Materials
DSIR	Department of Scientific and Industrial Research
DST	French Security Service
DTA	Directorate of Tube Alloys
FBI	American Federal Bureau of Investigation
FCD	KGB First Chief Directorate
FAECT	Federation of Architects, Engineers, Chemists and Technicians
G-2	U.S. Army Military Intelligence Branch
GRU	Soviet Military Intelligence Service
ICI	Imperial Chemical Industries
JIC	Joint Intelligence Committee
KGB	Soviet Intelligence Service

MAP	Ministry of Aircraft Production
MED	Manhattan Engineering District
MI5	British Security Service
MI6	Secret Intelligence Service
MIT	Massachusetts Institute of Technology
NDRC	National Defense Research Committee
NKVD	Soviet Intelligence Service
NSA	National Security Agency
OSS	Office of Strategic Services
PNG	Persona non grata
PSB	Personnel Security Board
RCMP	Royal Canadian Mounted Police
RDX	Research Department Explosive
SAM	Substitute Alloy Material
SED	Special Engineering Detachment
SI	Secret Intelligence Branch of OSS
SIS	Secret Intelligence Service
SOE	British Special Operations Executive
SVC	Science for Victory Committee
SVR	Russian Foreign Intelligence Service
SWP	Socialist Workers Party
TASS	Telegraph Agency of the Soviet Union
UNESCO	United Nations Educational, Scientific, and Cultural Organization
XY	NKVD Atomic *Rezidentura*
YCL	Young Communist League

Preface

ENORMOZ was the codeword assigned by the NKVD to a Soviet intelligence operation that was truly to change the world. It directly enabled the Kremlin's scientists to detonate an atomic weapon two years before anyone in the West expected them to, and heralded an era in which the superpowers confronted each other with nuclear warheads, a tense but essentially peaceful stalemate that was to become known as the Cold War. Ethel and Julius Rosenberg were to be executed in Sing Sing Prison, Dr. Robert Oppenheimer was to be accused of disloyalty, and the Anglo-American scientific community was to be riven for decades by suspicions about precisely who had spied for whom, and why.

Much has been written about Soviet efforts to acquire the Allies' atomic secrets, but it is only in recent months that it has been possible to tie up many of the loose ends, and solve some of the remaining mysteries that have baffled investigators since that fateful afternoon in September 1945 when Igor Gouzenko, a cipher clerk based at the Soviet embassy in Ottawa, traded a batch of purloined files in return for a secure future for himself, his pregnant wife and children. Gouzenko's defection led to the arrest of Allan Nunn May, a Cambridge-educated physicist, who confessed to having passed atomic secrets to a Russian contact in Canada in 1944. Dr. Nunn May was imprisoned in 1946, and since then there has been much speculation about the identities of his colleagues on the Manhattan Project who collaborated with the NKVD.

Nearly four years after the conviction of Dr. Nunn May, another physicist, Klaus Fuchs, confessed to having spied for the Soviets. Unlike Nunn May, Fuchs had worked at Los Alamos and had been a key member of the British team of scientists that had been sent to the United States to work on the bomb. His arrest led directly to the identification of his principal contact in the U.S., Harry Gold. Gold in turn incriminated David Greenglass who compromised his sister and brother-in-law, Ethel and Julius Rosenberg, then running an extensive spy ring that included nearly a dozen agents. The Rosenbergs continued to protest their innocence until their deaths in the electric chair on June 19, 1953, while Morton Sobell, Al Sarant, Joel Barr and the Cohens—Morris and Lona—fled abroad to Mexico. Forcibly returned to the FBI by the Mexican police, Sobell received a prison sentence of thirty years.

Hitherto it has been widely understood that Fuchs was politically naïve, and was virtually duped into making his confession. The reality, revealed in recently declassified documents, is that Fuchs not only cooperated with his interrogators, but also identified a colleague, Ronald W. Gurney, as a security risk. Gurney and his wife were investigated, and although no direct evidence of espionage was ever found, his subsequent career was blighted by the accusation.

Shocked by the arrest of his colleague Klaus Fuchs, the Italian-born physicist Bruno Pontecorvo took a vacation from the Atomic Energy Research Establishment at Harwell and in September 1950 flew via Helsinki to the Soviet Union with his family.

Even the most experienced British and American investigators, well used to poring over surveillance reports, monitoring telephone conversations and eavesdropping on conversations in homes and restaurants using sophisticated listening devices, were amazed by the breathtaking scale of Soviet penetration of the Manhattan Project and the sophistication of the espionage network. This, of course, was at a time when neither the U.S. nor Canadian governments possessed any centralized overseas intelligence-gathering organizations, and the celebrated Secret Intelligence Service was relatively small in comparison. While it would be several decades before the full picture could be pieced together, the Anglo-American authorities only gradually realized the huge scale and effectiveness of the effort devoted by the Soviets to stealing the secrets of the atomic bomb. Even before Igor Gouzenko defected in September 1945, the FBI had become aware, through conventional, routine surveillance, that the Soviets were engaged in an espionage offensive, concentrated in the NKVD *rezidenturas* at New York, Washington DC, San Francisco, Ottawa and Mexico City. Although the FBI eventually deployed considerable resources to keep some of the main espionage suspects under observation, it was not informed about the exact nature of the Manhattan Project, incredibly, until October 1944 because secrecy had been considered paramount. At that time the New York Field Office, headed by Alan H. Belmont, was staffed by more than a thousand special agents, of whom only fifty or sixty were assigned to Robert Granville's Soviet espionage section, some of whom were stationed permanently in the Pierre Hotel, overlooking the Soviet Consulate. The New York Field Office's espionage branch, designated Division 5, would eventually be organized into separate teams, with Squad 34 producing a weekly *Intelligence Digest*, monitoring the much-feared Line KR counterintelligence specialists. Sub-units concentrated on other suspects, with Squad 341 working the Soviet Mission to the United Nations and the Line N illegal support officers; 342 watching the UN Secretariat; 343 was assigned Amtorg, *Izvestiia* and other official fronts like TASS; 331 looked at the GRU and 332 kept NKVD personnel in the Soviet Mission to the UN under observation. For particular operations, Squad 344 could deploy more than a hundred special agents on physical surveillance duties. A file known as a "105" was opened on each Soviet professional, while a "65" file was reserved for Americans suspected of espionage.

The Bureau's initially slow reaction to the Soviet challenge is contrasted sharply by the meticulous nature of the molehunts conducted in the postwar era, with apparently unlimited FBI resources devoted to comprehensive round-the-clock physical surveillance of suspects, mail covers, telephone intercepts, the use of covert listening devices, the recruitment of informants, and the relentless interviewing of potential witnesses. The sheer depth of J. Edgar Hoover's search for traitors is revealed in the thousands of surveillance reports, wiretap transcriptions and field office reports submitted to headquarters that are now, half a century later, partially available to researchers.

The FBI was not alone in reacting slowly to the evidence of Soviet espionage. As Anthony Blunt reported to his astonished

NKVD controllers in 1941, MI5 made no effort to watch Soviet intelligence personnel attached to the embassy, and the RCMP's resources were even more limited. As there had never been a verified case of Soviet espionage in Canada, the RCMP's Special Branch consisted of a staff of five led by a junior inspector. The only significant example in Britain in recent years, which had centered on a group of Woolwich Arsenal employees in 1938, had not involved any diplomatic premises meaning these were spies run by illegals, not diplomats. The situation was not dissimilar in the United States, where there was a very large Russian émigré population, and a significant Soviet colony, with Amtorg at 210 Madison Avenue, at the corner of 36th Street, employing a staff of some 2,500. Not surprisingly, the FBI's counterespionage squads were more preoccupied by the threat from Germany and Italy. The first clue the FBI received, on August 7, 1943, was an anonymous letter, addressed to J. Edgar Hoover and typewritten in Cyrillic script, which described Colonel Vasili Zubilin's clandestine organization. This led to him being placed, belatedly, under constant surveillance. Hitherto, the best evidence of the FBI's attitude to the Soviet threat can be found in a complacent memorandum, dated October 24, 1940, from the Director to the White House, in which Hoover effectively dismissed the problem and cited not a single case of domestic Soviet espionage. He concluded by claiming that "the movements, contacts and financial transactions" of "those Consular representatives whose conduct is reported to be detrimental to the United States" in "a most discreet and careful manner" are "the subject of constant observation and study."[1]

Once the FBI had been indoctrinated into the research being undertaken by a total workforce of more than 129,000 scientists and technicians, among them a dozen Nobel laureates, at Berkeley, California, Chalk River Laboratories in Ottawa and Montreal in Canada, Oak Ridge in Tennessee, Hanford in Washington, and Los Alamos in Santa Fe, New Mexico, it was better able to grasp the implications of the Soviets' activities and take precautions to limit the loss of vital information.

The joint MI5 and FBI investigation into Soviet penetration of the Manhattan Project was eventually aided by information from defectors, interrogation reports from suspects, physical surveillance which occasionally included clandestine searches of sensitive premises, and a highly secret source codenamed BRIDE, but known within the Bureau as "Source 5." Now better known by the generic cryptonym VENONA, this material originated with decrypts of Soviet intelligence communications, and offered a tantalizing glimpse into NKVD and GRU methodology. VENONA also provided corroboration for the testimony of Elizabeth Bentley, a crucial defector who, in August 1945, had made a tentative approach to the FBI, and in November had begun giving the FBI a very detailed statement about her involvement with an NKVD "illegal" network in New York and Washington DC. Although her credibility came under sustained attack over many years, only the FBI was in a position to compare her recollection of her contacts and activities with what was disclosed in the sometimes acrimonious reports submitted about her between December 1943 and December 1944 by the New York *rezident*, Vasili Zubilin, and decrypted by the Armed Forces Security Agency (later the National Security Agency) at Arlington Hall in Washington DC. Some of this information overlapped with reports from other FBI informants, such as the former CPUSA official Louis Budenz, the double agent Boris Morros (the subject of the FBI's MOCASE investigation), and the former spy Hede Massing, thus enabling J. Edgar Hoover's G-men to piece together the story of Soviet espionage.

Although Elizabeth Bentley was not directly involved in atomic espionage, she was able to supply snippets of information that proved helpful in incriminating Julius Rosenberg and Harry Gold, who also appeared in the VENONA traffic, their identities concealed under the covernames ANTENNA and ARNO, respectively. The Soviet precaution of disguising individual sources with cover names was to lead MI5 and the FBI on a long odyssey of discovery in their search to identify the spies, and in particular to establish the real names of those who had been recruited from within the Manhattan Project. Some of the mysteries remain unresolved but, with the declassification of several Soviet archives, the release of FBI, CIA and NSA files in the United States, and the willingness of a few crucial NKVD and GRU witnesses to reveal what they know for the first time, it has only now become possible to put together most of the components of one of the most significant intricate jigsaw puzzles in history. What emerges is a clandestine conflict among scientists such as Hans Bethe, Ernest Lawrence, Philip Morrison, Luis Alvarez, Rudolf Peierls, and Albert Einstein, who were suspected of betraying atomic secrets to the Soviets, on one side; the British and American counterintelligence personnel deployed to plug the leaks, and their Soviet adversaries in London, New York, and Moscow who struggled to cope with the veritable windfall of classified information from the heart of the two-billion-dollar Allied nuclear weapons development program, on the other.

The challenge of fitting together the various pieces of evidence should not be underestimated, for it has been complicated by deliberate efforts to obscure what really happened. The catalyst for the disinformation campaign was the unexpected publication in April 1994 of *Special Tasks: Memoirs of an Unwanted Witness* by General Pavel Sudoplatov,[2] Lavrenti Beria's notorious henchman who, before being imprisoned for fifteen years, headed the NKVD's Department S after the war. Relying entirely upon his failing memory, the elderly Sudoplatov, who died in September 1996, named several distinguished physicists, among them Leo Szilard, Enrico Fermi, George Gamow and Robert Oppenheimer, as having been spies, and revealed that Klaus Fuchs had been codenamed MLAD ("YOUNG"). He also claimed that they had "helped us plant moles in Tennessee, Los Alamos, and Chicago as assistants in those three labs" and that Niels Bohr had given the NKVD atomic secrets in an interview conducted after the war. He was particularly emphatic that Oppenheimer, Fermi and Szilard "were knowingly part of the scheme."[3]

Sudoplatov's book, co-authored by his son and the American journalists Jerrold and Leona Schecter, caused consternation within the international scientific community, and especially in Moscow, where *Izvestiia* reported that *Special Tasks* had been quite wrong about the "big four" physicists, but confirmed that six such individuals in the United States, and four in Britain, had spied for the Soviets.

Shortly thereafter another rebuttal appeared, purporting to be an authoritative inside account of Soviet atomic espionage, researched by a former KGB officer, Vladimir M. Chikov, and American writer Gary Kern entitled *Stalin's Atomic Spies, KGB File No. 13676.*[4] Based on access to a file that supposedly had been read by only six people in the past half century, it was finally translated and published in French in 1996 as *Comment Staline a volé la Bombe Atomique aux Américains,* to clear Fermi and Oppenheimer of Sudoplatov's charges of espionage, refute some of his other allegations and introduce a new set of characters, all protected by codenames. Some, such as PERSEUS, turned out to be invented; others, like OLD, were authentic.

The problem for Chikov and his co-author, the American academic Gary Kern, was that they could not have anticipated the declassification and release by the U.S. National Security Agency of the VENONA texts, which provided a new and entirely authentic cast of codenames, and convincingly demonstrated that in the NKVD's wartime communications Klaus Fuchs had been known first as REST and then CHARLES, that OLD had been Saville Sax, and that his friend YOUNG had been Dr. Theodore Hall, who was then living in Cambridge, England, and not in America as the authors had claimed.

The VENONA documents constituted compelling evidence against Dr. Hall and prompted Joseph Albright and Marcia Kunstel to write *Bombshell* in 1997,[5] which gave a detailed account, along with a partial confession, of the physicist's espionage as the spy codenamed YOUNG. However, it did not solve the problems that had been created by the publication of the previous books on the same topic. To what extent had Sudoplatov's revelations been discredited? How much of Chikov's contribution had been fabricated deliberately in Moscow to protect Ted Hall? Who were the other spies, as yet undetected?

From Moscow's perspective, with the country in turmoil and the KGB's successor organization, the SVR, struggling to pick up the pieces and reassure its inherited sources of continued support and loyalty, the priority was to convince Ted Hall and others like him that their commitment to the cause would be neither forgotten nor betrayed. Hence Chikov's intervention to muddy the waters over precisely who had given away what atomic secrets to whom, and when. That effort would undoubtedly have proved completely successful if the late Senator Patrick Moynihan had not fortuitously mounted a campaign to have the VENONA project declassified. It is therefore only now that the full story of Soviet atomic espionage in Britain and America can be told for the first time.

Chapter I

The Frisch-Peierls Memorandum

Dark hints will be dropped and terrifying whispers will be assiduously circulated, but it is to be hoped that nobody will be taken in by them.

Winston Churchill, August 5, 1939

The first step in the development of the atomic bomb can be traced to the memorandum written at the University of Birmingham by Professors Otto Frisch and Rudolf Peierls, who had studied the delicate question of the critical mass of uranium or, in layman's terms, the point at which uranium would support a chain reaction and create the explosive energy associated with nuclear fission. Both men were German Jews, and leaders in their field. Born in Berlin, Peierls had left Germany for Zurich in 1929 and had moved to Cambridge four years later on the second half of his Rockefeller Scholarship. He was later appointed a Research Fellow at Manchester University, and then worked at the Mond

Laboratory in Cambridge for two years under (Sir) John Cockcroft, who had split the atom in 1932, before being appointed Professor of Mathematical Physics at the University of Birmingham.

Much work had been undertaken internationally in this field, particularly in Paris at the Joliot-Curie laboratory run by Frédéric Joliot where a team, consisting of Hans von Halban from Austria, Lev Kowarski from Russia, Francis Perrin of France, and Bruno Pontecorvo from Italy, had experimented in chain reactions. In March 1939 their article, "Liberation of Neutrons in the Nuclear Explosion of Uranium," was published in the journal *Nature*. On February 15, 1939, a paper written in Copenhagen by Niels Bohr, winner of the 1922 Nobel Prize in physics, and a young American, John Wheeler, appeared in the American journal *Physical Review*, in which the fissile characteristics of the uranium isotopes U-235 and U-238 were discussed. This was read with interest in Birmingham by Otto Frisch, an Austrian physicist who had moved to England from Gothenburg in Sweden shortly before the outbreak of war, and was now lecturing in Birmingham in the university's physics department. In Warsaw a young (Sir) Joseph Rotblat was seeking a chain reaction, and was later to come to Liverpool University to work under (Sir) James Chadwick. Similar and parallel work was underway at the Physio-Technical Institute in Leningrad and the Kaiser Wilhelm Gesellschaft in Berlin. One pioneer in the field, the Hungarian refugee Leo Szilard, had actually patented a design in London for an atomic explosive in 1934, before moving to New York to continue his research at Columbia University.

Initially, the official view of the possibility of a uranium bomb of "devastating power," according to Lindemann, was considered unlikely. On the recommendation of Professor Frederick Lindemann (later Lord Cherwell), advisor to the War Cabinet, Winston Churchill, anxious that Prime Minister Neville Chamberlain should not be bluffed by Hitler's frequent public boasts of secret weapons, informed Chamberlain in August 1939 that a uranium bomb "might be as good as our present day explosives, but it is unlikely to produce anything very much more dangerous." Nor was there anything particularly secret about the research being undertaken, for even H. G. Wells had predicted a world war would be fought in 1956 with "atomic bombs" in his novel *The World Set Free*. More recently, the editor of *Discovery*, C. P. Snow, wrote in the September 1939 edition that it was common knowledge that work was feverishly apace in the United States, Germany, France, and England to produce an atomic bomb, with some leading physicists believing that "an explosive a million times more violent than dynamite" would be produced within months for military use. If true, warfare would be forever changed.

Similarly, Professor J. B. S. Haldane, a covert Communist who had done much to popularize science (and was incidentally himself a Soviet spy operating for the GRU, later to be exposed by the VENONA decrypts), had also discussed the possibility of building an atomic weapon in March 1939 in one of his regular weekly columns in the *Daily Worker*. While Haldane publicly expressed the view that uranium bombs could not be developed quickly, and was willing to bet against any immediate success in the research, in private he told friends that a lump of uranium "the size of a walnut would be able to destroy an area from Piccadilly to Hampstead."

Behind the public debate there was considerable disquiet about the implications of developing such a device, manifested initially by Leo Szilard and Victor Weisskopf, who telegraphed Hans von Halban in Paris and urged him not to make any further public pronouncements on the subject for fear it would encourage and assist German research, and perhaps "give a dangerous bomb" to "a certain government." Szilard, a Hungarian, had long been convinced that such a weapon was feasible, but having failed to persuade Lord Rutherford when he wanted to join the Cavendish Laboratory, he teamed up with Weisskopf, a refugee from Germany, at Columbia University in New York.

Churchill's skepticism about the practicality of a bomb was partially shared by Rudolf Peierls, the theoretical mathematician who calculated that an explosive fission was technically possible, but that many tons of uranium would be required to achieve critical mass. Francis Perrin had fixed the quantity as being forty-four tons of natural uranium, nine feet in diameter, which could be reduced to thirteen tons if surrounded by a "tamper" constructed of iron and lead. While Peierls believed he could improve on Perrin's formula, he acknowledged in a paper, *Critical Conditions in Neutron Multiplication*, delivered to the Cambridge Philosophical Society in June 1939, but not published in its *Proceedings* until October, that the device would still weigh several tons and "there was of course no chance of getting such a thing into an aeroplane." He concluded that the design had "no practical significance," which was why his contribution was published after war had been declared.

Frisch, however, after further research with Peierls on the properties of U-235 and despite his previously expressed belief that a superbomb was "if not impossible, then at least prohibitively expensive," made the startling discovery that the quantities of uranium required were not several tons but just a couple of pounds, and that the chain reaction would generate heat of a temperature found only in the center of the sun. Both men were stunned by their figures, for while there was no chance of separating sufficient U-235 from scarce uranium ore to accumulate the several tons previously presumed necessary to reach critical mass, it was definitely practical, and perhaps could be accomplished in a matter of weeks with enough separation tubes, which would have to number about a hundred thousand in order to produce a pound or two of reasonably pure U-235 from U-238.

Thus, although Niels Bohr had foreseen the theoretical consequences of fission, he had not believed the process would ever be realized. To adopt his figures and create a viable bomb would have required a huge quantity of a scarce ore and an industrial process that would undoubtedly prove far too great an economic strain for any one country to sustain. However, with the method proposed by Frisch and Peierls, the same outcome could be achieved with only a fraction of the quantities contemplated by Bohr. "I worked out the results of what such a nuclear explosion would be," recalled Peierls. "Both Frisch and I were staggered by them."

"At that point we stared at each other and realized that the atomic bomb might after all be possible," noted Frisch, even though his calculations would demand investment on a scale that would bankrupt most countries. Based on what they had discovered, Frisch and Peierls wrote a two-part memorandum in March 1940: *On the construction of a "super-bomb" based on a nuclear chain reaction in uranium* and *Memorandum on the properties of a radio-active super-bomb*. The first document described the energy released in an explosion of a five-kilo bomb as being the equivalent of "several thousand tons of dynamite," while the second speculated that it was possible similar work had been undertaken in Germany. In the absence of any shelter to protect a civilian population, "the most effective reply would be a counter-threat with a similar weapon." The effect of the two papers was to demonstrate that previous assessments of the fissionable qualities of U-235 had been flawed, and that, mathematically speaking, even a one-kilo bomb "would still be formidable," with the resulting radiation likely to be "fatal to living beings" for long after the detonation. In fact, their assessment of minimum critical mass as being 600 grams proved to be vastly underestimated by a factor of twenty-five, but the error was insignificant in that there was nobody to contradict the two physicists. Yet their conclusion had certainly caught people's attention.

Having completed the memorandum, typed it themselves, and retained a single carbon copy, the two scientists realized they had no idea how or where to send it. They consulted their Australian colleague, Professor Marcus Oliphant, then head of Birmingham's physics department and himself occupied with developing a magnetron valve for what was then termed "radio direction finding." Oliphant stated that "I am convinced the whole thing must be taken rather seriously," and ensured that it was sent to Sir Henry Tizard, the chairman of the government's Aeronautics Research Committee. The Air Ministry had funded the development of radar, and as any atomic weapon was likely to be dropped from an aircraft, departmental responsibility was automatically given to the Royal Air Force.

At the end of the First World War, Lieutenant-Colonel Tizard had been the RAF's Assistant Controller of Experiment and Research, and in recent months had been concentrating on radar. Despite his earlier skepticism, based on the conclusion of research undertaken at the Imperial College of Science and Technology by (Sir) George Thomson, Tizard instantly grasped the implications of the Frisch-Peierls document. Thomson, an Imperial College Professor of Physics since 1930, had been engaged in military applications of science ever since he served in the Royal Flying Corps during the Great War, and later had worked on aerodynamics at the Cavendish Laboratory. He too had read the Joliot-Curie article in *Nature,* and in May 1939 he joined with Professor (Sir) William Bragg of the Cavendish to prevail on Tizard to use his influence to acquire some uranium oxide, perhaps from Belgium. As it turned out, Professor David Pye, then the Air Ministry's Director of Scientific Research, had a ton of pitchblende stored in an RAF warehouse in Hammersmith. This was used by Thomson and Professor P. B. Moon of Birmingham University, working at the Royal Aircraft Establishment at Farnborough, to investigate the phenomenon of a chain reaction. Thomson's verdict, which he came to regret, was that the possibility "seemed likely, though not certain" of using heavy water, which was unavailable in any large amounts, and that the military value "seemed too remote to justify further work in wartime," with odds of 100,000 to 1 against success. As he later remarked, "If this conclusion now seems disgraceful blindness, I can only plead that to the end of the war the most distinguished physicists in Germany thought the same." Indeed, he was convinced that the prospects of a superbomb were so poor that he recommended to Tizard that "we should let it be known to the enemy by various means that we had, in fact, got encouraging results; that the experiments were progressing favorably, and that great things were expected of them." Fortunately, this particular idea went no further.

In the absence of any other suitable body in Whitehall to consider such matters, Tizard gathered together a committee of scientists to examine the claims made in Birmingham. It met in the main committee room on the ground floor of the Royal Society, at Burlington House, on April 10, 1940. Among those present were John Cockcroft, Assistant Director of Research at the Ministry of Supply; Professor Alexander Hill, secretary of the Royal Society; James Chadwick; and Thomson, who acted as secretary. In addition to examining the Frisch-Peierls memorandum, the committee also heard evidence from Jacques Allier, of the French Ministère de l'Armament (Ministry of Armament), who warned of German interest in nuclear research, and pleaded the case for intensive Anglo-

French cooperation. Allier's appearance before the committee, recommended by Dr. H. J. Gough, the Director of Scientific Research at the War Office, alerted the membership to the advanced stage of research being conducted at the Collège de France.

A former bank official who had been called up for service in the Ministère de l'Armament with the rank of lieutenant, Allier had led a clandestine mission in March 1940 to Norsk Hydro at Vemork, about five miles west of Oslo, to buy up the hydroelectric company's stocks of heavy water, a valuable product widely believed to be an essential ingredient in nuclear fission. Norsk Hydro, partly owned by the French bank for which Allier had worked, was the world's only source of significant quantities of heavy water, which was distilled from vast volumes of ordinary water but designed to make ammonia for fertilizer. Accompanied by three other Deuxième Bureau (French Intelligence) officers—Captain Muller, Professor Mossé of the Sorbonne, and Lieutenant Knall-Demars—Allier had negotiated the sale of 185 liters of the precious commodity with Hydro's general manager, Dr. Alex Aubert. At this point, however, Allier learned that his assignment had been compromised and that a source in Paris, possibly a decrypted German telegram, had indicated that Allier was to be intercepted by the Nazis. Allier stored the thirteen metal containers in a house owned by the French embassy in Oslo and then arranged for a flight to Edinburgh from Fornebu, Oslo's main airport, after having confirmed their original reservations on a flight to Paris via Hamburg and Amsterdam. Allier and Mossé were diverted to Montrose, but were joined the following day in Edinburgh by Muller and Knall-Demars, who took the next flight and accompanied the remainder of their precious cargo. They then took a train to London and had the drums stored overnight at the headquarters of the French Military Mission, before completing their journey to Paris, where they arrived on March 16. The heavy water was deposited in the cellars of the Collège de France.

In his discussions with Aubert, Allier found out that the Norwegians had only recently declined a similar offer from the huge industrial combine I. G. Farben to acquire the same rare liquid, on the grounds that the Germans would not disclose the reason for their interest. Allier claimed that the original I. G. Farben order for heavy water had mentioned a purchase of up to two tons, and asserted that Aubert had told him that the Germans had cross-examined him about French atomic research. Allier concluded that this could only mean that the Nazis were researching a bomb, and he even offered a list of German scientists whom French Intelligence believed were already at work on the project.

The prevailing atmosphere at Tizard's sub-committee, chaired by Thomson, was one of healthy skepticism, and Tizard himself told the Cabinet Office that the "probability of anything of real military significance is very low." There was a natural bias against diverting valuable war resources away from more promising projects, such as radar and the submarine detection system known by the acronym ASDIC. When the committee held its meetings in Oxford, away from the threat of enemy bombing, the Air Ministry's Director-General of Research and Development, Air Marshal Arthur Tedder, dubbed it "the Balliol Beagles" because, in his opinion, "it was always letting loose fresh hares before it had caught the first lot."

By the time the Thomson committee met for a second time two weeks later, on April 24, 1940, the attitude of mild skepticism had disappeared. James Chadwick, one of those present, sheepishly admitted that he had started experimenting with fast-neutron fission with his new cyclotron in Liverpool, and had reached the exact same conclusions as Frisch and Peierls, but had been reluctant to say so until he had conducted further research. Originally he had believed it would take thirty or forty tons of uranium to achieve critical mass. In effect, the two German scientists, who were now sharing a house in Birmingham, had filled a gap in the work Chadwick had embarked on, and accordingly the committee "generally was electrified by the possibility" that a uranium bomb was a truly practical proposition after all. Its first directive was to instruct Alexander Hill, the distinguished physiologist who had won the Nobel Prize in medicine in 1922 and was then about to embark on an official mission to the United States to collect scientific intelligence and discuss future cooperation, to extend his enquiries to American research on uranium.

The principal scientific obstacle to the acquisition of U-235 was the production process. A narrow debate ensued among the few physicists indoctrinated into the theory about the best method of separating the uranium isotope. Frisch had contemplated a gaseous thermal diffusion method involving tens of thousands of Clusius tubes, at astronomic cost, while (Sir) Franz Simon at the Clarendon Laboratory in Oxford, who had emigrated to Britain from Germany in 1933 and become a naturalized subject, favored other options, including ordinary gaseous diffusion. In June 1940, as the Wehrmacht established itself across northern France, Peierls consulted Professor Lindemann and attempted to persuade him "the whole thing should be taken seriously."

Although Lindemann was yet to be convinced, the Thomson committee received some disturbing news from Copenhagen where Lise Meitner had been visiting as the Nazis had invaded. Viennese-born, beautiful and Jewish, Lise Meitner was a former X-ray technician during the Great War. She had headed the physics department at Otto Hahn's laboratory in Dahlem until July 1938 when, in fear of persecution, she had secretly moved to Stockholm via Holland, after having been denied an exit visa by the Nazis. She was also Otto Frisch's aunt. Her escape had been engineered with Hahn's knowledge, and the help of Paul Rosbaud, the scientific editor at the Springer Verlag publishing house. Minimally protected by her Austrian passport, she had promptly returned to Sweden from whence, on April 9, she sent an innocuous telegram, but containing an apparently hidden meaning, to a friend in England:

> MET NIELS AND MARGARETHE RECENTLY BOTH WELL BUT UNHAPPY ABOUT EVENTS PLEASE INFORM COCKCROFT AND MAUD RAY KENT

The message had been relayed to John Cockcroft at the Cavendish Laboratory in Cambridge who had understandably placed the worst possible interpretation upon it. He read it to mean that Niels Bohr was anxious about the work being undertaken by the Nazis, and he believed the clue was contained in the seemingly inexplicable reference to "MAUD RAY KENT." He realized this to be a partial anagram for "RADIUM TAKEN," doubtless an ingenious warning intended to alert Cockcroft to the fact that the Germans were collecting radium for a bomb development project. Chadwick agreed with the anagram theory, which coincided with other reports that the Nazis were gathering physicists at the Kaiser Wilhelm Institute in Berlin, and concluded that the enemy had begun a race to build an atomic bomb. As a direct consequence, the Thomson Committee renamed itself the MAUD Committee and prepared a detailed report for the War Cabinet.

This episode is doubly extraordinary because, in fact, Lise Meitner had not concealed any sinister message in her telegram. She had merely wanted to inform both Cockcroft and Maud Ray, the Bohrs' English governess who had taught their sons English and was now living in Kent, that the Bohrs were still in Copenhagen. That particular mystery remained unsolved until Bohr escaped to England in October 1943 and decoded it himself.

In the meantime, the MAUD Committee submitted a lengthy report in October 1940 to Lord Hankey, the Minister Without Portfolio, in the War Cabinet. His private secretary was a brilliant young Scot, John Cairncross, on temporary transfer from the Foreign Office. Precisely what this report said, and how it was handled, is not only crucial to understanding how the British government authorized the TUBE ALLOYS project, but also how the Soviets were tipped off to the possibility of an atomic bomb in the first place.

The MAUD Committee supervised research work across the country, coordinating the activities in just three centers—Liverpool, Oxford, and Birmingham—of a handful of physicists seeking to plumb the deep mysteries of atomic fission, while some simultaneously undertook their usual teaching duties. Frisch moved to Liverpool to collaborate on the basic nuclear data with Chadwick, who was supported by M. H. L. Pryce, with additional help from Norman Feather at the Cavendish. Peierls remained in Birmingham, working on his own with just a part-time secretary he shared with the university's engineering department, until May 1941 when he acquired Klaus Fuchs from Edinburgh as a talented assistant, and was authorized to recruit a group of mathematics graduates to operate some desk calculators provided by His Majesty's Stationery Office.

In Cambridge Hans von Halban and Lev Kowarski, having escaped from Paris with the Collège de France's stock of Norwegian heavy water, were concentrating on a chain reaction using deuterium as a moderator, a substance used for slowing down neutrons in a nuclear reactor. They had left Paris in May, storing their valuable commodity in a dozen jerry cans, first in the Banque de France vaults in Clermond-Ferrand, and then in the women's prison at Mont Dore. The heavy water finally ended up in the cell for condemned prisoners at Riom prison while von Halban, accompanied by his wife and baby daughter, set up a temporary research laboratory in the Clair Logis, a villa at Clermond-Ferrand. The Collège de France's plans to continue its work was interrupted by the swift German advance on Paris in June 1940; a decision was made to evacuate von Halban and Kowarski to Bordeaux where arrangements had been made for a British coaler, the *Broompark*, to take them to England. With Joliot and Allier electing to remain in France, the rest of the party made contact in Bordeaux with a British intelligence officer, the Earl of Suffolk, who had been sent to France on a mission from the Ministry of Supply to recover France's strategic stocks of industrial diamonds, specialist machine tools and heavy water. Escorted by Suffolk, along with his secretary and chauffeur, the twenty-five Collège de France physicists disembarked at Falmouth and went by train to Paddington where they stayed at the Great Western Hotel before being invited by (Sir) Ben Lockspeiser and (Sir) Solly Zuckerman, on behalf of the MAUD Committee, to be reunited with their heavy water at a small building just inside the Cavendish Laboratory's compound.

In Oxford the German spectroscopist Heinrich Kuhn and the Hungarian Nicholas Kurti from Breslau University joined Kurt Mendelssohn, an expert on low temperatures, at the Clarendon where Franz Simon had been established since 1933. Born in Berlin, Simon had been wounded twice during the Great War, had been gassed by the British and had won the Iron Cross, a decoration that had exempted him from many of the Nazi anti-Semitic employment restrictions and had allowed him to continue as Professor of Physics at Breslau. The objective of Simon's team at Oxford, supported by a £5,000 grant from the Ministry of Aircraft Production (MAP), was to design a gaseous diffusion plant for producing a kilo of U-235 a day. In mid-December 1940 it circulated a comprehensive report describing precisely what was required for the task, how many people would be required to run the industrial plant, and a projection of the costs involved. According to Simon's estimates, the process would cover forty acres and consume 60,000 kilowatts of power. The paper was personally delivered by Kurti and Simon to Thomson at Cambridge. Almost simultaneously, von Halban and Kowarski submitted a study showing a 95% certainty that a nuclear reactor was practical. Thomson recalled that "if Halban's paper had been published, it would have been enough to convince almost any nuclear physicist that the thing would work." The only component missing from the report was an answer to the minimal requirement of six tons of heavy water and several tons of uranium oxide, but this would be addressed at the next meeting of the Technical Committee at Nobel House, now occupied by the Ministry of Aircraft Production. In attendance were ICI's Research Controller, Dr. R. E. Slade, as well as von Halban, Kowarski, Simon, and the Swiss physicist Egon Bretscher, who had been working at the Cavendish before being drawn into the MAUD Committee by Cockcroft.

As a first step, ICI was awarded a contract to produce uranium hexafluoride, a highly corrosive gas that hitherto had been a key to fission research. The company set up an internal unit to liaise with the MAUD Committee. Five months later, in May 1941, Metropolitan-Vickers was contracted to build a pilot gaseous-diffusion plant at Rhydymwyn in North Wales. To keep the local population in the dark, a plausible cover story was concocted that the heavily guarded site, part of a Ministry of Supply factory making mustard gas, was engaged in the manufacture of synthetic rubber. Thus Britain was firmly committed to the first steps in a project, staffed by a truly cosmopolitan collection of physicists, chemists, and engineers (but without any Americans), intended to develop the world's first atomic bomb.

A significant influence over this coordinated research was the dramatic change of atmosphere in Whitehall created when Chamberlain was swept from power and Churchill's administration created the Ministry of Aircraft Production (MAP) to eliminate bureaucratic obstacles to the efficient preparation of Britain's defenses. The MAUD Committee was switched from the Air Ministry to Lord Beaverbrook's MAP, and Frederick Lindemann, now ennobled as Lord Cherwell, was given unrestricted, unsurpassed access to the Prime Minister, and began attending MAUD meetings himself. Having co-authored a paper on isotope isolation more than twenty years earlier, he was initially dubious about the possibility of a superbomb, but his views were to change. Despite the secrecy surrounding the MAUD deliberations, public speculation about the implications of atomic research continued when a feature entitled "Is Atomic Power Near?" appeared in the January 1941 issue of *Fortnightly*. The article revealed that a uranium bomb might be built from a particular isotope that could be extracted from just three percent of the world's annual production of uranium, estimated at 570 pounds. "One might think that it would be quite hopeless to try to separate this sensitive sort of uranium from the rest. But the possibilities are so remarkable that it might be worthwhile, even if very difficult. Suppose that this 570 pounds were separated, and portions of it were bombarded with neutrons. These can be obtained from a cyclotron. They might act as triggers for starting a chain of atomic explosions, making an atomic bomb…"

By the summer of 1941 the MAUD Committee had concluded that a uranium bomb was feasible, and had speculated about a 25-pound uranium device that would be the explosive equivalent of 1,800 tons of TNT, warning that the Germans were probably on the same track: "We know that Germany has taken a great deal of trouble to secure supplies of the substance known as heavy water… It appears in fact that its usefulness in the release of atomic energy is limited to processes which are not likely to be of immediate war value, but the Germans may now have realized this, and it may be mentioned that the lines on which we are now working are such as would be likely to suggest themselves to any capable physicist."

This first MAUD report was studied by Professor Lindemann, who was persuaded to change his views. On August 27 he wrote to the Prime Minister about the "super-explosive," explaining that "a great deal of work has been done here and in America, and probably in Germany, and it looks as if bombs might be produced and brought into use within, say, two years." Lindemann still believed the odds of success were slim at best, but urged the Committee nevertheless to press ahead with production of the bomb, for the prospect of the Germans developing the process before them would have been "unforgivable."

On September 16 the MAUD Committee outlined what was required to develop a working device within three years. ICI would have to make the project a priority. A representative from Woolwich Arsenal named Ferguson claimed that it would only take a few months to construct a bomb fuse. The race was now on full bore against the Germans to develop the bomb first. It was already known that one prominent German physicist, Professor Hahn, had researched the question of uranium disintegration for the past few years. To make the situation even more dire, it was believed that about eight tons of uranium oxide had fallen into the hands of the Germans when Belgium was invaded on May 10, 1940.

In fact, the Nazis had acquired hundreds of tons of uranium oxide, far more than the MAUD Committee had ever realized, from the Czech mines at Joachminsthal, and had also embarked upon an ambitious atomic research program. The initial incentive had been an Abwehr (German military intelligence) report describing various foreign research projects, which had been discussed at a meeting held at the War Office on Hardenbergstrasse on September 16, 1939. It was attended by Kurt Geiger, inventor of the eponymous radioactivity monitor; Otto Hahn, who had discovered fission and in December 1938 had split the uranium atom; Siegfried Flugge, who had published an article in *Die Naturwissenschaften* ("Natural Sciences") in June 1939, predicting uranium's vast potential for developing atomic energy, and had also written a news feature in *Deutsche Allgemeine Zeitung*; and the physicist Josef Mattauch. Also present was a representative of the Wehrmacht's Ordnance Research Department, Dr. H. Basche, along with the chemists Paul Harteck, Walther Bothe, Heinrich Hoffmann, Kurt Diebner, and Erich Bagge. It was decided at this meeting that bomb research should be accelerated under the authority of the *Heereswaffenamt* (Army Weapons Office), and assisted by Werner Heisenberg who should be drafted immediately into military service. Thus began the Nazi project, which had been feared and predicted by the MAUD Committee.

On September 20 the British Chiefs of Staff gave their formal approval to the plan recommended by MAUD, and to the decision to build a plant to manufacture the bomb in England. Five days later, on September 25, Anatoli V. Gorsky of the NKVD *rezidentura* in the Soviet embassy in London, alias attaché Anatolii Gromov, sent the complete report to Moscow under his codename, VADIM, crediting his source as LISZT. Gorsky had joined the NKVD in 1928 at the age of twenty-one, and had been in London since 1936, first as deputy *rezident* to Ivan Chapsky, alias Second Secretary Anton Schuster, and then, following the latter's recall and execution in 1937, to Grigorii B. Grafpen, alias Grigorii Blank, who in December 1938 was to be recalled and imprisoned himself for five years in a labor camp. Gorsky, too, had been withdrawn in February 1940, but had made the long return journey, via Alaska and New York, in December as *rezident*, ready to run LISZT, and his report was circulated in Moscow by Yelena Potapova, an NKVD officer with a good grasp of English and science:

> VADIM transmits a report from LISZT on a meeting of the Uranium Committee held on 16 September 1941. The meeting was chaired by THE BOSS.
>
> The following points were made at the meeting:
>
> A uranium bomb can definitely be developed in the space of two years, especially if the Imperial Chemical Industries firm is contracted to make it in the shortest possible time.
>
> A representative of the Woolwich Arsenal named Ferguson said the bomb's fuse could be made within several months. It is neither necessary nor possible to achieve the minimal velocity of the relative movement of the explosive mass at 6,000 feet per second. The explosion process would occur prematurely. But even in this instance

> the force of the explosion would be tremendously greater than that of an ordinary explosive.
>
> Until most recently, calculation of critical mass has been made only theoretically, since there have been no data on the size of the cross-section of U-235. But as regards fast neutrons there have been indications that the cross-section of U-235 does not differ greatly from that of ordinary uranium. It is assumed that the necessary measurements will be made by December.
>
> Experiments are scheduled for the near future to determine the density of neutrons in the space between adjoining masses of U-235 so as to achieve the most effective explosion.
>
> Three months ago the Metropolitan-Vickers firm was given an order for a 20-stage apparatus, but permission for it was granted only recently. The order has been given top priority.
>
> The Imperial Chemical Industries firm has a contract for producing uranium hexafluoride, but has not yet begun production. Not long ago a patent was granted in the USA for a simpler method of production using uranium nitrate.
>
> At the meeting it was stated that information on the best type of diffusion membranes could be obtained in the USA.
>
> The Chiefs of Staff Committee passed a resolution at its meeting on 20 September 1941 to begin immediate construction of a factory in England for the production of uranium bombs.
>
> VADIM requests an evaluation of LISZT's materials on uranium.[1]

When the full text of LISZT's message was first declassified and released in Moscow in 1993, General Pavel Sudoplatov (or his co-author Jerry Schechter) made a fundamental mistake that was to cause considerable confusion and lead to accusations of obfuscation. Whoever translated the document interpreted LIST as the Russian word for LEAF and therefore the source codenamed LIST was transformed into LEAF, which prompted two further errors. First, there was no Soviet agent codenamed either LIST or LEAF, and second, LEAF was incorrectly attributed to Donald Maclean. In fact, the true explanation is that Lord Hankey's secretary John Cairncross had two successive codenames, MOLIERE and LISZT, with the latter being written in some of the translated original

NKVD documents as LIST. Both codenames had a connection with Cairncross, for he was a Molière scholar, and Lizst was his favorite composer. Having put that complication to one side, one can see that Cairncross removed the paper from the Cabinet Office registry, and in Gorsky's message there is a reference to Lord Hankey as BOSS, which is a further indication of the relationship between the source and his superior. Of course the SVR, as the declassification authority, was unenthusiastic about naming Cairncross as the source of this important document, especially as he had specifically denied having even seen it. Instead, it suited them to perpetuate the myth that Maclean, who was by then dead, had been responsible, and thus the unnecessary confusion was allowed to continue.

Gorsky's message represented the first leak of atomic information from Britain, and was followed on October 3 by a seventeen-page report prepared by his NKVD colleague, Vladimir B. Barkovsky, on the British estimates of achieving critical mass, and an account of the difficulties experienced in separating U-235 by gas diffusion. Born in 1913 in Belgorod, Barkovsky had started life as a locksmith and in 1935 had begun a four-year course at Stankin, Moscow's Institute of Machine Tools, joining the NKVD upon his graduation in 1939. He had intended to become a pilot, and had undergone a military induction course in which he had learned to parachute and ride a motorcycle. However, unexpectedly, he was ordered to report to a training unit at Starya Ploshchad and in June 1939 embarked on an intensive English language course at Malakhovka, a tiny village about 50 miles southeast of Moscow. He was then assigned to the English Department, which at the time consisted of just three officers and a single typist, because "at that time intelligence had been unbelievably weakened by the repressions and, essentially speaking, had to be completely rebuilt." Barkovsky also spent a month's probationary period at the Ministry of Foreign Affairs, and by the end of the year had been posted to London under his own name, where he remained until 1946, first as an attaché and later as Third Secretary, using the codename JERRY. His journey to England, via Japan and Hawaii, took 74 days. When he arrived in February 1941, he found a tiny *rezidentura.*

"There were only three of us... but plenty of work." The other two were Gorsky and "another greenhorn like myself who had arrived in England in March 1940. A week after my arrival in London I established contact with my first agent."[2]

Gorsky's source for the MAUD Report was John Cairncross, who had been recruited by a spy codenamed MAYOR, the CPGB activist James Klugmann, in 1937. Although Cairncross later protested in his autobiography, *The Enigma Spy*,[3] of any involvement in compromising British atomic secrets, documents released in Moscow attributed to his codenames LISZT and MOLIERE demonstrate that the socially insecure Scot, who had achieved an unequalled record by taking first place in both the home and foreign civil service examinations, had wormed his way into Lord Hankey's confidence by befriending his son and pretending to be a fellow vegetarian.

Gorsky had been sent to London in December 1940 to rebuild the networks he had been ordered to abandon in February when Lavrenti Beria feared hostile penetration. His paranoia, in fact, was groundless. During 1941 Gorsky received a total of 3,449 documents from Cairncross, who enjoyed complete access to Lord Hankey's registry inside the Cabinet Office where, among many other secret papers, the minutes of the Committee of Imperial Defense and the War Cabinet were secured. Barkovsky was responsible for photographing the documents and recalls that "I was the only person at our *rezidentura* who photographed all the mail to be sent to Moscow. I knew all of them excellently, but only externally and by their codenames, and by who was providing what kind of material."[4] As well as handling information from Cairncross, Barkovsky insists that Donald Maclean also supplied atomic secrets to Gorsky. "He brought in the minutes from sessions of the English Uranium Committee. It turned out that the idea of creating an atomic bomb had managed to obtain the approval of the Combined Committee of the Chiefs of Staff. Moreover, the generals were in a hurry: get it to us in two years. Maclean obtained completely concrete information about how the English saw the design of the atomic weapon. The documents contained precise diagrams, formulas and figures... there were sixty pages there. I slaved over them all night, but I prepared the survey. I started reading them and for me it was a dense forest. After many difficulties I managed to prepare only two telegrams giving a survey of the situation."[5]

When the NKVD's Leonid Kvasnikov reported on these documents to Beria, the latter believed it to be disinformation from the Germans or British to get the Soviets to deflect their manpower and material resources into a hugely expensive project. Still, Beria sent the documents to an unknown independent expert, although certainly a physicist, for review. As Kvasnikov related in an interview on Belgian television, Beria told him, "I'll get you into the cellars if this turns out to be disinformation."

At this early stage Kvasnikov was almost entirely dependent for his information on the London *rezidentura*, headed by Gorsky, and staffed by Barkovsky and a third officer, Pavel D. Yerzin. Under sheer pressure of work, their numbers were increased by the addition of Andrei Graur, who arrived in 1941 under cover of first secretary and was employed there using his own name, and Boris Krotov (codenamed BOB). The other, declared NKVD officer in London was Ivan Chichayev, who acted as a liaison officer to Special Operations Executive. In 1943 Konstantin Kukin was transferred to London, and a year later he was to take over as *rezident* upon Gorsky's departure to Washington DC in September 1944.

Paradoxically, the British intelligence authorities were rather less concerned about Soviet activities than with what the Nazis were planning, and SIS possessed only one officer, Commander Eric Welsh, with any scientific experience. He also enjoyed strong Norwegian connections, having married a Norwegian wife, and having managed a paint factory outside Oslo before the war. His first task was to assess the enemy's nuclear development program, for which he relied on three sources of information: advice from recently arrived refugee scientists, articles published in academic journals and secret information derived from SIS channels. The task was not as daunting as it might seem because the international community of physicists was somewhat akin to an exclusive club where the members met regularly at conferences, married into each others' families, collaborated on research and maintained contact through letters and scholarly periodicals. With help from Rudolf

Peierls, Welsh compiled a list of sixteen German scientists who were either known to be researching the subject, or were considered to be good candidates: Otto Hahn, Werner Heisenberg, Heinrich Hoffmann, Fritz Strassmann, Siegfried Flugge, Carl-Friedrich von Wiezsäcker, Josef Mattauch, Karl Wirtz, Hans Geiger, Walther Bothe, Rudolf Fleischmann, Klaus Clusisu, Gerhard Dickel, Paul Harteck and G. Stetter. With the exception of Gustav Hertz, who had been dropped because of his Jewish origins, all were subsequently shown to have participated in the German project.

Thus, by the middle of 1941, British research into bomb development was leading the field, with assistance from the Collège de France, while similar work was being undertaken in Germany and Leningrad. Whereas there was close collaboration between almost all the refugee scientists based in Britain (with the exception of Professor Max Born of Edinburgh University, who disapproved of what he perceived to be the inevitable consequences of a super-bomb), their counterparts in Berlin, Leningrad, and the United States were scarcely at the starting gates. The acceptance by the Cabinet's Scientific Advisory Committee of the recommendations of the MAUD Report was a watershed, ending what might be termed the period of tentative research, and the beginning of an era of commitment to the actual manufacture of a bomb. The MAUD Committee itself continued for a few months under the MAP so as to ensure continuity, but a new body, established under the Department of Scientific and Industrial Research (DSIR) and known as the Consultative Council, was created, consisting of Sir John Anderson, Sir Henry Dale, President of the Royal Society, Lord Cherwell and Sir Edward Appleton.

The other result of the MAUD Report, which was submitted to Colonel John Moore-Brabazon MP, the Minister for Aircraft Production, was the creation of the Directorate of Tube Alloys, headed by (Sir) Wallace Akers, the research director of ICI, and his deputy, the chemist Michael Perrin, who were released from the company on October 18 for the duration of the war, and installed in an office at 16 Old Queen Street, only a few yards from the headquarters of the Secret Intelligence Service in Queen Anne's Gate. The cabinet minister with overall responsibility for the project was Sir John Anderson, until recently the Home Secretary, and now Lord President of the Council, who was a physical chemist himself. His Ph.D. thesis at Leipzig University, coincidentally, had been on the chemistry of uranium. A technical subcommittee, consisting of Peierls, Chadwick, Simon, and von Halban, was created to take the research into the development stage. It met for the first time on November 6, 1941.

By this time ICI and Metropolitan-Vickers had taken the TUBE ALLOYS project from the realm of the theoretical into practical, industrial application. The problem of isotope separation was being addressed at ICI's Metals Division at Witton, just outside Birmingham, where the Research Manager, S. S. Smith, was engaged on the manufacture of membranes, which would be components of the equipment being constructed by Metropolitan-Vickers in Manchester and ICI at Billingham. The company's General Chemicals Division built a uranium refinery at Widnes, and its production of 200-pound ingots of the pure metal were delivered to Witton for final fabrication. At Oxford, Franz Simon's small research team grew to almost forty, and occupied much of the Clarendon Laboratory, as well as Jesus College's chemistry laboratory, with additional work on isotope separation being undertaken by Dr. Arms in the Physics Laboratory at Birmingham. The membranes, developed at Lund Humphries in Bradford, were put into production at Sun Engraving in Watford, and the entire enterprise was focused at Rhydymwyn, near Mold in North Wales, where the various components were assembled.

The site selected for the TUBE ALLOYS project, remote and secretive, was then in use by ICI as an underground storage facility for high explosives and the highly toxic chemical ingredients of mustard gas. The entire area of the Alyn valley was dotted with abandoned lead and zinc mines and quarries, amounting to some eighty miles of passages and connected workings. In September 1938 the Ministry of Supply began tunneling into the limestone at Hendre to construct a series of deep chambers, initially to store up to 10,000 tons of TNT. By October 1940 2,200 miners had dug four shafts into the hillside 30 feet wide and 760 feet long, and fitted them with air vents, blast doors and two 2-ton cranes to carry the munitions. In addition, a separate facility, codenamed WOODSIDE, was constructed nearby as an overflow. Those engaged in building the complex were sworn to secrecy and told that it was intended to store the nation's art treasures, whereas in fact they were actually deposited some distance away at a different quarry, at Grange, in the same county of Clwyd.

The site became operational in June 1940 when ICI delivered the first consignment of chemicals, accompanied by massive army and police escorts, with a mobile decontamination unit, and stored them temporarily in a surface facility codenamed ANTELOPE, while the runcol (the blistering agent in mustard gas) was transferred into massive lead-lined underground tanks. During the last months of 1941, when there were already 262 workers based in the compound, the TUBE ALLOYS staff began to arrive, with contingents from ICI at Randle and Billingham, together with technicians from Metropolitan-Vickers and the Clarendon Laboratory. At the height of its activity there were more than a thousand people on the site, with 120 of them categorized as engaged on atomic research in the surface laboratories, the remainder assembling millions of smoke shells and other munitions, as well as processing the acids required for chemical weapons.

Rhydymwyn remained the TUBE ALLOYS secret center until 1944, by which time the American Manhattan Project had all but consumed the entire organization and any intention of fabricating an atomic weapon in England had been abandoned. The decision had already been taken to establish a Canadian plant at Chalk River, conveniently close to the country's vast uranium deposits. George Thomson had been despatched to Ottawa to open a liaison office soon after the Directorate of Tube Alloys had been created. The first proposal was for close cooperation at Chicago but as there were American objections, Michael Perrin opened negotiations with the Canadian government and visited the Canadian Minister of Munitions and Supply, C. D. Howe, and a Canadian physicist, Dr. C. J. Mackenzie, who had undertaken some early research into fission at McGill University with Lord Rutherford. The British suggestion, endorsed by Prime Minister Mackenzie King, was to begin work jointly in Montreal under the umbrella of the Canadian National Research Council, which would exercise administrative control and meet all the costs except the salaries of the British scientists.

In February 1942 Peierls, von Halban, Simon, and Akers left for a tour of the United States, but only after the U.S. Attorney General had pledged that Akers would not be subpoenaed upon his arrival in America to give evidence in unconnected anti-trust litigation being brought against ICI. By the time the party had returned to England in April, the only way to prevent time-wasting duplication was total Anglo-American collaboration. Two months later, on June 20, 1942, Churchill stayed with Harry Hopkins and Roosevelt at the president's magnificent home in Hyde Park, New York, and "strongly urged that we should at once pool all our information, work together on equal terms, and share the results, if any, equally between us."[6] Thus it was informally agreed that they would proceed with an Anglo-American bomb on the basis of an equal partnership but, perhaps surprisingly, given the gravity of this agreement, no record of it was kept, and the understanding of precisely what had been accepted by both sides was to cause more than a few difficulties in future months. Indeed, Thomson complained that "by the end of the year I realized that I was being shut out," and Churchill was forced to raise the matter at the Casablanca conference when he was reassured by Harry Hopkins that the British had not been deliberately excluded, but merely had fallen victim to the very strict security policy of compartmentalization, or "need to know" exercised by the U.S. Army. On September 17, 1942, the Army was placed in overall control of the weapons project and run by General Leslie Groves' Manhattan Engineering District (MED), then based in New York's Empire State Building.

The first step in the collaboration was von Halban's move to Montreal in September 1942, followed by the rest of his team from Cambridge in December. However, these first steps faltered, probably due to the growing suspicion among the American scientists that Britain and Canada were more interested in developing sources of industrial atomic energy for the postwar era, and were thus allowing the Americans to make a colossal investment in the bomb project that would not have the same economic impact after an Allied victory. This was the message delivered by Henry Stimson during a visit to London in early 1943. The conflict was finally resolved by a written agreement, drawn up by Sir John Anderson, and signed by Roosevelt and Churchill at the Quebec conference in August 1943 in which the Americans effectively agreed to pay for the project in exchange for the British relinquishing any commercial advantage.

Chapter II

Anglo-American Cooperation

> Why start on a project which, if it was successful, would end with the production of a weapon of unparalleled violence, a weapon of mass destruction such as the world had never seen? The answer was very simple. We were at war and the idea was reasonably obvious; very probably some German scientists had had the same idea and were working on it.
>
> *Otto Frisch*

The American atomic bomb program originated with a lecture tour undertaken by Enrico Fermi in Washington DC in March 1939. Fermi had won the Nobel Prize in physics the previous year, and had moved from Rome with his Jewish wife Laura to Columbia University when Mussolini passed Italy's anti-Semitic laws. While in Washington Fermi made a visit to the Navy Department with colleagues from Columbia, carrying a letter from a skeptical physicist George Pegram addressed to Admiral S. C. Hooper in the office of the Chief of Naval Operations. While noting his reservations, Fermi explained that experiments had suggested that

> [t]he chemical element uranium may be able to liberate its large excess of atomic energy, and that this might mean the possibility that uranium might be used as an explosive that would liberate a million times as much energy per pound as any known explosive. My own feeling is that the probabilities are against this, but my colleagues and I think that the bare possibility should not be disregarded.

The result of Fermi's lobbying was a $1,500 grant from the Naval Research Laboratory for fission research at Columbia. As this was hardly adequate for what the physicist had in mind, Leo Szilard and Eugene Wigner approached Albert Einstein and in June obtained his support for a plea to be made directly to the White House. Their intermediary was one of Roosevelt's personal friends, Alexander Sachs, who was then economic adviser to the New York investment bankers Lehman Brothers. After having persuaded Sachs, Szilard and Wigner enlisted the help of a third Hungarian physicist, Edward Teller, who helped draft a letter addressed to the president. Dated August 2, 1939, Einstein explained that "it may become possible to set up a nuclear chain reaction in a large mass of uranium" and

> [t]his new phenomenon would also lead to the construction of bombs, and it is conceivable—though much less certain—that extremely powerful bombs of a new type may thus be constructed. A single bomb of this type, carried by boat and exploded in a port, might very well destroy the whole port together with some of the surrounding territory. However, such bombs might well prove to be too heavy for transportation by air.

Einstein also outlined the problem of finding sufficient uranium ore and recommended that the president appoint "a person who has your confidence and who could perhaps serve in an unofficial capacity" to liaise with the government and raise the necessary funds from private donations to speed up the research. In closing, the physicist warned that Germany had taken over the source of uranium in Czechoslovakia, and that "the son of the German State Secretary von Weizsäcker is attached to the Kaiser Wilhelm Institute in Berlin where some of the work on uranium is not being repeated."

Einstein's prescient warning was all too true. Apart from minor deposits in Norway, Sweden, and Russia, the best uranium mine in Europe was at Joachimsthal in Czechoslovakia. There were further deposits at the Eldorado Mine near the Great Bear Lake in Canada's frozen arctic, and some limited amounts of ore that could be recovered from the tailings of carnotite (used to refine vanadium) in Colorado and New Mexico. However, the very best reserves were undoubtedly at the Shinkolobwe mine in the Upper Katanga region of the Congo, currently exploited by the Belgian firm Union Minière du Haut-Katanga. All the calculations made hitherto suggested that several thousand tons of the rare ore known as pitchblende would be required to refine enough uranium to carry the research forward. The issue of speed was emphasized by Einstein because of the fear that the Nazis had taken control of the main Czech mine and had commenced similar, parallel work in Berlin under Carl-Friedrich von Weizsäcker, younger son of Ernst von Weizsäcker, the State Secretary of the German Foreign Ministry between 1938 and 1942, later convicted of war crimes at Nuremberg in April 1949.

While Einstein was right about the shortage of uranium ore, and had correctly identified Professor von Weizsäcker as an eminent German physicist working at the Kaiser Wilhelm Institute for Physics at Berlin-Dahlem, he was premature in his concern about the work undertaken there. In fact, the Institute would not be taken over by the Wehrmacht's Ordnance Corps until October 1939, which proved the catalyst for its Dutch director, Peter Debye, to move to the United States in January the following year, after refusing to take German citizenship. His replacement, Dr. Kurt Diebner, was not highly regarded by his colleagues, and although plans for the construction of an experimental pile in the grounds of the Institute began in July 1940, no German reactor was ever to come even close to achieving critical mass or a chain reaction. Nevertheless,

Einstein's reference to von Weizsäcker was enough to exacerbate the fear that the Allies were engaged in a race with the Nazis for a viable nuclear bomb. In reality, the most progress was made in Leipzig by Professor Werner Heisenberg, who pursued a completely mistaken route to fission based on heavy water.

Einstein's letter evidently impressed the president. On October 12, Roosevelt invited Sachs to breakfast at the White House and then ordered his military aide, General Watson, to take the necessary action. Instead of appointing a single individual to supervise a bomb project, an Advisory Committee on Uranium was formed, consisting of a representative from the army and navy's ordnance divisions, chaired by Lyman Briggs, the Director of the U.S. National Bureau of Standards. Briggs promptly invited Szilard, Teller, and Wigner to explain their case. The result was the authorization of $6,000 in February 1940 for the purchase of fifty tons of uranium ore and four tons of graphite. Soon afterwards, Einstein wrote a second letter to the White House, dated March 7, again raising the spectre of a German uranium bomb, based on information about top secret research being carried out by another of the Kaiser Wilhelm Institutes, the Institute of Physics, he had received from Dr. Debye, who reached the United States the following month.

Peter Debye's news caused alarm in both London and Washington, prompting a long article in the *New York Times* by William Laurence, entitled "Vast Power Source in Atomic Energy Opened by Science" which described how the Kaiser Wilhelm Institute in Berlin was now the center of Nazi research into uranium and that, moreover, the greatest German physicists, chemists and engineers had been ordered to drop whatever they were doing and devote themselves entirely to atomic energy research.

However, the reality was that the United States had produced only a few grams of uranium metal, and many scientists were highly critical of Briggs's failure to grasp the initiative. For example, Robert Serber complained that, although Briggs had given support to Fermi and Szilard, "he gave nothing at all to John Dunning and Eugene T. Booth for their gaseous diffusion experiments at Columbia. The project was limping along and, in fact, Vannevar Bush, the chairman of Scientific Research and Development was thinking of closing it down completely, until the British came along and saved the day."[1]

The project also suffered from excessive secrecy. When Samuel Allison first joined, he had not been told that the project's ultimate goal was the development of a bomb. "This aspect was played down. We weren't told. I thought we were making a power source for submarines."

Within five months the Briggs Committee, which had only met twice, was absorbed into a new National Defense Research Committee, headed by Professor Vannevar Bush of the Massachusetts Institute of Technology, and became known as the "S-1 Section," sponsoring university fission research projects at Columbia, Princeton, Cornell, Johns Hopkins, Virginia, Chicago, Minnesota, Iowa State, and California (Berkeley), with a budget that by December 1941 would escalate to $300,000. The key event in the transformation was a visit made by Harvard's Professor Kenneth Bainbridge to London in April 1941. Bainbridge, who by coincidence had undertaken some research himself the previous year into isotope separation, had been sent to England by Bush to exchange information on radar, reciprocating the first Tizard mission the previous September, but Cockcroft had invited him to a special meeting of the MAUD Committee convened at Burlington House on April 9. Unexpectedly, Bainbridge had been confronted by Oliphant, Peierls, Frisch, Thomson, von Halban, Kowarski, Chadwick, Simon, Lockspeiser, Tuck, and a single American, Dr. H. S. Arms, and had received the most comprehensive account of their accomplishments to date. The conclusion was that Britain had achieved the technical skill to make an atomic bomb within three years. Although the country, gripped in a desperate war for survival with Nazi Germany, lacked sufficient electricity to produce either graphite or heavy water as moderators, Canada had plenty of resources. There was hydroelectric power in abundance, no shortage of cold water, uranium from the Eldorado mine, refining facilities at Port Hope on Lake Ontario, and heavy water from an electrolytic hydrogen plant at Trail in British Columbia. The Committee proposed a similar exchange of information along the model established by Tizard on radar, and offered to send von Halban to Washington DC to brief the NDRC.

Even before the Tizard mission, which arrived in Halifax on the *Duchess of Richmond* early in August 1940, there had been informal contacts between members of the MAUD Committee and the Americans. Alexander Hill, during an official visit to America, had been asked by Thomson "to find out if anything of interest is going on in the United States"; in June 1940, Lord Rutherford's son-in-law, Professor R. H. Fowler, was asked to make overtures to the Canadian and American authorities while he was in Ottawa, and see whether von Halban and Kowarski could continue their research into heavy water in Canada.

During the voyage across the Atlantic, Cockcroft was invited to lecture to the other passengers, mainly Royal Navy seamen on their way to crew American Lend-Lease destroyers. Because of the very classified nature of the Tizard mission, which concentrated on technological breakthroughs such as sonar and microwave radar, he chose what he regarded as a completely safe scientific topic—atomic energy. In his address, Cockcroft defined a measurement of nuclear energy as the amount required to lift a 50,000-ton battleship one foot into the air, and claimed that there was sufficient potential energy in a single cup of water to break the back of such a warship. Cockcroft reassured his audience that "there was no hope at all that such a thing would be achieved during the present war."

Cockcroft and Fowler met the Briggs Committee in Washington on October 7, 1940, to discuss the separation of U-235, still regarded as "a long-term project," and the acquisition of uranium ore. The two scientists then joined the Canadian physicist A. G. Shenstone to meet Fermi and Szilard at Columbia in November, before Cockcroft flew back to London on December 1, noting that Fermi "was convinced that no uranium mixture could ever be any use as an explosive owing to the long relaxation time of the fundamental process concerned." Although atomic fission was not intended to be a key part of the Tizard exchange of technical information, the mission did have a lasting impact on Canada by establishing a route for coordinating research on atomic issues. On November 22, Cockcroft and Fowler, preoccupied with radar, met two Canadian National Research Council physicists, G. C. Laurence and

E. W. Stedman, and put them in direct contact with Fermi and his colleagues in America. Soon after Cockcroft's return to England, Laurence met Pegram, Harold Urey and Briggs in New York, and drafted a report on American research for London.

After the Tizard mission, a copy of all MAUD Committee minutes was sent to Fowler in the U.S. to circulate to his contacts, and in February 1941 the president of Harvard, James B. Conant, opened an NDRC office in London. By September he had learned enough to be persuaded that the British had made tremendous progress, as Arthur Compton, then the University of Chicago's Dean of Physical Sciences, recalled:

> Ernest Lawrence of the University of California met President Conant of Harvard and me in our house here in Chicago. He told us of calculations indicating that an atomic bomb of great effectiveness could be made using much smaller amounts of U-235 than had previously been thought necessary. The British scientists responsible for these calculations were so convinced of their significance that they were eager to get going on a full-scale effort to produce the required U-235 to make the bomb.[2]

Lawrence, who had been using his invention, the 37-inch cyclotron (for which he had been awarded the 1939 Nobel Prize in physics), at the Radiation Laboratory on the university's campus at Berkeley, disclosed that his colleague Glenn Seaborg was confident that his new man-made element, plutonium, had excellent potential as a bomb metal. Thereafter, Compton promptly undertook a tour across the country, calling in at Columbia to hear Fermi estimate that critical mass could be achieved with less than a hundred pounds of uranium, and learn that Harold Urey and John Dunning were concentrating on methods of isolating the U-235 isotope. At Princeton he discussed the construction of a reactor or pile with Wigner, and discovered that Louis Turner had suggested one built of plutonium. In California Glenn Seaborg assured Compton that once a reactor had begun to "cook" uranium fuel rods, it would only be a matter of weeks before sufficient plutonium could be extracted to make a bomb.

On October 3, George Thomson gave copies of the final MAUD report to James Conant and Vannevar Bush; within the week the latter was describing to President Roosevelt and Vice President Henry Wallace how a bomb could be built. Roosevelt authorized Bush to consult only General Marshall and Secretary of War Henry Stimson regarding future policy on atomic weapons. Two days later, on October 11, Roosevelt wrote to Churchill, suggesting that future efforts "might usefully be coordinated or even jointly conducted." Later the same month Pegram and Urey arrived in London and were greeted by Akers at Old Queen Street to be introduced to Appleton and Perrin and briefed on the TUBE ALLOYS project. Thus, for the first time, two ostensible neutrals from a non-belligerent country were allowed to learn virtually everything about the British atomic bomb project. Almost nothing was held back. The two Americans were escorted to Liverpool to have Chadwick explain his progress with neutrons, and then visited Bradford where the Lund Humphries printing works had come up with an ingenious solution to the problem of manufacturing membranes for isotope separation with sufficient accuracy. Michael Clapham, chairman of ICI's Metals Division, had been searching for an efficient method of isolating the heavier U-238 isotope, and had previously worked at Lund Humphries as a printer. Recalling the principles of the offset-litho process, which depended on chemically altering thin films of copper with tremendous precision, Clapham had successfully applied the idea to make membranes that separated the valuable U-235. The Americans then continued their journey to Oxford to discuss the theoretical dimensions of the project with Simon and Peierls before traveling to Birmingham to meet Professor W. N. Haworth of the university's Chemistry Department, who demonstrated how he was refining pure uranium. Finally, on November 4, they saw von Halban and Kowarski in Cambridge, and Urey, who had discovered heavy water but had only seen the liquid in microscopic quantities, was shown the Collège de France's collection of jerry cans.

Impressed by what they had witnessed, Pegram and Urey had a final meeting with Akers and Appleton in London on November 5 and began to draft their report, which acted to reinforce the conclusions of the MAUD report already circulating in Washington DC, and a further study undertaken by Arthur Compton under the auspices of the U.S. National Academy of Sciences. According to Conant, "enthusiasm and optimism reigned."

Although Urey's visit to London was supposed to be top secret, news of it was reported to the NKVD's acting *rezident* in New York, Pavel Pastelnyak, who was under consular cover after coming to the U.S. in 1938 to supervise security arrangements for the Soviet pavilion at the World's Fair the following year. Pastelnyak's source was Dr. Emil Connison, a well-known New York Communist physician with a controversial medical reputation and links to Urey. On November 24, 1941, Pastelnyak, codenamed LUKA, cabled Moscow that Urey had gone to London to work on "an explosive of enormous force," but when the Center sought confirmation from Cairncross through the London *rezidentura,* speculating that this was connected to uranium research, Gorsky replied that Urey had already returned to the United States.

On November 6, 1941, Compton reported to Vannevar Bush that, based on his discussions, a bomb could be made within three to five years. "The possibility must seriously be considered that with a few years the use of bombs such as described here, or something similar using uranium fission, may determine military superiority." It would cost $300 million and be 300,000 times more powerful than TNT, making a bomb of a hundred pounds the equivalent to 15,000 tons of high explosive. Impressed by Compton's conclusions, Bush took them to Roosevelt on November 27, together with a copy of the British MAUD report. In his cover letter, Bush explained that Compton's verdict was "somewhat more conservative than the British report."

> The present report estimates that the bomb will be somewhat less effective than the British computations showed, although still exceedingly powerful. It predicts a longer interval before production could be started. It also estimates the total costs much higher than the British figures.[3]

Despite Compton's conservatism, Bush received immediate authority to use the president's own secret funds of several million dollars to support a further six months of research. If, at the end of that period, the prospects looked good, S-1 was promised unlimited financial backing.

On the morning of Saturday, December 6, 1941, Bush gathered together the S-1 team and outlined the next six months. Briggs would remain as chairman, with Columbia's Pegram acting as his deputy, but Conant would supervise both on behalf of Bush. As for the direction of the research, Urey was to continue to work at Columbia on isolating U-235 by mechanical means, incorporating the high speed centrifuge method adopted by J. W. Beams at the University of Virginia, and the spectrographic method developed by A. O. Nier at the University of Minnesota; Lawrence would experiment with electromagnetic separation in California, using his Calutron device, which could produce one microgram (one 500-millionth of a pound) of U-235 an hour, leaving the bomb design to Compton in Chicago. A newcomer to the team, Eger Murphee, then Director of Research at Standard Oil, would plan the engineering required for a pilot manufacturing plant. The atmosphere at the meeting was entirely relaxed, and some of those assembled moved on to the exclusive Cosmos Club for lunch, little realizing that as they sat down to eat a Japanese carrier force was steaming towards the Hawaiian Islands, preparing to launch a surprise air raid on Oahu's naval base at Pearl Harbor.

Luckily, the S-1 team's search for uranium ore went no further than a warehouse on Staten Island, New York, where 1,140 metric tons of high-grade pitchblende from Katanga had been stored by Union Minière since its arrival in June 1940, following an unsuccessful bid to buy it by the British the previous year. On that occasion Sir Henry Tizard had approached two Union Minière directors, (Sir) Edgar Sengier and Lord Stonehaven, formerly a Parliamentary Under-Secretary for Air. Through his friendship with the Belgian ambassador, Baron Cartier, and Stonehaven's connections with the RAF, Tizard had attempted to acquire an option on the Katanga deposits, but his request had been turned down. Disappointed, Tizard had warned Sengier, "you have in your hands some thing which may mean catastrophe to your country and mine if it were to fall into the hands of a possible enemy."

In fact, Sengier had accepted an order from America, from Alexander Sachs, on behalf of the Uranium Committee, who had shipped his purchase in 2,000 steel drums from Lobito Bay, in Portuguese Angola, in October and November 1940, but then allowed it to be unloaded and forgotten. Colonel Kenneth Nichols of S-1 purchased all of it for a price of $1.35 a pound, significantly less than the cost of the lower quality Canadian ore at more than $6.00 a pound, and shipped it by rail to MIT at Cambridge, Massachusetts, where it was processed into an oxide for the next leg of the journey to Fermi's laboratory in Chicago.

In June 1942 Arthur Compton undertook a further review of the progress achieved by the S-1 scientists and set out the scale of the challenge ahead. The Columbia team had accomplished much with its attempts to perfect gaseous diffusion; although Lawrence had hit some obstacles with his magnetic separation system. Seaborg was developing larger samples of plutonium, and Fermi's calculations about a reactor looked promising. There was nothing approaching a breakthrough but there was more than enough optimism to justify continuation of the project. What remained daunting was the astronomic size of the investment required, with miles of pipe, a huge power source and thousands of vacuum pumps required to implement Denning's porous diffusion system, which was just one of three under trial, each likely to cost around $300 million. The president, however, was unconcerned by the estimates and on June 17, 1942, approved Compton's recommendations and authorized the U.S. Army Corps of Engineers to start the enormous undertaking.

In the new War Department in Washington DC, Colonel J. C. Marshall took over a suite of offices designated "Development of Substitute Materials" and effectively began an engineering project under the command name Manhattan, using the Boston industrial design consultants Stone & Webster to select a suitable site on which to construct the centrifuges, apparently on behalf of Standard Oil. The first choice was eighteen miles northwest of Knoxville in Tennessee on the banks of the Clinch River, which, besides isolation, promised water and power in abundance, and was to become known as the Clinton Engineer Works.

Despite this elaborate commitment, nobody had actually gone beyond the theoretical study of fission, and by November 1942 Compton had decided not to wait for the completion of the Argonne site. Instead, he arranged for the improvised laboratory in a squash court under one of the stands of the University of Chicago's unused football field on Ellis Avenue to be converted into an experimental reactor built with a brown dioxide of uranium, a metal of impressive purity achieved by Mallinckrodt Chemical Works of St. Louis. Six tons of the valuable uranium were carried into the basement of the west stand of Stagg Field where Enrico Fermi directed the construction of the world's first atomic pile, a spheroid of graphite shaped like a doorknob. On the afternoon of December 2 the control rods were removed under the supervision of George Weil and critical mass was achieved, with the instrument monitors showing the start of a chain reaction. Norman Hilberry, Compton's assistant, was poised over the core with a control rod dangling on the end of a rope, an axe in his hand, ready to cut the line and drop the rod into the heart of the pile in case the reactor became dangerous, but the experiment was concluded safely, much to the delight of Wigner, who offered Fermi a bottle of Chianti in celebration. Watching from the gallery were Crawford Greenwalt of du Pont, the youngest member of S-1, and Compton. As the control rods were replaced, restoring the pile to a dormant state, Compton telephoned James Conant in Cambridge, Massachusetts, and informed him that "the Italian navigator has found the New World." Worried about the consequences of such an experiment in the center of Chicago, and not deep in the Argonne Forest as originally intended, Conant asked if "the natives were friendly." "Everyone landed safely and happy," replied Compton, beaming with delight. Paradoxically, when the Manhattan Project got underway, Compton would find it difficult to obtain a security clearance because of an earlier flirtation with radical politics and the leftist Teachers' Union.

Fermi's success, achieving a controlled chain reaction with U-238, demonstrated that unseparated uranium could be transmuted into plutonium, an entirely new element that was itself fissionable. Although this did not in itself advance the development of a bomb (for the calculation was that the pile would have to run for 70,000 years to produce sufficient plutonium), the way was now open to concentrate on the mass production of plutonium of which only a few millionths of a gram then existed.

One of the first consequences of S-1's transformation into the Manhattan Project was the introduction of military style security. Security had previously been tight, though it consisted of not much more than the showing of a movie, *Next of Kin*, which was intended to explain the importance of maintaining complete silence about any war-related work of a confidential nature. Under the military regime a three-hundred-strong Counter-Intelligence Corps (CIC), detachment known as "the creeps," under the command of Colonel John Lansdale, a recent graduate of Harvard Law School, began the arduous task of screening the thousands of technicians recruited to work on a project so secret that not even the security experts were allowed to know about it. Lansdale himself had only learned of the project when he was assigned by James Conant to undertake an undercover mission on the Berkeley campus, masquerading as a left-wing law student to check on rumors of lax security around the Radiation Laboratory. Over lunch at the Faculty Club, Lansdale was appalled when Lawrence was pointed out to him, with the remark that the physicist was "trying to split the atom to make a bomb." It was, of course, almost impossible to conceal the central truth that the widespread research into isotope isolation was intended to result in a bomb, as was described by Pollard and Davidson in their 1942 book *Applied Nuclear Physics*:

> The separation of the uranium isotopes in quantity lots is now being attempted in several places. If the reader wakes some morning to read in his newspaper that half the United States was blown into the sea overnight he can be rest assured that someone, somewhere, succeeded.

At this stage there were "five different horses running neck and neck": separation of U-235 was being pursued by centrifuge, diffusion, and electromagnetic methods, and plutonium production was planned with a uranium-graphite pile and a uranium-heavy water pile. On May 14, 1942, Conant reported to Bush that "while all five methods now appear to be about equally promising, clearly the time to production… by the five routes will certainly not be the same but might vary by six months or a year because of unforeseen delays. Therefore, if one discards one or two or three of the methods now, one may be betting on the slower horse unconsciously."

By August 1943 the horserace had been reduced to three, the centrifugal method proving too difficult, and heavy water abandoned as a moderator for lack of sufficient quantities. Plutonium production continued with a pilot graphite pile, and gaseous diffusion and electromagnetic separation showed great promise under the management of the U.S. Army's DSM project, with the U.S. Navy supplying the facilities for pilot plants at the Naval Research Laboratories at Anacostia and Philadelphia. It was at this stage, moving from research into production, that Roosevelt and Churchill agreed at Quebec on a Combined Policy Committee (CPC), consisting of Secretary for War Henry Stimson, with Conant and Bush to represent the U.S.; British interests were entrusted to Field Marshal Sir John Dill and Colonel J. J. Lewellin, with the Minister of Munitions, C. D. Howe, representing Canada. The CPC's technical subcommittee was composed of just three men: Richard Tolman of CalTech for the U.S., Chadwick for Britain, and C. J. Mackenzie for Canada. The CPC's purpose was to formalize the exchange of information and silence the critics, among them Henry Stimson and General Groves, who wanted to limit British participation and were suspicious of a recent, secret Anglo-Soviet agreement on assistance to develop new weapons. Churchill had demanded full collaboration but, in recognition of local sensibilities and fearing a complete shutout, had agreed not to share atomic knowledge with any third party without American consent.

* * *

The first British mission to reach the United States, by flying boat from Lisbon in late 1941, consisted of Sir Wallace Akers and Franz Simon, with Hans von Halban traveling by sea, because of his heart condition, and Rudolf Peierls flying separately to Canada by bomber from Prestwick because he was considered too well known to the enemy, and therefore a possible target for abduction in Portugal. A B-24 Liberator carried Peierls on the sixteen-hour flight to Newfoundland for refueling, and then on to Dorval, outside Montreal, before he finally arrived in Ottawa for a briefing given by George Thomson, head of the British Scientific Liaison Office. After a short stop to gather together in New York, members of the delegation individually, or as a group, made a tour of the American facilities, visiting Harold Urey, Enrico Fermi, and Karl Cohen at Columbia University in New York, before moving on to Chicago to see Arthur Compton and then Berkeley so that Peierls could see his old friend Robert Oppenheimer, with whom he stayed overnight. Peierls returned from California to discuss centrifuges with Jesse Beams at the University of Virginia in Charlottesville, and then made a second visit to Compton in Chicago.

The second stage of cooperation was the establishment by von Halban, taking his heavy water research team, of a laboratory outside Montreal, leaving his rival Lev Kowarski in charge in Cambridge.

In August 1942, following Churchill's meeting with President Roosevelt at Quebec, a second team of British scientists, consisting of James Chadwick, Mark Oliphant, Simon, and Peierls, crossed the Atlantic. This time they flew together by flying boat from Foynes in Ireland, and upon their arrival in Washington met General Leslie Groves, now in military command of the Manhattan Project, and held a meeting with Oppenheimer, "who was not allowed to tell me everything," recalled Peierls. "He was accompanied by a senior colleague, evidently as a witness to what he was telling me."[4] The group also visited several laboratories, where the staff had been baffled by Groves, who had instructed that the foreigners "could be told everything, but must not be shown anything."

Peierls returned to England by bomber, and on December 3, 1943, returned to the USA on the troopship *Andes*, accompanied by the main group of British scientists, among them Otto Frisch, who was to go to Los Alamos, Frank (later Lord) Kearton, and Tony Skyrne. After their arrival at Newport News, Virginia, they went by train to Washington DC and then New York, where the theoreticians were given offices on the twenty-fifth floor of the British Supply Mission headquarters on Wall Street, conveniently close to the Kellex Corporation's design group based in the Woolworth Building.

Peierls later moved to Los Alamos, where there was a large British contingent headed by James Chadwick. Among them were Joseph Rotblat, Egon and Hanni Bretscher from Cambridge, James Tuck from Oxford, and Ernest Titterton and Philip Moon from Birmingham. In addition, Niels Bohr made several visits, the 1944 Nobel Prize-winner Isador Rabi called in occasionally, the Hungarian mathematician John von Neumann was a resident periodically, and the others included an Etonian, Tony Skyrne, and Ronald Gurney, the Princeton-educated scientist who would become Chief Physicist in the Theoretical Nuclear Physics Division.

Peierls was asked to head the hydrodynamics group and shared an office with his friend Klaus Fuchs. This relationship was to become the focus of what the FBI subsequently called the FOOCASE, a lengthy investigation into Soviet espionage at Los Alamos which, when combined with the leads supplied by Harry Gold, would result in more than forty-five cases for the FBI. Among the first was Ronald Gurney, the British-born physicist who had landed at Seattle in January 1941, while attempting to make his way back to England from Sweden via Russia. Instead of completing his journey, he was employed from June 1943 as an expert on ballistics at the Aberdeen Proving Grounds in Maryland, and in October 1946 moved to the Argonne Laboratory. Fuchs had been friendly with Gurney and his wife Natalie in Bristol before the war, and he described them both as potential security risks, citing in particular her membership in the Society for Cultural Relations with the USSR. Natalie had worked for the British Purchasing Commission in Washington DC between 1941 and 1943, and had acquired a reputation as a left-winger. She was also a member of South-East Asia Institute and some other organizations officially designated subversive by the Attorney General. Fuchs's accusation was enough to ensure that Gurney's application to join Harwell was rejected on security grounds by MI5.

There was never any evidence that Gurney had engaged in espionage, but coincidentally the other two VENONA spies identified simultaneously with Fuchs, although entirely unrelated to him, proved to have been part of the Soviet espionage network headed by Gold and Abe Brothman. The historic FBI memorandum from Lish Whitson, dated September 1949, which exposed Fuchs as the spy codenamed REST, also named Theodore Heilig and suggested that Arthur P. Weber might be GOOSE. With help from NSA cryptographers, Whitson had narrowed the field to Fuchs because of a single VENONA text, dated June 15, 1944, which referred to an Atomic Energy Commission document, the file copy of which, MSN-12, had been written by Fuchs. It was entitled "Fluctuations and the Efficiency of a Diffusion Plant; Part III specifically referred to "The Effect of Fluctuations in the Flow of N2." The letters MSN stood for documents prepared by British scientists who were in New York City working on atomic energy research. "The author of this document is K. Fuchs, who is actually Emil Julius Klaus Fuchs, who is usually known as Karl Fuchs. He is a top ranking British atomic scientist. Information concerning REST indicated that he was a British scientist, inasmuch as he had also furnished to the Soviet intelligence information concerning British participation in the atomic energy development. It is also indicated that he has a sister in the United States. There are indications that REST was actually the author of the document."[5]

This was the deduction that was to seal Fuchs's fate, but it also cast suspicion on Heilig and Weber. Born in Jersey City in August 1897, Heilig had started his own chemical company, the Tadlee Chemical Corporation, in November 1942, and had won some important government contracts. Like Weber, he had been closely associated with Abe Brothman, who would be recognized as a key figure in the NKVD's organization. Originally from Brooklyn, Weber was a skilled chemist who had worked for Brothman, first from February 1941 in the Henderick Manufacturing Company, following his graduation from CCNY, and then between June 1942 and July 1944, in Brothman's Cheturgy Design Corporation. Their business was the manufacture of aerosol filling machines, aerosol dispensers, and the chemical DDT, but Heilig, Brothman, and Weber were to fall out as partners, following several fraudulent invoicing scams. According to Brothman, Heilig offered to obtain a draft deferment for Weber if Brothman would sign over to Heilig the rights to his automatic filling machine. Brothman refused; Heilig was indicted by a Federal Grand Jury in New York on fraud charges in March 1948, based on testimony from Weber.

Significantly, Weber joined Kellex Corporation as a chemical engineer in July 1944 and remained there, save for a gap of one month in March 1946, until the end of October 1949, when the FBI tentatively identified him as GOOSE, although this later turned out to be Harry Gold's codename. Suddenly, from this moment, MI5 and the FBI were in a position to mount a counteroffensive against Moscow. The identification of Klaus Fuchs had been the result of a long and complicated comparison between the movements of the VENONA spy codenamed REST (and CHARLES), his leave in 1944 and his rendezvous in Albuquerque. The records were searched for the leave applications and movements of every scientist at Los Alamos, so they could be compared with the information disclosed by the VENONA texts, until the field was narrowed to Fuchs alone, who made an exact match. His subsequent identification of Harry Gold as his contact was to be the second breakthrough in a sequence that would eventually expose most, if not all, the ENORMOZ spies.

Chapter III

Beria's XY *Rezidentura*

Whoever gets this first will win the war.
James Conant

The Soviet atomic weapon project can be said to have begun with a memorandum written in 1939 by a thirty-six-year-old physicist, Igor V. Kurchatov, who described the military potential of nuclear fission, noting that it was likely that Nazi scientists had already embarked on research in the field. Having headed a major laboratory for almost a decade, Kurchatov commanded considerable respect in Moscow, but Stalin was preoccupied with other distractions. When the Germans invaded in June 1941, only minimal work had been undertaken by Kurchatov, despite support from the eminent Piotr Kapitsa, who had studied at Cambridge under Ernest Rutherford, and in October 1940 had described to an audience of selected scientists an atomic bomb that in theory could "easily annihilate a great capital city having a few million inhabitants."

The Nazi attack forced an evacuation of the laboratory from Moscow to Kazan, a town about four hundred miles to the east. Once established there, Kurchatov's team was ordered to concentrate on less theoretical devices. Kurchatov devoted himself to countermeasures for the enemy's magnetic naval mines, which were taking a heavy toll on Allied shipping. It was not until Lavrenti Beria realized the advances made in Britain that he assembled a subcommittee of the State Defense Committee, which included Abram Joffe and Piotr Kapitsa, to advise on how the Soviets should join the nuclear race for a uranium bomb. Beria's committee recommended an immediate start, and in February 1943 Kurchatov was brought back to Moscow to be placed in charge of a new research facility, known only as Laboratory No. 2, located in an abandoned farm overlooking the Moscow River and neighboring an artillery range. By mid-1944, his institute had acquired about fifty staff, of whom just twenty were physicists, but none of his subordinates, including his confidantes Kikoin and Alikhanov, were allowed to know for many years that his apparently inspired instincts were greatly assisted by information supplied by the NKVD's 10th Section of the Fifth Department, which had been given responsibility for the collection of scientific and technical intelligence in 1938. In May 1940 this office was headed by Leonid R. Kvasnikov, a graduate of the Institute of Chemical Engineering who had worked in the security service since 1939, and had just returned from a mission to Poland, lasting several months, where he had been attached as an intelligence officer to the commission for resettlement in the eastern part of the country, occupied by the Red Army. In his new role Kvasnikov monitored scientific developments in the atomic field. Seeing the military potential, he prepared a questionnaire to collect relevant information from the countries he considered most likely to be engaged in the military application of atomic power, with the exception of America. Kvasnikov recalls that "the questionnaire was not sent to the U.S. because there was nobody to send it to, Ovakimyan having been detained by the American authorities." (See Chapter VI.)[1]

The first to react to Moscow's questionnaire was the London *rezidentura*. On September 25, 1941, Anatoli V. Gorsky reported that a meeting of the Uranium Committee, a Cabinet subcommittee, had taken place in London, at which it had been concluded that it was "quite feasible to develop a uranium bomb, especially if Imperial Chemical Industries (ICI) undertakes to do this in the shortest possible time. The representative of Woolwich Arsenal, Ferguson, stated that the bomb fuse could be constructed in a matter of months." The telegram contained certain scientific and technical information suggesting that the development of the atom bomb was already in progress in the USA, and concluded with a report that "the Chiefs of Staff, at their meeting on 20 September 1941, had taken the decision to start on the construction of a plant in Britain for the manufacture of a uranium bomb." On October 3, 1941, Gorsky sent another message on the work of the Uranium Committee, which contained information on the proposed magnitude of the critical mass of uranium in the bomb, and the problems connected with the industrial separation of uranium-235 by gas diffusion. The full report, delivered to the London *rezidentura* by John Cairncross, was sent by courier and in translation consisted of seventeen pages of extremely valuable data. Vladimir B. Barkovsky prepared the subsequent encoded reports to the Center. Barkovsky was then twenty-eight, and had been selected by the Deputy Chief of Intelligence, Pavel A. Sudoplatov, for work in Britain immediately after he had graduated from the School for Special Assignments. This was a facility set up in 1938 to train a new generation of intelligence officers to replace the heroes of the "golden decade," who had been purged by Yagoda and Yezhov at the end of the 1920s and the first half of the 1930s. Barkovsky remembers how Gorsky summoned him late in the evening, presumably immediately after he returned from his meeting with John Cairncross, and ordered him to prepare synopses from the original English material. Barkovsky was, of course, unfamiliar with the subject of the reports and had worked hard throughout the night to understand what it was all about, although Gorsky did not disclose his source. Within six months of his sleepless night poring over the first reports, he had become sufficiently familiar with atomic theory to be able to run other sources, but before he was able to do so he still had to overcome some serious obstacles. "Gorsky brought me materials, and they contained technical terms, overlays and other drawings. And he would tell me, 'You're an engineer. You figure them out. Prepare information for a telegram giving a survey of the situation… I must admit that at that time I had no idea of what we were dealing with. For me it was ordinary technical information like, for example, radar or jet aviation. Later on, when I really got into the problem properly and had specialized sources, I began to understand everything.'"[2]

In March 1942 the NKVD prepared a memorandum for Stalin on the West's development of an atomic bomb. Apart from the descriptive element, this paper contained proposals for what the Soviets should do next, suggesting that a consultative body on atomic problems should be set up and attached to the State Committee for Defense, and that prominent experts should be allowed to study the NKVD's material so it could be evaluated and exploited.

In February 1942 the Plenipotentiary for Scientific Affairs of the State Committee for Defense, Sergei V. Kaftanov, learned of the discovery during a raid on the Ukrainian town of Taganrog of the body of a German engineering officer named Vandervelde. He had been carrying a briefcase containing an exercise book filled with incomprehensible notes. Experts who studied the pages concluded that they were of considerable value, because they indicated that work was in progress in Germany on a military atomic project. As Taganrog is in the heart of a mining area, Kaftanov concluded that the officer had been prospecting for uranium and reported this to the State Committee for Defense. It was this German interest that finally convinced the normally suspicious Beria of the feasibility of developing an atomic bomb, prompting him to submit the information received from the London *rezidentura* to Stalin.

The Soviet physicist Georgi Flyorov, who had volunteered for the armed forces at the beginning of the war, and was attending a course at the Air Force Academy in Yoshkar-Olu near the border with Mongolia, had always been convinced of the possibilities offered by atomic energy, and he confided in Igor V. Kurchatov, a member of the Committee for Defense, as well as to the Director of Kazan's Physical-Technical Institute, Abram Joffe. In May 1942, while in Voronezh and browsing through scientific literature in the university library, he noticed that foreign publications on atomic issues had disappeared. This was a clear sign that research in this field had become classified. He wrote another letter to the State Committee for Defense, raising the question of developing an atomic bomb. This second letter, which contained the sentence "It is essential to manufacture a uranium bomb without delay," was passed on to Stalin and coincided with Beria's submissions and those made by Kaftanov. Flyorov's timely intervention hastened the decision to tackle the problem of building a Soviet atomic bomb, thus ensuring the collection of relevant intelligence. According to Barkovsky, "a conference occurred in Stalin's office, with the same Joffe, Semyenov, Khlopin and Kapitsa participating. They were acquainted with the available information. The decision was made to begin work on the atomic problem immediately."[3]

On November 26, 1942, a special questionnaire was sent to New York, and another went to London two days later, containing instructions to assess the chances of acquiring new sources. It so happened that on the day after receiving the questionnaire, Gorsky was able to report that Professor James Chadwick, together with three young scientists, had left for Canada to work on the atomic project.

In order to carry out their new task, the NKVD set up a special sub-*rezidentura* in New York, designated "XY" for scientific and technical intelligence and headed by Kvasnikov, who was to become a great enthusiast for the atomic project and was posted to Amtorg between March 1943 and October 1945, ostensibly as an engineer, leaving Lev Vasilevsky in his place. Moscow Center's work on the atomic problem, codenamed ENORMOZ, was supervised by the Head of the 3rd Department of the NKVD's First Directorate, and later by the Deputy Head of Intelligence, Gaik Ovakimyan, while a staff intelligence officer, Major Yelena M. Potapova, was directly responsible for the processing and translation of all the material. At certain stages she was assisted by Andrei Graur, a 3rd Department officer who had been implicated in an espionage case in Sweden before the war, and had fled London in

June 1943 following the arrest of Douglas Springhall, a CPGB activist and one of his key sources in London. According to the NKVD archives, Yelena Modrzhinskaya, Dmitri F. Ustinov and an aide named Cohen were initiated into certain purely operational aspects of the case, while Ovakimyan reported on all operational questions and intelligence material received directly to the Head of the First Directorate, Pavel Fitin. Either through him, or the head of the NKVD, Vsevolod N. Merkulov, all the material reached Beria, who coordinated the entire project.

Outside the NKVD only three civilians knew about the collection of atomic intelligence: the Deputy Chairman of the Council of People's Commissars and People's Commissar for the Chemical Industry, Mikhail G. Pervukhin; his personal secretary, A. I. Vasin; and, of course, Kurchatov. The concentration of the NKVD's efforts brought its first results in the beginning of 1943 when Barkovsky established contact with a valuable source, codenamed ERIC, of information on atomic research in Britain. The Center had learned of ERIC in December 1942 when the *rezidentura* had reported that a Communist sympathizer had passed a detailed report on atomic research in Britain and America. The unnamed scientist intended to send the material to the CPGB but it had been relayed to the Soviets, which suggested that the scientist had been ideologically motivated. With ENORMOZ in mind, Gorsky had asked the Center for permission to establish direct contact with this scientist; when approval had been given, Gorsky asked his contact to meet the scientist again and ask him to agree to a meeting with a Soviet intelligence officer. In a letter to the Center dated March 10, 1943, the *rezidentura* reported on the meeting with ERIC, recalling that "At first he hesitated, saying that he would have to think it over and that he saw no need for meeting anybody since he had already written all he knew about the atomic problem. Later in the conversation his attitude changed and he said that he hoped it would not be an Englishman since his English comrades were very careless. Finally, after assurances that everything would be properly organized, he said that he would be glad to meet our comrade."

The meeting took place in January 1943 at a London tube station, and after the usual signs and passwords had been exchanged, the scientist was judged to be straightforward and friendly, although obviously nervous. He verified all the arrangements for the meeting, which lasted more than an hour and a half, during which nothing was called directly by its name, but "ERIC knew with whom he had agreed to cooperate." Barkovsky remembers that when he met his new source for the first time he had been asked whether he understood nuclear physics and, upon receiving an unsatisfactory reply, the scientist said that he wanted his contact not to be just a transmitting channel, but to understand what it was all about. He urged the intelligence officer to study *Applied Nuclear Physics* by Pollard and Davidson. Barkovsky took his advice, and was grateful to ERIC for insisting on this as the American textbook turned out to be a great help to him in running his source. "He told me, 'We'll go through the book together, and then it will be considerably easier for you to deal with me.' I also did not see any other way out. I was completely swamped with work, but I started poring over the textbooks."[4]

ERIC passed on the secret material to which he had direct access. Being of a daring nature and something of an adventurer, he took what was kept in the safes of his colleagues. Barkovsky recalls how, when the scientist told him about this opportunity, and brought him the impression of a door key, a duplicate was required. It was too dangerous to have this work done in a local shop, and it would take too long to send the impression to the Center, as the wartime diplomatic bag had to be sent via the USA and the Far East before it finally reached Moscow several months later. However, as a young man Barkovsky had been a sixth grade fitter, and he did the job himself, fashioning a duplicate that fit perfectly.

> As a result of the decision taken by us we manufactured a copy of the key for ERIC and worked out arrangements for meetings so that we can contact him three times a week in London without prior notification. As a result we managed to remove from ERIC all the available American materials ... and other interesting materials on ENORMOZ.

ERIC's importance as a source is confirmed by a reference to him in an internal NKVD memorandum entitled *On the composition of the agent network for ENORMOZ of the First Directorate of the NKVD of the USSR (as of August 1945)*:

> During the period of his cooperation with us he supplied an enormous quantity of most valuable, genuine documents in the form of American and British reports on the work on ENORMOZ and, in particular, on the construction of uranium piles.

Describing ERIC's relationship with the NKVD, Barkovsky noted in a letter to the Center that he had been motivated by ideology, and was scrupulous when it came to money:

> ERIC as before works for us with enthusiasm, but still turns down the slightest hint of financial reward. Once we gave him more to cover his expenses than he had asked for. He showed his displeasure and stated that he was suspicious of our desire to give him financial help. He asked us to stop once and for all our attempts to do so. In view of this we fear that any gift to him as a sign of gratitude for his work would have a negative effect. ERIC is completely unselfish and extremely scrupulous in regard to anything that might appear as "payment" for his work.[5]

Although ERIC's true name has not been disclosed, it is highly likely that, based on recent Russian efforts to conceal his original codename, and the poor security exercised at the time of the choice of cryptonyms which was left to the often limited imaginations of individual Soviet case officers, that it was indeed "Eric." According to Barkovsky, ERIC was a young physicist and CPGB member who volunteered information from inside the British atomic research program, but also had access to data from the U.S., and was able in 1943 to assert that "the Americans are far ahead." He was "a person who had come to us by himself, without any recruitment. He wanted to help and correct the injustice."

> In his opinion, justice lay in preventing Russia's allies from knowing very important work of a defense nature. At our first meeting he began explaining something to me with much enthusiasm, but I had

> only the slightest idea about the structure of the nucleus... He not only gave me technical data, but explained the sense of it, so that I could comprehend what we were discussing. I prepared my own glossary that proved to be extremely useful. All the terms were new ones that no one had ever heard of before. And these people did not cost the treasury one pound. They were our kind of people, brave people with initiative who considered that giving aid to the Soviets was a moral and political duty. Understandably this pertains, I hope, not only to atomic scientists.[6]

There has been speculation, based on the need to make a duplicate key for him, that ERIC was a relatively junior technician who enjoyed excellent access to classified documents. Barkovsky describes him as "extremely well informed about the most diverse aspects of the work that was being done by the English in that area. He is the person with whom I worked... He was an excellent person and it was very pleasant to work with him. I remember him with gratitude... He was two years older than me."[7]

Despite Barkovsky's description, there is belief in the scientific community that ERIC was Professor Sir Eric Rideal, one of the most distinguished chemists of his generation, and a wartime colleague of the Marxists J. D. Bernal and J. B. S. Haldane. Born in 1890 and educated at Oundle and Trinity Hall, Cambridge, Rideal was the son of Dr. Samuel Rideal, who was also an admired research chemist and a leading authority on drainage and sanitation. During the Great War, Eric Rideal had served in the Royal Engineers and had been gassed in France. Later he was known to be an admirer of Conrad Noel, "the red vicar of Thaxted," and was part of the group of anti-war scientists that had gathered around Bernal. As Professor of Colloid Science at Cambridge between 1930 and 1946, he was closely associated with atomic research and an expert on heavy water. Thus he was certainly in a position to supply sensitive information to the Soviets, although there is no direct evidence to confirm he was indeed the mysterious ERIC. Nearly fifty at the outbreak of the Second World War, he was hardly a young man, nor even close to Barkovsky's age. Nevertheless, there is one other tantalizing clue to the scale and membership of the GRU's network in England, which is known from VENONA to have been run jointly by Colonel Ivan Sklyarov's legal *rezidentura* at the embassy, and by the illegals Ruth and Leon Beurton. The GRU *rezident*'s spy ring, known as the "X Group," consisted of Professor J. B. S. Haldane (codenamed INTELLIGENTSIA), the Hon. Ivor Montagu (NOBILITY), a Czech intelligence officer named Karel Sedlacek (BARON) and Colonel Kenneth G. Post, a territorial Royal Artillery officer attached to the Ministry of Supply as a tank expert (RESERVIST). Working in parallel was Ruth Beurton, née Kuczynsky (codenamed SONIA), who ran Klaus Fuchs and a handful of other agents. According to her memoirs, *Sonia's Report*, her husband "also had contact with a chemist who gave him information."[8] This may have been Eric Rideal.

Another of the London *rezidentura*'s sources, codenamed MOOR and also run by Barkovsky, passed on information about the separation of uranium-235 and the efforts made by the Americans and British to find new deposits. A third ENORMOZ source in Britain was KELLY who, like ERIC, supplied important atomic documents and in June 1945 handed over more than 35 reports and scientific correspondence on atomic developments. "Computations and a technical description of the device itself were received from America. But we compiled all the necessary information for its industrial manufacture. The atomic bomb is, after all, materials that did not exist previously, the methods to obtain and process them, and new technological processes. The English provided all of that to us. Our agent network consisted of volunteers. The people genuinely wanted to help us. No one had to be urged to do so. A very large amount of information came flowing in… We were interested in everything: engines, radar, chemistry, microbiology, innovations in aviation, shipbuilding, etc." When asked to quantify the amount of documents he handled, Barkovsky replied, "That would be hard to do. I think about 5,000 pages of technical documentation were collected."[9]

Barkovsky has suggested that he was personally responsible for running between fifteen and eighteen different sources in London, and has described his recruitment of an unnamed radio engineer:

"He did not have an idea of who I was or what I was planning to ask him about. He told me, 'Our Royal Navy has created a special anti-magnetic system to protect ships against German mines. You will encounter the same problem so I have brought you detailed information about how this is done, and what material is used. Here are the diagrams, the blueprints...'"[10] Barkovsky will identify neither MOOR nor KELLY, but says that they were introduced by prewar agents.

Having started the ENORMOZ project in the autumn of 1941 on the basis of John Cairncross's reports, the London *rezidentura* remained Moscow's main source of Allied atomic secrets at least until the end of 1944, as confirmed by an assessment entitled *A Plan of Measures for the operational exploitation of the ENORMOZ agent network*, prepared for the NKGB leadership and dated November 5, 1944:

> The positive results which have been obtained in the exploitation of the ENORMOZ agent network as a whole have come mainly from the London *rezidentura*. In spite of the participation in the work on the ENORMOZ problem of a large number of scientific organizations and scientists in America, according to most of the information reaching us from agent sources, developments there are slow which is why the greater part of information on that country does not come from the *rezidentura* in the USA but from the *rezidentura* in Britain. On the basis of information received from the London *rezidentura*, the Center has repeatedly sent guidelines on its work to the New York *rezidentura* and also sent a trained agent. The New York *rezidentura* has, however, not fully taken advantage of these possibilities. During the whole period of the work on ENORMOZ, they have recruited only one agent and his access is limited.

An example of such guidelines, prepared on the basis of ERIC's material and sent to the U.S., is a letter from the Center, dated July 27, 1943, targeting atomic weapon facilities:

1. The group of Professor A. Compton, the head of the entire Manhattan Project in the Research Committee for National De-

fense where regular reports are received on the results of the work of all research and project groups.

2. The Columbia group of which Professor Dunning and Professor Urey are members.
3. The Chicago group.
4. The California group.
5. The Kellogg Company.

Even in 1945, when the "XY" sub-*rezidentura* in New York had acquired a number of sources, London's importance remained undiminished. A report dated August 1945 from Pavel Fitin, Chief of Intelligence, to Vsevolod Merkulov, People's Commissar for Security, praised the London *rezidentura* for its accomplishments:

> Extremely valuable information on the scientific developments of ENORMOZ reaches us from the London *rezidentura*. The first material on ENORMOZ was received at the end of the 1941 from Cairncross. This material contained valuable and highly significant documentation, both on the essence of the ENORMOZ problem and on the measures taken by the British government to organize and develop the work on atomic energy. This material formed the point of departure for building the basis of, and organizing the work on, the problem of atomic energy in our country.
>
> In connection with the reception in Britain of American and Canadian material on ENORMOZ, in accordance with the exchange program of technical information, we are receiving material from the London rezidentura which throws light on the state and course of the work on ENORMOZ in three countries: Britain, the USA and Canada.

Vladimir Barkovsky, who is the best informed KGB officer on the history of the Soviet bomb, distinguishes between the information obtained in the USA and in Britain up to the end of 1945: "In the USA we obtained information on how the bomb was made and in Britain of what it was made, so that together they covered the whole problem."

The *rezidentura* reported that the work on rapid neutrons was conducted in Liverpool by Professors Chadwick, Fish, and Joseph

Rotblat, and on the separation of isotopes by Franz Simon, while in Cambridge Professors J. B. S. Haldane, Lev Kowarski, and Allan Nunn May were concentrating on slow neutrons. It was also noted that some of the scientists had been moved to Canada, together with Professor Chadwick and Niels Bohr, who had escaped from Denmark with the help of SIS. According to a report from Kim Philby dated November 20, 1945, SIS had set up a new section with the symbol TAL (Tube Alloys Division) to disseminate information on atomic research undertaken abroad, principally the Soviet Union. Headed by Commander Eric Welsh RNVR, formerly the head of SIS's Norwegian section, it was located at SIS's London headquarters in Broadway, Victoria. Philby's illuminating report served to remind the Soviets that it was essential to surround the work being carried out in the Soviet Union with the strictest secrecy.

In July 1943, the newly promoted head of the 3rd Department of the NKVD's First Chief Directorate, Gaik Ovakimyan, now expelled from the USA, prepared a memorandum for the head of the security apparatus, Vsevolod Merkulov, while the Chief of Intelligence, Pavel Fitin, submitted a more detailed paper on August 11, 1943, together with a review of work on the atomic problem. Both documents suggested handing over all the work on ENORMOZ to the First Chief Directorate, a proposal prompted by the need to coordinate and concentrate all the atomic intelligence. The principal recommendation was to transfer the GRU's sources to the NKVD. Merkulov gave his approval on August 13, noting that the GRU chief, Leonid Ilyichev, "does not object in principle. You should arrange a meeting with him to discuss the details." This solution proved to be timely because soon after the conversation between Merkulov and Ilyichev, the secret lines of the NKVD and the GRU accidentally crossed in London, a muddle caused by Klaus Fuchs.

In the beginning of 1943 the London *rezident*, Konstantin M. Kukin, codenamed IGOR, reported that when checking a list received from ERIC of people working on ENORMOZ, his attention had been drawn to Klaus Fuchs, a refugee who unexpectedly turned out to be an illegal member of the German Communist Party. According to ERIC, Fuchs was working on rapid neutrons at

Birmingham University. When the *rezident* investigated, he learned that Fuchs was known to Jurgen Kuczynsky, the German émigré Communist leader codenamed KARO. Kuczynsky, however, who was not a formal agent, categorically refused to talk about Fuchs and behaved so strangely that it was concluded that KARO knew Fuchs was working for the Soviets. This prompted Kukin to ask the Center to check on Fuchs, an inquiry that, at the end of November 1943, revealed that Fuchs had been a GRU agent since August 1941, when he had been approached on Kuczynsky's recommendation through the Soviet ambassador, Ivan Maisky. According to the GRU file on Fuchs, Maisky was not on good terms with the NKVD *rezident* Ivan Chichayev, so he passed on Kuczynsky's information to the GRU *rezident* Ivan Sklyarov who ordered his secretary, Semyon Kremer, to meet Fuchs. Kremer had been born in Gomel in February 1900 and at age seventeen had joined the Gomel section of the Red Guard. In November 1918 he enlisted with the Red Army and became a Party member in 1919, fighting on the western front during the Civil War. He graduated from the Frunze Military Academy in 1934 and joined the GRU in 1936. The following year the then head of the GRU, General Uritsky, personally had selected him for a posting in London as the military attaché's secretary.

When Kuczynsky next visited the embassy, Maisky introduced him to Kremer who arranged to meet Fuchs with him in a quiet side street. Maisky later recalled, "I am quite clear that Fuchs never came to the embassy. We agreed via Dr. Kuczynsky how and where to meet, and did so on a quiet street in west London at night. I took great care in preparing for the meeting and kept checking for surveillance on my way there." This encounter was described in a VENONA text transmitted to Moscow in August 1941 by Colonel Sklyarov, codenamed BRION:

> On 8th August BARCh had a meeting with a former acquaintance, Doctor FUCHS who [1 group unidentified] that [10 groups unrecovered] in Birmingham [34 groups unrecovered] in three months time and then all the material will be sent to CANADA for industrial production, [1 group unidentified] the fact that in GERMANY, in

LEIPZIG [9 groups unrecovered] Professor HEISENBERG [34 groups unrecovered] 1000 tons of dynamite. Report when opportunity occurs. BRION

At the meeting Fuchs told Kremer that work on building the atomic bomb had started in the U.S. and UK. Asked by Kremer why he had decided to disclose this information, he replied that it was imperative for the Soviet Union to have its own bomb to ensure its own security. In the statement he made to the police in January 1950, Fuchs explained that "at that time I did not have the slightest doubt that Soviet foreign policy was correct and I was convinced that the Western allies were consciously doing their utmost to see that the Soviet Union and Germany would completely exhaust themselves in their struggle to the death. I never had the least hesitation about passing on to the Soviet representatives all the information in my possession though I tried, at least at the outset, only to tell them about the results of my own research."

At his next meeting with Kremer, again on a quiet London street, Fuchs handed him a large notebook with information on the British Tube Alloys project. For the most part, these were his own research notes and copies of reports and papers he had written. Kremer took it all back to the *rezidentura*, from whence it was sent to Moscow by diplomatic bag. The response was a cable ordering contact with Fuchs to be maintained, but in the spring of 1942 it was lost, partly because of conflict that had broken out between the GRU and NKVD *rezidenturas*. Kremer, caught up in the infighting and at one point openly threatened by one of the KGB staff, took advantage of a visit to London by the new GRU Chief, General Golikov, to wangle himself a rapid transfer back to Moscow. Having lost touch with Kremer, Fuchs made a second approach to Kuczynsky; this time the latter put him in touch with his sister, Ursula Beurton. She and Fuchs had their first meeting in the summer of 1941. She ran him until November 1943, passing back his material to the *rezidentura* through Nikolai Aptekar, codenamed SERGEI, the military attaché's driver.

While Ursula Beurton was running Fuchs, she was also responsible for handling another atomic source, codenamed TINA, whose ability to filch secrets from the TUBE ALLOYS project must have been unexpected. Born Melita Sirnis, the daughter of a Latvian émigré, she had long worked as a Soviet agent, having been recruited in 1937, and was mistakenly thought by Moscow to have been compromised when Percy Glading was arrested in 1938 and convicted of running a spy-ring inside the Woolwich Arsenal. Although there were clues to her name in Glading's notebook, MI5 failed to pursue them and when she married a Communist mathematics teacher named Norwood, Melita seems to have dropped from MI5's sight, perhaps while she had a baby in 1943, until the end of the war, apart from being logged as a CPGB member. She was able to join the British Non-Ferrous Metals Research Association in May 1944 as a typist and, as secretary to the chairman, handled atomic data, which she passed to Ursula.

Fuchs received his U.S. visa on November 22, 1943. On the same day he met Ursula to tell her he was going to America. At their next encounter she briefed him on how to get in touch with his American contact, "Raymond," in New York on the first Sunday in February 1944. When revealing the GRU's role in recruiting Fuchs, General Ilyichev reported that Fuchs was to be accompanied to America by a group of other British nuclear physicists, and that arrangements for meeting him in New York had been made already.

The agreement between the NKVD and the GRU to coordinate their atomic espionage conceals more than it reveals, but indicates that each case would be handled separately, depending upon the operational requirements. During the period of his cooperation with the GRU, Fuchs passed on a number of theoretical papers on fission of the atom and construction of a uranium bomb, which were sent to Sergei Kaftanov, and later to the Deputy Chairman of the Council of People's Commissars, Mikhail Pervukhin. A list of the reports received from Fuchs shows that the first were received in Moscow on September 22 and 30, 1941, while Cairncross sent material to Moscow on September 25 and October 3. After a lull, Fuchs became active again in May 1943, only six months after ERIC's original tip, and in Moscow his material was handled by the

NKVD's Directorate S, specifically by three senior officers: Makhnev, Zaveniagin, and Zenov.

According to his file in the NKVD's archive, Fuchs passed information to Ursula Beurton twice in September 1941, and five times in 1943, until his departure for America in November. Once he arrived in the United States on December 7, 1943, responsibility for handling Fuchs passed from the GRU to Semyon Semyonov of the New York *rezidentura*, who deployed Harry Gold as a courier and intermediary, but the two men were unable to meet until February 5, 1944, as Gold subsequently reported:

> We took a long walk after dinner and he explained the FACTORY set-up: He is a member of a British mission to the US working under the direct control of the US Army.
>
> The work involves mainly separating the isotopes of FACTORY and this is being done thus: The electronic method has been developed at Berkeley, California, and is being carried out at a place known only as CAMP Y – K believes it is in New Mexico... Simultaneously the diffusion method is being tried here in the East... Should the diffusion method prove successful, it will be used as a preliminary step in the separation, with the final work being done by the electronic method. They hope to have the electronic method ready early in 1945 and the diffusion method in July 1945 but K says that the latter estimate is optimistic. All production will be done in the US; only preparatory work is being carried on in England. K says that the work will be done in "watertight" compartments, but that he will furnish us with everything in his and Peierls' divisions and as much of the other as possible; Peierls is K's superior, but they have divided the work between them.
>
> The two countries had worked together before 1940, and then there was a lapse until 1942. Even now, K says there is much being withheld from the British. Even Niels Bohr, who is now in the country incognito as Nicholas Baker, has not been told everything.

This account of the meeting was followed on February 9 by a VENONA cable from Leonid Kvasnikov, addressed to General Fitin:

> On 5th February a meeting took place between GOOSE [Harry Gold] and REST [Klaus Fuchs]. Beforehand GOOSE was given a detailed briefing by us. REST greeted him pleasantly but was rather cautious at first, [1 group unrecovered] the discussion GOOSE satisfied himself that REST was aware of whom he was working with. REST arrived in the COUNTRY [America] in September as a member of the ISLAND [British] mission on ENORMOZ. According to him the work on ENORMOZ in the COUNTRY is being carried out under the direct control of the COUNTRY's army represented by General SOMERVELL and STIMSON: at the head of the group of ISLANDERS is a Labour Member of Parliament, Ben SMITH.
> The whole operation amounts to the working out of the process for the separation of isotopes of ENORMOZ. The work is proceeding in two directions: the electron method developed by LAWRENCE [71 groups unrecoverable] separation of isotopes by the combined method, using the diffusion method for preliminary and the electron method for final separation. The work [46 groups unrecovered] 18th February, we shall report the results.

Gold met Fuchs for a second time on Madison Avenue on February 25, and again on March 11 in Woodside, Queens. The physicist handed over fifty pages of information about the Manhattan Project, but complained about unnecessary duplication, having been asked to provide information he had already given the GRU in England. After this third encounter, Gold reported to Semyonov that Fuchs "asked me how his stuff had been received, and I said quite satisfactorily but with one drawback":

> References to the first material, bearing on a general description of the process, were missing, and we especially needed a detailed diagram of the entire plant. Clearly he didn't like this much. His main objection, evidently, was that he had already carried out this job on the other side, and those who receive these materials must know how to connect them to the scheme. Besides, he thinks it would be dangerous for him if such explanations were found, since his work here is not linked to this sort of material. Nevertheless, he agreed to give us what we need as soon as possible.

At another meeting, on March 28 in Central Park, Fuchs told Gold that "his work here is deliberately being curbed by the Americans, who continue to neglect cooperation and do not provide in formation" and speculated that he might have to return to England by July, or be transferred to CAMP Y. Gold's regular fortnightly meetings with Fuchs continued uninterrupted in Brooklyn's Borough Hill Park, although the New York *rezidentura* was concerned about the attention that Kvasnikov and Semyonov had attracted from the FBI:

> For the time being ANTON and TWAIN are not being shadowed anymore but shadowing of CALISTRATUS [Alexander Feklisov] has started. One is forced to the conclusion that the GREENS [FBI] is carrying out trial surveillance.

On May 8, 1944, the New York *rezident* Stepan Z. Apresyan described how Fuchs had revealed a policy disagreement between the British and American scientists on the future of the weapons development program:

> REST advises that the work of the Commission of the ISLANDERS [British] in the COUNTRY [America] is not meeting with success in view of the unwillingness of workers of the COUNTRY to share secrets with the ISLANDERS.
> It will be proposed to REST that he should either return to the ISLAND or work at the special laboratory-camp for study [35 groups unrecoverable] the work of REST from the two indicated.

The next month, on June 15, Apresyan expanded on the crisis that Fuchs claimed had hit inter-allied relations on the project:

> [1 group unrecovered] received from REST [Klaus Fuchs] the third part of Report 'SN—12 Efferent Fluctuation in a Steam [37 groups unrecoverable] Diffusion Method—work his specialty. REST expressed doubt about the possibility of remaining in the COUNTRY [USA] without arousing suspicion. According to what REST says, the ISLANDERS [British] and TOWNSMEN [Americans] have fi-

> nally fallen out as a result of the delay in research work on diffusion. The TOWNSMEN have told the representatives of the ISLAND that construction of a plant in the ISLAND "would be in direct contradiction to the spirit of the agreement on ENORMOZ signed together with the Atlantic Charter" At present the ISLAND's director in CARTHAGE [Washington DC] is ascertaining the details of the transfer of work to the ISLAND. REST assumes he will have to leave in a month or six weeks.

This telegram was followed on July 25, 1944, by Apresyan's proposal to pay Fuchs for his six months of cooperation:

> Almost half a year of contact established with REST [Klaus Fuchs] has demonstrated the value of his work for us. We consider it necessary to pay him for this half year the due reward of 500 dollars. He fully deserves this sum. Telegraph consent.

However, the *rezident* never got the chance to pay Fuchs, for neither his cut-out Harry Gold, nor his new handler, Anatoli A. Yatskov of the 8th (Economic) Directorate, alias Anatoli Yakovlev (codenamed ALEKSEI), had managed to make contact as scheduled on August 5. In a telegram to Moscow on August 29, 1944, Apresyan gave an account of Gold's mission to find Fuchs and his visit to his sister, Kristel Heineman, who was then living in Cambridge, Massachusetts:

> In July when it became known that REST [Klaus Fuchs] might be leaving for the ISLAND [Britain], instructions were given to ALEKSEI [Anatoli Yakovlev], and by the letter to GOOSE [Harry Gold], to arrange a password for meeting with REST in case he was leaving. On 5 August REST did not appear at the meeting and GOOSE missed the next meeting. When he checked on REST's apartment, GOOSE was informed that REST had left for the ISLAND. In order to re-check, I sent GOOSE to REST's sister, she and her husband the departure up to 20 September [67 groups unrecoverable] should check his arrival. I did not have time to hand over to REST the 500 dollars authorized by you.

The reason for Semyonov's withdrawal from New York in September 1944 has not been disclosed, but upon his return to Moscow he is known to have described, in a memorandum dated November 1944, the very extensive scope of the FBI's surveillance, and it may be that, because he was forced to abandon some meetings with agents, his operational usefulness was considered at an end. There may also have been a disciplinary reason, for certainly there was some dissatisfaction in Moscow with what was evidently considered the rather casual approach taken by Gold in his handling of Fuchs, as demonstrated by this complaint, dated July 28:

> At one time, when we instructed GOOSE [Harry Gold] to establish contact with REST [Klaus Fuchs], we drew special attention to the need for detailed accounts of REST's work. After establishing his liaison with REST, we receive his information in every mail, but we do not have a single report from GOOSE about his work with REST or about REST himself. Missing also are precise data about where REST works, his address, how and where meetings take place, GOOSE's impressions of REST, etc. Nor do we have the conditions of meeting REST adopted by himself and GOOSE in case of sudden loss.

Clearly Fuchs's disappearance had given Apresyan and Moscow some cause for serious concern, especially as Gold had failed to turn up for their next scheduled meeting. Then Fuchs missed a third rendezvous, as is indicated by a VENONA cable, dated September 22, 1944:

> GOOSE [Harry Gold] will travel to REST's sister on 26th September. The sister has not been traced by means of external surveillance; her whereabouts are unknown; she was to have returned after the 20th. We shall report the outcome of GOOSE's journey immediately.

A telegram from Moscow on November 16, 1944, showed that Gold (now referred to as ARNO, following a comprehensive change in codenames) had discovered that Fuchs (now known as

CHARLES) had not gone to England, as had been anticipated, but had been transferred to New Mexico:

> On ARNO's last visit to CHARLES's sister it became known that CHARLES has not left for the ISLAND [England] but is at Camp No. 2 [Los Alamos]. He flew to Chicago and telephoned his sister. He named the state where the camp is and promised to come on leave for Christmas. He is taking steps to establish liaison with CHARLES while he is on leave. The assumption that CHARLES has left for the ISLAND was due to [40 groups unrecoverable]

On February 27, 1945, Moscow asked the New York *rezidentura* for details of Fuchs's work in Chicago:

> Advise forthwith: exactly where and in what capacity CHARLES is working in the RESERVATION; the object of his trip to CHICAGO and whom he met there; what has he been doing since August; why has the meeting with him been arranged only in June; why did he not have a discussion [2 groups unrecovered] and by what [4 groups unrecovered]. ARNO, CHARLES's sister (henceforth ANT); how [6 groups unrecovered] ARNO about CHARLES's arrival, how in detail their meeting went off; what materials were received from CHARLES.

On March 31, Moscow noted Fuchs's value, referring specifically to the Manhattan Project's K-25 gaseous diffusion plant at Clinton, Tennessee:

> We are sending herewith an evaluation on ENORMOZ. Referenced are materials from CHARLES about the FUNICULAR:
>
> 3. 5/46 [31 groups unrecovered]
> 3. 5/60 [6 groups unrecovered]—contains an interesting method of calculation, which will be used during the design.
> c) 5/62 technical data on the FUNICULAR and 12 groups unrecovered]
> d) 7/83, paragraph 1—about the degree of separation of the membrane offers substantial interest.

3. 7/84 paragraph 1—about tests of the membrane and information about the layout of the plant—is of interest. What is needed is [7 groups unrecovered] plan of the plant.
3. 7/83 and 84—on the theory of the stability of the FUNICULAR together with CHARLES' materials on this question received earlier they form a full and valuable place of information.
3. YOUNG's [Theodore Hall] report about work [4 groups unrecovered]. [1 group unrecovered] great interest.

The value of Fuchs's information became clear in a VENONA cable from Moscow dated April 10, 1945, in which the topic of interest was not just uranium separation, but also the method of detonation:

> CHARLES's information under No. 2/57 on the atomic bomb (henceforth BALLOON) is of great value. Apart from the data on the atomic mass of the nuclear explosive and on the details of the explosive method of actuating BALLOON it contains information received for the first time from you about the electro-magnetic method of separation of ENORMOZ. We wish in addition to establish the following: 1. What kind of fission—by means of fast or slow neutrons—[35 groups unrecovered] [281 groups unrecoverable]

It is clear from the two messages above that in March and April 1945 the New York *rezidentura* was receiving detailed, valuable information from, among others, Ted Hall and Klaus Fuchs from Los Alamos, at a critical moment in the development of the bomb. Tremendous progress had been made on the electric detonator, designed to initiate simultaneous explosions within a millionth of a second, and Hanford had reported that major deliveries of plutonium would begin in May. Accordingly, the pressure from Moscow to cultivate new sources became intense, and Kvasnikov recalls that there was a proposal "that Gold, accompanied by his elderly mother, would move to Santa Fe, to the very sanatorium essential for her treatment. The idea was that Santa Fe was close to Los Alamos where Fuchs could easily go for sightseeing or just to spend a weekend."

Compared to the work undertaken in London on gathering atomic intelligence, the initial effort in the United States was really of minimal significance, as Moscow often reminded the New York *rezidentura*. The NKVD's Moscow archives show that the issue was raised on March 27, 1942, when the Center directed:

> Currently they are working extremely hard in England, Germany and the US on the problem of extracting Uranium-235 and its use as an explosive to produce bombs of enormous destructive force. Therefore the problem seems close to practical solution. We need to take up this problem with all seriousness.

In the months that followed, little was achieved in New York, as the Center noted in a memorandum dated November 26, 1942:

> We attach great importance to the problem of Uranium-235 and although we are having some rather good opportunities to cultivate agents working on the problem in the U.S., we haven't yet begun such cultivation.

Actually, this report was not entirely accurate for there had been some progress made with Clarence Hiskey, then Professor of Chemistry at Columbia University, and an enthusiastic member of the CPUSA. In March 1942 Hiskey had described research then being undertaken at Columbia on an atomic weapon to his contact, Zelmond Franklin, codenamed CHAP, who in turn had relayed the gist of his information to the New York *rezidentura*:

> 1. That the Germans were far ahead in this bomb.
> 2. That his researchers, together with a number of leading chemists and physicists, were working with desperate haste.
> 3. The radioactive bomb had not been perfected in their laboratory, but considerable progress has been made.
>
> The Germans may be advanced sufficiently to be ready to use it.

Franklin, who had worked at the Soviet pavilion during the 1939 World's Fair, claimed that Hiskey had told him that "scientists in the Columbia research lab have advanced far enough to be planning to try it out in some vast desert area" and that there was a fear among those who knew of the project that "it might truly destroy millions of people at a crack."

On April 15, 1942, Moscow responded to the tip from Franklin and the New York *rezident*, Vasili Zarubin, was informed that:

> The matter of major American work on Uranium-235 is correct, though strongly exaggerated regarding achievements. They work intensively on the matter in England, Germany and the US. The problem of using uranium energy for military purposes is of great interest for us. We need the following data on the matter:
>
> 1. Isolation of the main source of uranium energy – Uranium-235 from uranium. Achievements of the Americans on this matter. Laboratory and factory methods of isolation. Industrial equipment for the isolation process.
> 2. At what stage of development is current research on the use of uranium energy in bombs?
> 3. By whom and where is the work carried out on elaborating the uranium bomb's shell?
> 4. The way to produce the uranium bomb's explosion – i.e., fusion.
> 5. Methods and protective measures from uranium radioactivity in the process of production.
> 6. What is known about the Germans' work on the uranium bomb, and what are their advantages in comparison with American work, as Hiskey says?
> 7. What is known about factory production of laboratory work on the uranium bomb?

This comprehensive questionnaire, doubtless drafted by Beria's scientists, formed the basis of the *rezidentura*'s continued contact with Hiskey, who was assigned the codename RAMSEY, and at one point suggested that Franklin should himself infiltrate Columbia's project, before rejecting the idea because such an attempt might attract unwelcome scrutiny from the FBI. Hiskey also advised that even if Franklin succeeded in penetrating the Manhattan Project, he probably "would not see the results. Only the leading personnel get to see the results."

Originally from Milwaukee, Franklin had fought with the Abraham Lincoln Battalion in Spain, but his usefulness as an agent came to an abrupt conclusion in 1947 when the managing editor of the *Daily Worker*, Louis Budenz, who had been a member of the CPUSA since 1935, converted to Catholicism and denounced the Party. In his autobiography, *This is My Story*,[11] Budenz named the man he had known as "Irving" Franklin as having operated as an NKVD agent in Canada, and correctly identified Franklin's ex-wife Sylvia Callen as a spy who had infiltrated the Trotskyites. In addition, Franklin was identified to the FBI as an NKVD agent by one of his contacts, James O. York, who recalled that Franklin had used the alias "Warner."

Hiskey, whose family name had been changed from Szczechowski, was also from Milwaukee. A first-rate physicist, he had earned his doctorate in 1939 from the University of Wisconsin, where he had met his wife Marcia Sand, also a CPUSA activist, and was granted a reserve commission in the Chemical Warfare Service. He was appointed director of research into rhenium at the University of Tennessee's laboratory at Knoxville, and in autumn 1941 had taken up a post teaching chemistry at Columbia University; the following year he joined Dr. Harold Urey's SAM project, concentrating on the gaseous diffusion method of separating uranium-235, which was to be incorporated into the K-25 plant at Oak Ridge, Tennessee. It was during this period in New York, working with Urey, that Hiskey was recruited by Franklin.

This work was moved to the Metallurgical Laboratory at Chicago in May 1943, where Hiskey continued his union activism on behalf of the Federation of Architects, Engineers, Chemists and Technicians (FAECT) and a CPUSA educational front, the Abraham Lincoln School, but his participation in atomic research was swiftly terminated in April 1944 after he had been compromised by holding meetings with a GRU illegal, Artur Adams (see Chapter VI). Hiskey had played a key role in developing the U-235 separation plant at Oak Ridge, and had worked on the Metallurgical Project at the University of Chicago.

Hiskey's link with Adams, with whom he was spotted on several occasions, was cut when the scientist was called up for military service, posted to the Quartermaster Corps and sent to a remote arctic base near Mineral Springs in Alaska where he sorted winter underwear. During a posting to Whitehorse, in the Yukon, he was the subject of a clandestine search, and was found to have "had in his effects a personal notebook which contained notes that he had made while working on the atomic bomb project at Chicago, Illinois, relative to the development of several components of the bomb."

After he protested about the waste of his talent, Hiskey was transferred to an army installation in Hawaii manufacturing soap for troops in the Pacific. He was discharged in May 1946 and began teaching analytical chemistry at the Brooklyn Polytechnic Institute in New York. In 1950, having refused to testify about Adams before Congress, he was indicted for contempt, but the charge was dismissed in April 1951. Similarly, Edward T. Manning, who worked as a technician on the Metallurgical Project at Columbia and Chicago, had been introduced to Adams by Hiskey but when they met in New York they must have been under surveillance, for he was suspended. In January 1945 he was drafted into the army and had one final meeting with Adams, who declared that it was still not too late for him to supply details from his former work. Manning angrily blamed Adams for wrecking his career, and later reported his encounter to the FBI.

Despite having established RAMSEY as a reliable source, albeit one that was going to come under intensive FBI and U.S. Army scrutiny, Moscow remained dissatisfied, and on July 1, 1943, protested to the New York *rezidentura* that although ENORMOZ was known to employ more than five hundred people, and be costing many millions of dollars, "the prolonged pace of agent cultivation in the U.S. is particularly intolerable." Six weeks later, on August 11, General Fitin acknowledged to Vsevolod Merkulov that "the state of agent cultivation on this problem and its prospects… [is] unsatisfactory, especially in the U.S."

Moscow's displeasure at New York's lack of performance was exacerbated by a curious incident which occurred in August 1944 when an anonymous donor handed in a package of secret Manhattan Project documents to the Consulate General at 7 East 61st Street.

The Center was unimpressed by the way the *rezidentura* had handled the unexpected gift and sent a rebuke, emphasizing its purported ineptitude in not seizing a recruitment opportunity:

> The receipt of material on ENORMOZ from a source unknown to you, first of all, reflects your unsatisfactory work on this subject, with available possibilities neither being discovered nor used by you, letting the cultivation of this primary problem drift. The tranquility or indifference with which you reported to us about this material and the circumstances of its receipt... surprised us very much. If somebody dared to make such a risky move to bring this most secret document to the PLANT (Consulate General), how could you... not take every step to determine who the unknown person was? We attach great importance to this event. The stranger's material is exceptionally interesting, and our data, received from other sources, support its contents. Therefore, take every measure to locate this person. Report the results immediately.

This episode is curiously reminiscent of an incident reported by Vasili Mitrokhin, who took notes of another anonymous donation, which he dated as sixteen months earlier, in April 1943. He says an anonymous woman delivered a letter to the Consulate General containing classified information, and then returned a month later with a further delivery detailing aspects of plutonium research. The *rezidentura* discovered that she was a nurse named Lucia, the daughter of a well-known left-wing Italian trade union leader. A meeting was arranged under the sponsorship of the Friends of the USSR Society, at which point Lucia had revealed that her sister Regina was married to an American scientist employed by Du Pont, who had used her as an intermediary to send information to the Soviets. He was given the codename MAR, and continued to supply secrets even after he had been posted to Hanford in October 1943. The *rezidentura* apparently assigned the codename MONA to Regina and OLIVIA to Lucia, although none of them appear in any of the VENONA traffic.

On November 5, 1944, Pavel Fitin made a further complaint about the indifferent results achieved in America, noting that the credit for recruiting Klaus Fuchs could not be taken by the New York *rezidentura*:

> Despite participation by a large number of scientific organizations and workers on … the problem of ENORMOZ in the U.S., mainly known to us by agent data, their cultivation develops poorly. Therefore, the major part of the data on the U.S. comes from the *rezidentura* in England. On the basis of information from the London *rezidentura*, the Center more than once sent to the New York *rezidentura* a work orientation and sent a ready agent too. The New York *rezidentura* didn't use those opportunities completely. For the period of cultivating agents on ENORMOZ, it drew only one agent—PERS—not having great possibilities.

Fitin's pessimism was not shared by Semyon Semyonov, who recorded in a November 1944 memo that "the agent situation for developing work on technical intelligence in America [is] more favorable than at the beginning of the war." His opinion may have been colored by his own direct involvement with the spy codenamed PERS, allegedly the sole recruitment accomplished by the New York *rezidentura* prior to November 1944. Originally codenamed VOGEL ("bird" in German), PERS was a young engineer and CPUSA member whose father had been close to the Party's General Secretary, Earl Browder. When asked for guidance, Semyonov had advised PERS to join the Kellogg Construction Company, then considered a target by the NKVD because of its involvement in contracts for ENORMOZ, and by June 1944 he had found a job with a Kellogg subsidiary, the Kellex Corporation. On June 16, Pavel Fedosimov reported to Moscow that VOGEL had supplied "two secret plans of the ENORMOZ plant." There is no obvious explanation for the sudden appearance of Fedosimov, who was also engaged at that time in handling Donald Maclean on his weekend visits to New York. Three months later, in September 1944, the *rezidentura* reported to Moscow that

> [i]n August we did not receive any materials from VOGEL. He informs us that his enterprises are moving indecisively forward. Construction of the ENORMOZ experimental plant is proceedings slowly as if by its own momentum. They say this happens because great changes and alterations in the plant's initial construction are expected.

By February 1945 VOGEL/PERS had rejected an invitation from Kellex to go to what he called "an atomic camp" which Feklisov thought was Los Alamos. All attempts to persuade him to change his mind failed, the young man protesting that he did not want to lose his comfortable apartment, and that there was insufficient accommodation at the new site for his wife and baby. He also insisted that he did not want to lose $20,000, which he said he had invested in a new business with another Communist, and even a meeting with Anatoli Yatskov on March 11 could not dissuade him. On this occasion he argued that his wife had fallen ill, and that, moreover, an offer to volunteer for Los Alamos would look suspicious because the posting was considered very unpopular among his colleagues. Apparently VOGEL/PERS produced some more ENORMOZ plans in May 1945, but thereafter simply dropped from sight, only to emerge again decades later as a tantalizing spy suspect for the FBI to try and identify in the VENONA traffic.

VOGEL/PERS may be the same person as a spy handled by Aleksandr Feklisov, who recounted in his memoirs, *The Man Behind the Rosenbergs*, that one of his star agents was VULTURE (*khvat* in Russian). In his book Feklisov changed the codename to protect him, but described him as not motivated by "any political or ideological reasons" and working "at the Du Pont chemical plant and passing us information on nylon and the latest varieties of gunpowder. He would hand over a large envelope full of documents to Semyonov during his meetings" and demand cash to pay for his home and his daughter's college education. Apart from the coincidence of the codename, with *khvat* being a bird, both agents were handled by Semyonov, and apparently motivated by money. The differences in their alleged backgrounds, such as VOGEL/PERS working for Kellex and VULTURE for Du Pont, may be a further deliberate attempt by Feklisov to conceal his agent's true identity.[12]

Another abortive source in New York during this early period was a chemist, William Malisoff, codenamed TALENT (and later HENRY), who ran Unified Laboratories Inc. from 1775 Broadway. One of Ovakimyan's agents, he had offered to expand his business, which developed lubricating process for war industries, with help from the Soviets but had been turned down, despite his protest that he had given them millions of dollars' worth of intelligence. Initially interested, the Center had been embarrassed by Malisoff's enthusiasm and lack of security. One of Malisoff's subsources, codenamed TAL-1, had been the subject of a report submitted by the NKVD's illegal *rezident*, Jacob Golos, who had been told by one of his contacts, Julius Rosenberg, that TAL-1 had introduced Malisoff as one of his financial backers, and had mentioned him as having been associated with Mikhail Kaganovich, the Commissar for the Aviation Industry. At that time, in early 1942, Julius Rosenberg had not been recruited by the NKVD and was merely a keen member of the CPUSA's industrial branch 16B and an organizer, albeit one who was in touch with Golos. Naturally the Center was appalled that Malisoff's covert links, and his role as an agent, should have been disclosed to people "who were not connected with us." Nevertheless, Malisoff appears to have been encouraged to meet "with a number of people working on the problem of ENORMOZ" and was particularly assiduous in his pursuit of Harold Urey and other Manhattan Project scientists. The FBI's investigation of Malisoff proved inconclusive because he died in November 1947.

Apart from RAMSEY, the other key figure in the New York network from the outset was Harry Gold, the Swiss-born biochemist who had been brought to the United States as a child by his Russian refugee parents, and had engaged in industrial espionage in and around Philadelphia, where he lived alone, for the Soviets since 1935, when he had been recruited by his friend Thomas L. Black. At the time he came under suspicion in 1950, he was working in the heart laboratory of the Philadelphia General Hospital, and in the first sixteen of his interviews with the FBI he emphatically denied any knowledge of Soviet espionage or of Klaus Fuchs. He finally cracked when he was confronted with incontrovertible evidence that, despite his many statements to the contrary, he had indeed traveled to Albuquerque in 1944. His subsequent confession was a vital breakthrough for the FBI, and his importance to the Soviets is demonstrated from the content of this VENONA text from the New York *rezidentura* dated December 13, 1944:

> We consider it risky to concentrate all the contacts relating to ENORMOZ on ARNO [Harry Gold] alone. This is good in that it limits the circles of [2 groups unrecovered] but it is dangerous to disrupt [1 group unrecovered] work on ENORMOZ [45 groups unrecoverable]

The implication is that Gold had been entrusted with a large part of the *rezidentura*'s atomic sources, and on that basis it is possible to reconstruct much of it. By December 1944 Gold was running Klaus Fuchs, but he was also in touch with several other sources with access to technology that the NKVD must have valued. First among them was Abraham Brothman, a chemist who had been supplying the Soviets with information since 1935 and had been introduced to Gold as "Frank Kessler" by the illegal *rezident*, Jacob Golos. Codenamed CONSTRUCTOR, Brothman was engaged in biological research, ran his own firm, the Republic Chemical Machinery Company in New York between 1938 and 1942, and had been a member of the Young Communist League (YCL) at Columbia University in 1932. According to a VENONA text from Apresyan dated October 1, 1944, Gold had reported that Brothman's business had suffered some setbacks:

> According to GOOSE's [Harry Gold] latest advice CONSTRUCTOR [Abraham Brothman] has stopped working at the Cheturgy Design Company where jointly with Henry GOLVINE and Art WEBER he was working on the production of BUNA-5. At the same time CONSTRUCTOR collaborated on the Aerosol problem (the work has partly been sent to you) with HENLIG. In both cases his partners cheated CONSTRUCTOR. They appropriated his work

> and chucked him out. Right now CONSTRUCTOR at his laboratory at 114 East 32nd Street with the help of the Grover Tank Company and the Bridgeport Brass Company has organized his own company and in the course of two or three weeks proposes to finish work on Aerosol and DDT and consolidate his position with these. According to GOOSE's advice he had known about the disagreements for three weeks or so but he considered them a temporary quarrel and did not [1 group unrecoverable] us [40 groups unrecoverable] sum of 100 dollars a month. Telegraph your decision. We shall advise in detail by post.

Despite the behavior of his untrustworthy partners, Brothman continued to act as a source of technical information for the New York *rezidentura,* although he was later to be compromised by Elizabeth Bentley who identified him by name as an agent run by Jacob Golos, and implicated his mistress, Miriam Moscowitz. Initially the NKVD believed that, even if Brothman came under investigation, Gold would be safe insofar as the younger man had masqueraded as "Frank Kessler," a married man from Philadelphia in all their dealings. Moscow would eventually learn in 1946 that Gold had abandoned his cover, had taken a job with Brothman's company, and together the pair had even visited the Soviet Purchasing Commission to negotiate the sale of some vitamin products, thereby eliminating the security precautions demanded by the NKVD's rules of *konspiratsiia* or tradecraft.

In June 1950 Gold told his FBI interrogator, T. Scott Miller, that in addition to holding regular meetings with Brothman, he had been assigned in August 1941 another highly motivated Communist chemist, Alfred D. Slack, codenamed AL, following the arrest of his regular handler, Gaik Ovakimyan. Slack had worked at Eastman Kodak at Rochester, New York, and had been collecting industrial secrets of proprietary film manufacturing processes since 1938, but in October 1944 had obtained a job in the Manhattan Project at Oak Ridge, Tennessee. This is the site the NKVD termed CAMP 1, although it was once later described in an NKVD report submitted by Merkulov to Beria as "Woods Hall, in the vicinity of Knoxville, Texas, where a factory is being completed to produce uranium-235."

Slack was arrested by the FBI at Syracuse, New York, on June 15, 1950, and admitted that while he had been working at the Helston Ordnance Works at Kingsport, Tennessee, in 1942, he had sold Gold, whom he knew only as "Martin," a sample of, and the formula for, the RDX explosive. He also named a colleague at Eastman Kodak, Richard D. Briggs, who had died in September 1939, as another of Ovakimyan's sources, and as his controller, codenamed DICK. Slack was subsequently convicted and in September 1950 was sentenced to fifteen years' imprisonment, having generated an FBI file running to 2,969 pages.

Having been identified as "Raymond" from a photograph by Klaus Fuchs, Harry Gold was arrested by Ernie van Loon in Philadelphia on May 22, 1950. His lawyer advised him to cooperate fully with his FBI interrogators, which resulted in his subsequent lengthy confession to Scott Miller and Dick Brennan. Apparently Gold had spent much of his adult life engaged in espionage; even his two years at Xavier University in Cincinnati had been paid for by the NKVD. Of all his Soviet controllers, he had been especially close to "Sam," an MIT graduate whom he identified from photos as Semyon Semyonov, and his various statements to the FBI, including a 123-page autobiographical account entitled *The Circumstances Surrounding My Work as a Soviet Agent*, led to dozens of leads. Among those implicated by Gold were Joseph Katz and his friends and fellow chemists Ferdinand Heller and Tom Black, who also confessed to having been recruited by Ovakimyan, and supplying industrial secrets to the Soviets. According to their statements, both men had approached Amtorg in 1935, volunteering to take their skills to Russia, and had encountered Ovakimyan who had persuaded them to remain in the United States and collect industrial intelligence. In turn, they implicated Vera Kane. In addition, Gold named Ben Smilg, an MIT graduate and aeronautical engineer at the National Aeronautics Center in Dayton, Ohio, and Al Slack.

Despite the euphoria that reigned, there was one aspect of Gold's confession that caused some alarm for the FBI. After having been abandoned by Yakovlev in 1946, because of his continued business ties to Brothman, contrary to instructions, he mentioned that he had been contacted quite unexpectedly in July 1949 and summoned to a meeting in a bar in New York in late July by "John," but nobody had turned up. Two months later, an unknown NKVD officer appeared in Philadelphia and quizzed him about the testimony he had given during the grand jury investigation of Brothman in 1947. They had a further meeting in New York in early October, at which Gold was warned to leave the country if the FBI interviewed any of his friends. Another meeting was planned for the end of the month, but the Russian had failed to turn up. Although Gold did not know his contact's true name, he helped the FBI identify him from its collection of diplomatic passport photos as Filipp Sarytchev, a member of the New York *rezidentura.*

The unavoidable implication of these events was that the Soviets had learned, at a very early stage, of a molehunt underway which finally led to Klaus Fuchs and Gold himself. The unpalatable interpretation was that there was a leak from somewhere inside the investigation and that the NKVD was able to monitor its progress. This view was compounded when David Greenglass, in a statement made on June 16, 1950, to Special Agents Leo Frutkin and John Lewis, recalled that he had been warned by Julius Rosenberg at about the same time (weeks before the arrest of Fuchs and months before the FBI's identification of Gold) that "something had happened" to jeopardize the network and he should prepare an escape plan. It would take another year, until May 1951, for suspicion to fall on Kim Philby, the newly arrived SIS liaison officer in Washington DC, as the likely culprit for the breach in security.

Behind the scenes, and unknown to the prosecution, VENONA had helped the FBI to secure the convictions of Harry Gold, the Rosenbergs, and Klaus Fuchs, where there can be no argument about the correct identifications of the relevant codenames, but there is a possibility that Armed Forces Security Agency (AFSA) analysts made an error in respect to the codename VEKSEL. It was translated by Meredith Gardner as BILL OF EXCHANGE. The codename occurs only in two VENONA texts, and one, from Leonid Kvasnikov dated May 26, 1944, contained information from Theodore Hall:

> A list of places where work on ENORMOZ is being carried out: 1. HANFORD, State of WASHINGTON, production of 49. 2.

State of NEW JERSEY, production of 25 by the diffusion method. Director UREY. 3. BERKELEY, State of CALIFORNIA, production of 25 by the electromagnetic method. Director LAWRENCE. 4. NEW CONSTRUCTION, administrative center for ENORMOZ; also production of 25 by the spectrographic method, Director COMPTON. 5. CHICAGO, ARGONNE Laboratories—nuclear research. At present work there has almost ceased. Director COMPTON. 6. The RESERVATION, the main practical research work on ENORMOZ. Director VEKSEL. 7. Camp [2 groups unrecovered] base in the area of CARLSBAD, State of NEW MEXICO, the place for the practical testing of the ENORMOZ bomb. 8. MONTREAL, CANADA—theoretical research.

This is a curious, and not entirely accurate list, naming Ernest Lawrence, Arthur Compton, and Harold Urey by name, and appears to identify VEKSEL as the director of the site known as the RESERVATION, taken by analysts to mean Robert Oppenheimer, but there is some doubt about precisely what was really meant. The sites mentioned are Hanford, New Jersey, Berkeley, Chicago, Los Alamos, and Montreal, with NEW CONSTRUCTION probably being Oak Ridge, Tennessee, but two prominent names, those of Robert Oppenheimer and Enrico Fermi, are missing.

In numerical order, the text links Urey to New Jersey, Lawrence to Berkeley, and Compton to an administrative center, codenamed NEW CONSTRUCTION, and also to the Argonne, leaving VEKSEL as the director of the RESERVATION, site of the "main practical research work" on the bomb. In addition, there is a reference to Montreal and "Camp" in New Mexico. The problem arises over the correct interpretation of RESERVATION because the identification of VEKSEL as its director depends upon it. If RESERVATION is meant to be Los Alamos, and the NSA's footnote is uncertain on this point, identifying it only as "possibly Los Alamos," then VEKSEL is Robert Oppenheimer. However, if RESERVATION is Chicago, then Fermi is a better candidate for VEKSEL. The only other reference to RESERVATION in the VENONA text, dated February 27, 1945 (see page 64 above), which refers to a visit Klaus Fuchs had made there, but as the very next sentence concerns whom Fuchs met in Chicago, it is by no means certain that the RESERVATION (*zapovednik* in Russian) definitely is a codename for Los Alamos, which appears in several other VENONA texts as "Camp-2."

In short, it is by no means certain that VEKSEL is definitely Oppenheimer. While there is no direct link between Los Alamos and a reservation (and it was not in or near an Indian reservation), the Argonne laboratory was indeed in the midst of a national park, which is the sense of *zapovednik*, an area where forestry is protected and animal hunting banned. Is it possible that RESERVATION is the codename for the Argonne? In any event, VEKSEL must be either Oppenheimer or Fermi.

The second VENONA reference to VEKSEL occurred in an earlier text from Moscow addressed to Leonid Kvasnikov, dated March 21, 1945:

> 3. In our Nos. 5823 of 9 December 1944, 309 of 17 January 1945, and 606 of 1 February 1945 instructions were given to send HURON to Chicago to re-establish contact with VEKSEL. Carry these out as soon as possible. HURON should also make use of his stay in CHICAGO to renew his acquaintance with Goldsmith, who is known to you and who is taking part in the work on ENORMOZ.

This second text suggests that HURON was to visit VEKSEL in Chicago, and also tends to implicate Hyman Goldsmith who is referred to as apparently "known to" Kvasnikov. There is no direct suggestion that Goldsmith was Kvasnikov's source, for if he was it is likely that he would have been assigned a codename. Nevertheless, whoever HURON was, there must be some doubt about identifying Oppenheimer as VEKSEL, as he was not based in Chicago in January and February 1945. On the other hand, there is a good case to be made for radically changing the identification of VEKSEL.

One possibility is that the NSA's translation of VEKSEL is fundamentally mistaken. The original translation as BILL OF EXCHANGE was very old-fashioned and not one ever used in modern, Soviet Russian. A better choice would have been "businessman's obligation" or "promissory note," which implies an element of compulsion. Whereas this description does not fit Oppenheimer, who owed the Soviets nothing, it might be relevant to Fermi, who was always short of money and had fled to the United States from Italy in December 1938, accompanied by his wife, two children, and nanny. After receiving his Nobel Prize in Stockholm, Fermi settled at Columbia, before moving reluctantly to Chicago in April 1942. Furthermore, Fermi had been named by Pavel Sudoplatov in his autobiography as a Soviet source. Could it be that the anti-Fascist Fermi had been assisted to leave Italy by the Soviets, and received a loan that had required repayment?

Chapter IV

Penetrating Los Alamos

In 1942 we were all obsessed by the fear that the Germans were on the same track, and perhaps ahead of us.

Bertrand Goldschmidt

The massive research undertaking, which was to become known by its cover title of the Manhattan District Engineering Project, would eventually employ almost 125,000 people, and be concentrated at five sites outside New Mexico. By far the largest was at Oak Ridge, a 59,000-acre estate in Tennessee, known mysteriously as "Site X" and populated by a staff of 78,000, making it the fifth biggest town in the entire state. The design work had been contracted out to the Kellex Corporation, a specially created subsidiary of the M. W. Kellogg Company, built by the J. A. Jones Construction Company of Charlotte, North Carolina, and operated by the Carbide and Carbon Chemicals Corporation. Oak Ridge also accommodated the enormous Y-12 electromagnetic plant set up by the University of California in what, at two million square feet, would be the world's largest factory building, housing five "racetracks," each containing up to ninety-six Calutrons, and staffed by 22,000 technicians. The hardware was manufactured to order by Westinghouse; the electrical control equipment by General Electric; and the ten-thousand-ton magnets by the Allis-Chambers farm machinery group. The Tennessee Eastman Company ran the whole operation under supervision from the University of Chicago. The initial objective was to build and run an experimental air-cooled graphite pile designed to produce a gram of plutonium a day.

Originally it also had been intended to build the main plutonium plant at Clinton, but the process was considered too dangerous, and a new site, designated "W," was established at Hanford, an area covering 670 square miles on the Columbia River in the state of Washington. The design and construction of the three water-cooled reactors, in separate valleys several miles apart, was entrusted to the E. I. du Pont de Nemours Company, which accepted the contract for a non-profit fee of one dollar. Work began in April 1943. The construction camp was to house a workforce of 60,000, and the town of Richland, developed to accommodate the operating staff, would grow to a population of 17,000, and produce plutonium by the kilogram. By the end of September 1944, the first pile had been initiated, and by Christmas two piles were operating at full capacity. The massively expensive K-25 plant did not become operational until January 20, 1945, following an investment of $200 million and the work of 55,000 people, drawn from three universities and no less than six of the country's largest industrial concerns.

In Canada the initial focus of the weapons project was the University of Montreal, although the arrival of von Halban's team did not go unnoticed by the local newspaper, *Montréal Matin*, which reported on January 8, 1943, that sixty foreign scientists "mostly of Jewish, Russian, French, Polish, Czech and even German origin" had gathered to conduct "intensive research of the highest importance on radioactivity, physics and physical chemistry, under the direction of the great French physicist Pierre Auger, and under the high patronage of the National Research Council." This was an egregious breach of security, for Montreal was the center of French Canada, which was largely sympathetic to Vichy France. The leak was traced to Dr. Henri Laugier, the university's distinguished physicist, who had provided the Tube Alloys team with their laboratories but had been excluded from much of the planning.

According to the GRU's archive, one of those who played a major role in the effort to penetrate the Manhattan Project in Canada was Yakov Chernyak, an experienced illegal who had moved to Canada in 1943 after operating in Europe. He ran a large number of agents, including "a world renowned scientist—now dead." The intelligence he sent to Moscow was considered very important, and on one occasion his despatch included "a report on progress on building the bomb, indicating the objectives of U.S. scientific research, and information on the bomb's precursor materials, together with a description of the uranium isotope separator, the process used to produce plutonium and the principles by which the 'device' was to be built, and how it worked; samples of uranium 233 and 235; and a report, complete with drawings, of the uranium pile was to be built and how it worked."

Within the Manhattan Project itself the focus of attention now shifted from the preparatory work undertaken at Hanford and Oak Ridge, to the weapon's assembly at Los Alamos.

Site Y, as Los Alamos came to be known, occupied a wooded area that formerly had been a boys' ranch school, and had been selected by Robert Oppenheimer because it offered suitable isolation in which a handful of scientists could conduct the top secret experiments that would result in the assembly of an Anglo-American atomic weapon. Oppenheimer was very familiar with the territory because his family owned a ranch in the Sangre de Cristo range, less than twenty miles away, across the Rio Grande valley, and had been a regular visitor. At an altitude of 7,300 feet, and at the end of a perilous, winding dirt road through the Jemez Mountains, the property was perched on a mesa known as the Little Bird Plateau and enjoyed impressive views across the desert of the Sangre de Cristo Mountains. When Oppenheimer and his wife Kitty arrived there in March 1943, the property having been seized by the government for a "demolition range," he anticipated that a few temporary buildings would be built to accommodate some fifty scientists, with their wives undertaking all the support jobs that would be required. In fact, Los Alamos was to expand dramatically to house a staff of nearly a thousand, and Site Y would eventually cover 54,000 acres and accommodate, in a hutted city thrown up in double-quick time by the M. E. Sundt Company, several thousand scientists, technicians, support staff and security personnel, including a Special Engineering Detachment (SED) of 1,300 enlisted men. Its numerous divisions and subdivisions were identified by letters, including Oppenheimer's T for Theoretical Division; TR for TRINITY (the codename for the test to be conducted at the 2nd Air Force's bombing range at Alamogordo); G for gadget, the euphemism for the bomb itself, and headed by Robert Bacher; E for explosives, headed by the White Russian, Harvard-trained chemist George Kistiakowsky, who was considered the world's leader in his field; and F for Ernico Fermi's alias, Eugene Farmer.

Although the food was good, the living conditions at Los Alamos were grim, prompting its description as "a luxurious prison camp." At least initially the scientists carried out their experiments with the minimum of raw materials. Until the spring of 1944 the total stock of U-235 amounted to just two grams, separated at Berkeley, and there were only 200 micrograms of plutonium, the very first of the product from the experimental pile at Oak Ridge. Later, as the supplies increased, this valuable commodity was transported across the country in a convoy of U.S. Army ambulances, accompanied by unmarked patrol cars equipped with radios, a far cry from the very first delivery, made by Glen Seaborg carrying it from Tennessee in a suitcase.

Security would become an obsession at Site Y, but that did not prevent some startling public leaks. In 1944 the *Cleveland Press* reported, under the headline "Forbidden City," that Los Alamos contained a secret government laboratory where "tremendous explosions" had been heard.

It is a curious irony that the very first occupants of Site Y were security suspects. Oppenheimer himself would become the subject of numerous investigations, as was his wife Kitty, his mistress Jean Tatlock, and his brother Frank. When they first arrived, Kitty and

"Oppie" took possession of what had been the headmaster's house, while their companions, Robert Serber and his wife Charlotte Leof, took over the Big House, the old boys' dormitory. This latter pair would also become security suspects, as both had a long history of involvement in left-wing politics. Serber's father, a Russian immigrant, had been Amtorg's lawyer in New York. Charlotte's father, Dr. Morris Leof, was a general practitioner and Russian immigrant whose home in Philadelphia had been a center of radical politics, and her brother Milt was a CPUSA member. Serber had spent four years working under Oppenheimer at Berkeley before being appointed Professor of Physics at the University of Illinois at Urbana in 1938. He had married Charlotte, a journalist and his cousin by marriage, in 1933, and she too had been appointed to a post at Los Alamos as a librarian. Formerly active as a secretary for a Republican medical charity during the Spanish Civil War, and in Russian War Relief, she was the only woman to head a section at the laboratory and was responsible for handling, preparing and filing all the classified scientific papers considered too sensitive to be allowed to leave the site. She also worked in Oppenheimer's own office, and therefore, like her husband, was exceptionally well informed about everything inside and outside the "technical area" at Los Alamos. Virtually all the scientists who worked at Los Alamos came into contact with Robert Serber because, as the T-2 group leader, he delivered the initial indoctrination speech to newcomers. He also invented the term "gadget" to avoid using the word "bomb," after Oppenheimer and John Manley decided to tighten security. In addition, it was his description of the implosion theory that entranced Seth Neddermeyer and prompted him to begin the implosion experiments. Serber's lectures, in a series of five and each an hour long, were typed by Charlotte, but considered so sensitive that *Los Alamos Report No. 1: The Los Alamos Primer*, was not declassified until 1965.

Security was taken seriously at Los Alamos from the outset, but few realized the scale of the espionage offensive launched by the Soviets against their target. Certainly General Groves remained conscious of a degree of threat, as did his subordinates, Boris T. Pash, William Consodine, and Peer de Silva. Pash, the son of

Moscow's Metropolitan Theophilus, had shortened his Russian name in 1932 from Pashkovesky. He was a White Russian immigrant and vociferously anti-Communist. Like many others, he became convinced that Oppenheimer himself was at the heart of an attempt to penetrate the project, and on September 2, 1943, his subordinate de Silva wrote, "Oppenheimer is playing a key part in the attempt of the Soviet Union to secure by espionage, highly secret information which is vital to the Soviet Union." De Silva speculated that Oppenheimer "must either be incredibly naïve and almost childlike in his sense of reality, or he himself is extremely clever and disloyal."[1]

Although he was to be heavily criticized after the war for lax security procedures, with Senator Brien McMahon memorably describing the MED as a "cafeteria service for enemy spies," Groves infuriated many of the scientists who found themselves under his military command by insisting on strict compartmentalization. They demanded an unimpeded flow of information at frequent open colloquia where ideas could be freely exchanged among cleared personnel, whereas the general insisted that contact between the various Manhattan Project sites should be kept to a minimum. He himself operated with a tiny staff, in a suite of six small offices on the fifth floor of the War Department building, and enforced a rigid discipline requiring the use of code letters for all the MED sites and pseudonyms for the senior physicists (Arthur Compton became "Mr. Comas"; Eugene Wigner was "Mr. Wagner"), with all papers locked away in large triple combination safes every night. Such precautions were no guarantee to airtight security, and in August 1943 the CBS correspondent Arthur Hale reported on his popular radio show on station WKBU out of Harrisburg, Pennsylvania, that "the Columbia Project" was "investigating the energy of the atom" and that scientists were confident "a blast based on this energy could destroy everything for a square mile." John Lansdale investigated that particular leak while Groves issued a countrywide directive banning all public use of the word uranium. Despite such lapses, Groves was convinced he had kept the lid shut on the Manhattan Project, with telephone calls monitored, outside visits restricted, mail intercepted and surveillance mounted on sensitive staff.

As for Capitol Hill, he personally briefed a handful of senior members of Congress to prevent intrusion by inquisitive staffers, and any unwelcome visitors were referred to Senator Harry Truman of Missouri, Chairman of the Military Expeditures Committee, who gave whatever assurances were required.

Groves, only forty-seven and the Corps of Engineers' Director of Operations when he received his promotion to the rank of major-general, was a West Point graduate and career soldier who had gained a reputation for circumventing bureaucracy and achieving results, his most recent responsibility being the construction of the Pentagon in Washington DC, a massive project which was ready for occupation in January 1943, just a year after work had begun on the foundations. Famously boasting more than seventeen miles of concentric corridors, the Pentagon was the largest office building in the world, and a veritable marvel of engineering for which Groves could take much credit. Described variously as sometimes charming, often dictatorial and graceless, he possessed an impressive, highly retentive brain and, despite his obesity, showed considerable energy and tremendous determination, apparently requiring minimal sleep and thereby exhausting two shifts of secretaries. He also enjoyed direct confrontation and traveled constantly, crisscrossing the county by train and, somewhat reluctantly, plane, to confer with scientists and contractors. While he clashed with several temperamental physicists, particularly Leo Szilard and Harold Urey, he developed an excellent working relationship with Oppenheimer, a man he recognized as entirely unsuitable to lead the project, saying "it was apparent to me that he would not be cleared by an agency whose sole responsibility was military security" if wartime expediency had not made his appointment absolutely essential.

Los Alamos was a major Soviet target from the moment it was selected by Edwin McMillan and Oppenheimer. Many of those working there were either politically active or held strong views about the morality of developing nuclear weapons. Opinions varied among the staff about whether atomic knowledge should be shared with the Soviets, a topic of conversation apparently often raised, but there was a further debate regarding the actual use of the weapon once it became clear that the Nazis were unlikely to achieve a viable device. Whereas many scientists had been persuaded by the "race against time" argument, justifying their research in order to deny Germany a monopoly of atomic power, they were equally anxious about entrusting such knowledge to the U.S. government. Indeed, the Association of Los Alamos Scientists advocated a policy of "total dissemination of all information regarding atomic energy and the discontinuance of the manufacture of atomic bombs."

The morality of actually using the bomb during the current war was to preoccupy many of those involved, especially the 150 scientists at the Metallurgical Laboratory. In Chicago, as the TRINITY test approached, a group known as the Met Lab Committee on Political and Social Implications drafted a document authored by the German refugee and pacifist James Franck, advocating a demonstration of the weapon before an invited United Nations audience. The Franck Report argued that America would not be able to "persuade the world that a nation which was capable of secretly preparing and suddenly releasing a weapon as indiscriminate as the robot bomb and a million times more destructive, is to be trusted in its proclaimed desire of having such weapons abolished by international agreement."

The Franck Report never reached President Truman, but instead was studied and rejected by the Interim Committee, a body set up, and chaired, by Stimson in May 1945 to advise on atomic policy. The Committee's first task had been to deal with Niels Bohr's persistent demands that the Soviets be included in the bomb program, after which it was confronted by Walter Bartky, Leo Szilard, and Harold Urey who had taken it upon themselves to lobby the President's personal representative on the Committee, James F. Byrnes, at his home in South Carolina. When Arthur Compton was asked by General Groves about this irregular lobbying, the deeply religious physicist explained that the Chicago scientists were troubled "by their own consciences for having faced the world with the existence of the new powers" and by the prospect of using the weapon against a civilian population. James Conant confided to Stimson that "they suppose that there has been no transmission of any information on this subject to our Russian allies, and they fear lest this fact endanger the future of our relations with that country and that we may soon be involved in a secret armament race with that nation, particularly if use should occur before the Russians were notified of the existence of the weapon." Certainly Szilard was shocked by the experience, for he had learned from Byrnes that the administration no longer regarded the bomb merely as a military weapon that would end the war in the Pacific, but as a diplomatic instrument that would ensure Soviet cooperation in Europe after the war.

The debate about the use of the bomb was widespread, with contributions from many of those indoctrinated into the secret. As for General Groves, his initial concern was that the weapon should be used against the Japanese and not the Germans, for fear of letting a bomb that failed to detonate fall into the hands of the Nazis. Having won that argument, on the basis that atomic research in Japan was lagging years behind their Axis partners, Groves recommended that a Japanese target be a deep water harbor, such as Truk Lagoon in Micronesia, where recovery of an unexploded bomb would be more difficult.

On May 31, 1945, the Interim Committee recommended that the bomb be dropped on a heavily populated Japanese city, without prior warning, and decided against giving advance notice to the Soviets in case they demanded active involvement. This was opposed by Fermi, Oppenheimer, Lawrence, and Arthur Compton, arguing that the Soviets should be informed. At a further meeting, on June 21, Byrnes reversed his position and Stimson agreed to advise the president that the Committee now believed that, in the interests of securing postwar controls on nuclear development, the Soviets should be told about the bomb at the upcoming Potsdam Conference.

In addition to the Franck Report, the Chicago scientists organized a petition, which Szilard addressed to President Truman via Arthur Compton, based on a poll of more than half the Met Lab's entire staff. The majority had opted for "a military demonstration in Japan to be followed by a renewed opportunity for surrender before such use." This was retained briefly by General Groves before he relayed it to Henry Stimson's office, in Washington DC, where it arrived just as Truman was about to leave Potsdam, and never went any further. Szilard urged his colleagues at Los Alamos to organize a petition advocating a demonstration for the Japanese, and the scientists held a meeting in Bob Wilson's laboratory to discuss the issue, at which Oppenheimer spoke, but the consensus was against Szilard and so no petition resulted.

The debates that were concentrated in Chicago occurred throughout the Manhattan Project, with scientists concerned about the bomb, its use against Japan and the likelihood of exercising control over atomic energy in peacetime. These were the issues, rather than necessarily pro-Soviet sympathies, that motivated some of those involved to cross the line between policy and research and encourage them to open independent channels of communication to the Soviets. While there was a genuine race to beat the Nazis to a viable weapon, even those who harbored doubts about the basic morality of the research felt justified, but when the evidence mounted that the Germans had made some fatal, fundamental mistakes, further work on the project seemed harder to rationalize. The evidence had come from the British SIS, which had recruited Paul Rosbaud in Berlin before the war; from Norway where German demand for heavy water suggested that the more practical graphite had been overlooked or mistakenly rejected as a moderator in nuclear fission; from independent analysis conducted by Philip Morrison, and from the Alsos Mission.

Because the Americans had never developed a centralized organization to collect, collate, and distribute intelligence, the Manhattan Project initially had been entirely dependent upon the British for information about what was happening in Germany. G-2 had no knowledge of nuclear issues and the FBI, despite Hoover's expansion of its intelligence-gathering role into Latin America, possessed no assets within the Reich. Thus when Hans Bethe and Edward Teller wrote to Oppenheimer in 1943 and expressed the view that "it is possible that the Germans will have by the end of the year enough material accumulated to make a number of atomic bombs, which they will then release at the same time on England, Russia and this country," General Groves was prompted to look into it for himself. G-2, he learned, was clueless, as John Lansdale lamented: "There was a total lack of awareness of the need for scientific intelligence." Having approached General George Marshall, Groves was given the responsibility of coordinating atomic intelligence, and he did so by commissioning David Alvarez of the Met Lab in Chicago to study air samples taken from planes flying over Germany, and dispatching Robert Furman to London to scrutinize SIS's evidence. While Alvarez conducted a search for minute traces of radioactivity and krypton gases in the skies above Berlin, using a filtering technique perfected by General Electric in Cleveland, Colonel Franklin Matthias, the army engineer who had supervised DuPont's construction of Hanford, created a model of a huge, newly built industrial plant with substantial railway links, massive input of raw materièl, but apparently minimal product, that could assist the aerial photography interpreters looking for a Nazi version of Oak Ridge. Reconnaissance flights were also made over the uranium mines of Joachminsthal to detect signs of activity but, encouragingly, there were none. For good measure, Groves also ordered Captain T. O. Jones of the CIC to check out what the Soviets were doing at Kharkov, concentrating on the activities of the leading men in the field, such as Georgi Flyorov, Piotr Kapitsa, and K. Peterzhak. As far as the Soviets were concerned, Groves concluded that they would not achieve a viable device for about twenty years, an opinion he was unwise enough to express publicly in September 1949.

One significant component of the picture developed by the Allies of German progress had been supplied by Niels Bohr, who had been visited at his home in Copenhagen by Werner Heisenberg in September 1941. Controversy surrounds what actually passed between the two physicists, who were old friends, but late in December 1943 Oppenheimer called a small conference in his office at Los Alamos, which was attended by Niels Bohr, his son Aage, Edward Teller, Hans Bethe, Robert Serber, and Victor Weisskopf to discuss a small sketch that had been drawn by Heisenberg. All those present agreed that the drawing was of a heavy water-moderated nuclear reactor, but not a bomb, and a few days later this analysis was included in a memorandum signed by Bethe and Teller for General Groves. Their conclusion was that the Germans had designed a pile not a bomb, but Groves was unconvinced and ensured that, in the face of rumors that the Nazis might deploy some kind of radioactive barrier on D-Day, some of the first troops ashore carried Geiger counters. Even when this mythical weapon failed to materialize, the general wanted better, positive proof, in the form of evidence from a German scientist.

The enthusiasm of the Secret Intelligence branch of OSS for acquiring information about Nazi atomic research led to the embarrassing fiasco of Operation SHARK, the intention of which was to infiltrate an agent into Rome in February 1944 to make contact with the Italian physicist Edoardo Amaldi, whose name had been provided by Enrico Fermi as a fervent anti-fascist. In fact, the designated agent never got farther than Algiers, where he was taken into custody by the U.S. Counter-Intelligence Corps on suspicion of being a German spy and found to be in possession of a mass of compromising documents.

Undeterred, OSS/SI then deployed Morris ("Moe") Berg, the Princeton baseball star, on a mission to Switzerland early in 1944 to cultivate the Swiss physicist Paul Scherrer who, according to Paul Rosbaud, was in touch with Werner Heisenberg. Rosbaud, who had been recruited by Frank Foley, SIS station commander in Berlin, had kept SIS informed about the Nazi atomic program since the spring of 1942 when he re-established contact with London through Norway, and in particular about the whereabouts of Nazi scientists after an air raid attack on the Kaiser Wilhelm Institute in Dahlem. R. V. Jones recalled that "his reports enabled us to follow the move of Heisenberg and his colleagues from Berlin to southern Germany."[2]

Berg, who had spent three months in Italy interrogating Italian scientists to learn of any technical breakthroughs, was armed with a letter of recommendation from Guy Suits, a General Electric physicist who had studied under Scherrer. In fact, Scherrer was not only completely cooperative but was also supplying technical intelligence, designated AZUSA, to the OSS representative in Berne, Allen Dulles. At OSS's suggestion, he invited Heisenberg to Zurich to give a lecture. Accompanied by Carl-Friedrich von Weizsäcker, Heisenberg arrived in early December 1944 and delivered the public address at the Federal Institute of Technology on December 18 to a small audience that included Berg. According to several writers describing this episode after his death in May 1972, Berg had been authorized by OSS to assassinate Heisenberg if he thought it expedient.[3] In fact, Berg attended a small dinner held by Scherrer after the lecture and heard Heisenberg express the view that Germany would lose the war, a remark interpreted by the American as meaning that the Nazi atomic weapon development program had run into insurmountable difficulties. Berg continued to collect atomic intelligence until the end of the war, and a proposal to infiltrate him into Hechingen was quashed when it was realized that his capture could compromise the knowledge that he inevitably had acquired of the Manhattan Project. Instead, he undertook a further mission to Sweden to interview Lise Meitner, but the real work on the enemy's atomic capabilities was undertaken by Alsos.

Headed by Boris T. Pash, Alsos was the codename, derived from the Greek word for "grove," for a highly secret unit created with the task of seizing the enemy's research, either by capturing documents, scientists or entire installations. The undeclared objective of the mission was to determine how far the Nazis had progressed in developing an atomic bomb. It was first deployed in Italy, where the Dutch physicist Samuel Goudsmit of MIT's Radiation Laboratory, who was the only member to be briefed on the Allied atomic program, concluded that the Italians had accomplished nothing in the weapons field. Evidently the Soviets were interested in Alsos, for a VENONA cable from the San Francisco *rezident*, Grigori Kheifets, dated March 18, 1944, reported some rather accurate information from an unidentified source codenamed BROTHER-IN-LAW:

> According to information from BROTHER-IN-LAW the chief of SOLT [G-2 military intelligence] in BABYLON [San Francisco] Lieutenant Colonel PASH left for Italy at the end of December. LYREBIRD [Anna Louise Strong] by agreement with the publishing house is preparing to go home for a period of two or three months.

The first Alsos mission, consisting of Colonel Pash, James Fisk of Bell Laboratories, John Johnson of Cornell, four other scientists, and a dozen military personnel, was assembled in Algiers in

December 1943. Upon their arrival in Naples, they moved into the luxurious Hotel Parco and established an office in the Banco di Napoli. Their task was to conduct searches in Brindisi and Taranto for a list of knowledgeable Italian scientists named by Enrico Fermi, among them Gian-Carlo Wick and Edoardo Amaldi. However, Pash and Fisk concluded in March 1944 that further work was pointless. Their best source had been a former Italian air attaché in Berlin, Major Mario Gasperi, who reassured his inquisitors that the Luftwaffe had absolutely no knowledge of any new devastating explosive. Similarly, the Italian Chief of Naval Ordnance, General Matteini, convincingly denied all knowledge of any Italian participation in atomic research. An expert on missiles and torpedoes, Professor Carlo Carlosi, also denied any knowledge of Heisenberg's work. Alsos uncovered not a shred of evidence to suggest that the Italians had collaborated on an Axis bomb project, and Pash returned to the United States empty-handed.

Although Alsos was directed from Washington DC, it established a liaison office in London, headed by Major Horace K. Calvert, and the Princeton physicist H. P. "Bob" Calvert, who worked closely with SIS's scientific adviser, Reg Jones, and the Directorate of Tube Alloys intelligence unit run by Eric Welsh. All Allied intelligence regarding German atomic research was filtered through the DTA's Technical Committee, and it was diverse. Early in 1942 SIS station in Stockholm had recruited a scientist at the university to report on news seeping out of Germany, and in June the same year a Professor Waller wrote from Sweden to a friend in London reporting that Heisenberg was supervising experiments into atomic fission. A month later Leo Szilard heard from a friend in Switzerland that the Germans were building "a power machine" and might use the radioactive fission product as a weapon. This was confirmed in August by a German professor in Norway who claimed that Heisenberg was working on a U-235 bomb and "a power machine."

The focus of the DTA's attention always remained the Vemork plant, where SIS had acquired some very detailed information. Initially this had come from Professor Leif Tronstad who had arrived in Britain in the autumn of 1941, but by March the following year

SIS had established contact, through Tronstad, with his friend Dr. Jomar Brun, the plant's chief engineer in charge of production and willing to communicate with London via letters hidden in toothpaste tubes and smuggled into Sweden. On April 23, 1942, the DTA, based on Brun's reports that the Germans had doubled the number of electrolysis cells to eighteen, recommended that the production of heavy water should be terminated, and by May 7 Special Operations Executive was examining the problem. However, it was not until October 18 that a small four-man SOE mission, codenamed SWALLOW and led by Jens Poulsson, parachuted into the area to guide in a larger force of commandos. This attempt ended in disaster in November when the two gliders carrying the raiders plunged into a mountain. One of the Halifax tow-aircraft was also lost, and the few survivors of the crash were murdered by Nazi occupation troops. A further, less ambitious operation, dubbed GUNNERSIDE, landed safely on February 17–18, 1943, to link up with the SWALLOW team; together they launched a successful raid on Vemork ten days later.

Alsos began its serious study of German developments in Paris as soon as the city was liberated, and concentrated on the Joliot-Curie laboratory, which had been used by German physicists. The only discovery to throw any light on German atomic weapon research had been the exposure of Cellastic, a front company operated by the Abwehr in what had been the prewar Venezuelan Legation in the rue Quentin Beauchart. Headed by a Dutch collaborator named Kleiter, Cellastic was a scientific intelligence organization with a strong interest in acquiring equipment for the enemy's physics laboratories. In addition, Alsos found another company, Société des Terres-Rares, that had been procuring stocks of uranium and thorium and shipping them to Germany. Just outside Toulouse an Alsos team recovered thirty tons of Union Minière uranium ore from the refinery at Oolen, which had been hidden from the enemy throughout the occupation.

In Brussels Alsos learned that Auer-Gesellschaft had been the conduit for more shipments of uranium, but the real breakthrough occurred in November 1944 when the University of Strasbourg was occupied and the first group of German physicists captured, among them Rudolf Fleischmann. Study of the interrogation reports and a cache of documents revealed that Werner von Heisenberg's Kaiser Wilhelm Institute for Physics had been evacuated from Berlin to the Grotz textile plant in the small Württemberg village of Hechingen. The Alsos office in London arranged for an aerial reconnaissance mission to be flown over the area and the resulting pictures showed that the buildings were nowhere near the scale required to process sufficient uranium for a nuclear pile. Despite this encouraging news, Goudsmit reported that "neither the military nor our civilian colleagues, initially, were as convinced as we were that their fears of a German A-bomb attack had been unfounded."[4]

Fear of being taken by surprise by the Nazis had been generated over a long period, fueled by reports, for example, that the physicist Pasqual Jordan had been located at Peenemünde, the center of the V-1 and V-2 rocket research, with the implied hint that he had been working on atomic warheads. The Germans had gained respectful recognition as the masters of establishing vital industries underground, and it was not forgotten that they had almost unlimited skilled labor, literally at their disposal. The visible expansion of a concentration camp at Bisingen, close to Hechingen, caused some concern that the area was being transformed into a Nazi version of Oak Ridge, but detailed photo-interpretation produced the reassuring analysis that it was supplying labor to a neighboring oil shale plant, unconnected with atomic research.

In March 1945 Alsos reached the University of Heidelberg and found Walther Bothe, who had destroyed his secret documents and declined to divulge any details of German atomic research. Nevertheless, evidence emerged of two further important sites, one of them being in the village of Thuringen, south of Heidelberg. When this was captured, a uranium pile laboratory was discovered in a bombproof cellar under an old schoolhouse, which had been the administrative headquarters of a Nazi atomic project headed by Walther Gerlach and Kurt Diebner. Although some of the equipment had been hastily removed by SS troops just before the arrival of General Patton's tanks, Alsos found sufficient documents to confirm that "the German uranium project was only in a very initial stage."[5] The entire German stock of uranium, 1,100 tons of Belgian ore hidden in a salt mine near Stassfurt, was found by an Alsos team headed by Sir Charles Hambro in an operation codenamed CALVERT, and removed before the arrival of Russian troops. The ore had been stored in rotting barrels that could not be moved but, fortuitously, a nearby barrel factory was pressed into service and 20,000 containers were produced to hold the ore so they could be transported by road to an airfield at Hildesheim, from where they were flown out of the country.

The other important site turned out to be an experimental centrifuge laboratory run by Dr. Willi Groth and located in a wing of a silk parachute factory in Celle. Its objective was not to separate U-235 for a weapon, but to produce slightly enriched uranium for a pile supervised by von Heisenberg at Haigerloch, near Hechingen. Overtaking the French colonial troops in the area, Colonel Pash entered Hechingen and the neighboring hamlet of Tailfingen on April 22, 1945. There he found a uranium pile in a natural cave, and took Otto Hahn and Karl Wirtz into custody. Apparently von Weizsäcker had departed by bicycle for his home at Urfeld in Bavaria two days earlier, leaving behind his staff, two tons of uranium, two tons of heavy water and ten tons of carbon. Pash was soon joined by Michael Perrin, who flew in from London, Eric Welsh and John Lansdale, and together they supervised the dismantling of the German pile. Having removed everything useful, the pit was destroyed by explosives so as to prevent the French from ever learning what had occurred.

The ten principal Alsos prisoners were flown to England and interned at a large country house, Farm Hall, at Godmanchester near Cambridge, where they underwent a lengthy interrogation, codenamed Operation Epsilon, lasting six months that revealed "the whole German idea of the bomb was quite different from ours and more primitive in conception." That the German scientists had not deliberately misled their captors became clear when the transcripts of their private conversations were studied following the BBC's announcement of the attack on Hiroshima. The candid, unrehearsed reaction of the astonished physicists proved beyond doubt that they had not even come close to developing a viable weapon, and this news tended to undermine the commitment of the Manhattan Project scientists who had been persuaded to compete in a "race for the bomb" against the Nazis. Samuel Goudsmit, who closed Alsos down in October 1945, recalled two years later that

> many of our scientific and military experts believed that we were engaged in a desperate race with the Germans for the secret of the atomic bomb, and it is only by a miracle, but a hair's breadth, that we got there first. To be sure we were engaged in such a race, but that race, as we now know, was rather a one-sided affair and the situation was not nearly so desperate as we supposed. The plain fact of the matter is that the Germans were nowhere near getting the secret of the atomic bomb.[6]

When, for example, had General Groves become satisfied that there was no plausible threat from a German atomic weapon? Certainly Philip Morrison, who made a study of the direction of German research, reached that conclusion in the late summer of 1944, and SIS, working with the benefit of information from Paul Rosbaud, the Austrian editor of German technical publications, endorsed that opinion. Married to Hildegard Frank, who was Jewish, Rosbaud had become an Anglophile while a prisoner of the British in Italy during the First World War and had been willingly recruited by Frank Foley in Berlin in 1933. A Roman Catholic, he was considered highly reliable and his messages were assessed to be especially significant and accurate because he regularly talked to Walther Gerlach, the physicist who was responsible for coordinating the entire project. According to R. V. Jones, SIS Scientific Adviser, "Rosbaud's wartime reports were particularly valuable because they helped us correctly to conclude that work in Germany towards the release of nuclear energy at no time reached beyond the research stage; his information thus calmed fears that otherwise might have beset us." Rosbaud had been trained as a physicist at the Technische Hochschule at Berlin-Charlottenburg and "although he did not have access to their work it was clear that this had no association with a large-scale effort such as the production of an atomic bomb would require."[7]

What makes the issue controversial is the widespread belief that the British authorities had become aware as early as the summer of 1942 that there was no chance of Hitler building an atomic bomb, but had suppressed the news on the grounds that the Allied scientists needed an incentive to complete their work. That estimate had hardened into policy by the middle of 1943, when the Directorate of Tube Alloys "concluded that, while the Germans were researching on atomic energy, their primary objective was not the production of a weapon but the development of power, and that the danger they would acquire an atomic weapon before they would be defeated could be discounted."

When Michael Perrin disclosed this to General Groves, the latter took the view that the matter would only be resolved with any certainty once German physicists had been interrogated. An official British report dismissing the prospect of a German bomb was annotated by an American hand: "In this conclusion it is felt the British are skating rather thin."

The issue was of great significance to many who had always harbored reservations about the morality and wisdom of secretly building a bomb and then dropping it on Japan without warning. If there was no prospect of a Nazi bomb, and there were anxieties about the indiscriminate carnage that would be the inevitable consequence of military use in the Pacific, the implication was that a future American administration could deploy it as a diplomatic lever against the Soviets. Such a scenario was too much to contemplate for some, and Joseph Rotblat left Los Alamos as soon as he realized the danger from Germany had evaporated. He recalls a conversation with Groves in which the general gave the impression that he had always regarded the Soviet Union as a future target. This dismayed some of the scientists. The realization that Groves and the Pentagon perceived the atom bomb as a military opportunity precipitated much alarm, and may have been the catalyst for espionage. Indeed, Leonid Kvasnikov has described four key "very valuable" Soviet spies, whom he identified by the codenames BULL, CAT, SHOT, and TIFF:

> They were not motivated solely by their pro-Communist views and Soviet sympathies, as is commonly believed. They realized to a large extent that nuclear weapons were turning science fiction, substantiated as it might be, into an awful reality. Many of them began to see that one nation's monopoly of nuclear weapons, whether the USA or Britain, could bring the world to the brink of nuclear blackmail and disaster. Not only Klaus Fuchs who had made this choice, but some others too, took to thinking of passing nuclear weapons secrets to Russia.[8]

The NKVD and GRU personnel working on ENORMOZ cared little whether those supplying them with information were dupes, politically naïve or ideological zealots, but is clear from scrutiny of the archive files that have been made available to independent researchers in Moscow that virtually every Communist Party member in Britain and the United States with useful access was approached or "pitched" to "work for peace." The big issue was who these individuals were.

Chapter V

The XY *Rezidentura*

This business will never cease to be both unpleasant and fascinating at the same time.

Bruno Pontecorvo

In almost all Soviet intelligence installations overseas, both the NKVD and the GRU were represented, but the relative strengths of the competing organizations varied considerably, partly because of local conditions, but often it was a reflection of past experience or maybe nothing more complicated than the individual personalities involved. History had played a role in the virtual elimination of the NKVD *rezidentura* in London, where Stalin's purges had taken an awful toll by 1940. Despite the impressive recruitments conducted in England during the "golden era" of famous illegals such as Arnold Deutsch, Theodore Maly, Dmitri Bystrolyotov, and Alexander Orlov, the purges had depleted the ranks of professionals and left the networks isolated. By the end of November 1940, when Anatoli Gorsky returned to London as *rezident*, his task had been to reestablish contact with the old sources and rebuild the NKVD's presence in London, albeit without the help of any illegals. In contrast, the GRU had developed a thriving infrastructure and, on the basis of what is known from VENONA and the illegal Ursula Kuczynsky, was in control of nearly forty active and productive agents.

In Canada the situation was not dissimilar, with Vitali Pavlov complaining in his memoirs, when he arrived in Ottawa in August 1942 to take up his post as NKVD *rezident*, that the GRU had acquired the country's best potential sources of information. In the United States, the scene was rather more complicated, chiefly because of the activities of a single man, Gaik Ovakimyan, the Armenian who was to play a crucial role in ENORMOZ.

Urbane, sophisticated, with a good command of English and a doctoral degree in chemistry, Ovakimyan had been in the NKVD since 1931, and in the United States, attached to Amtorg under "purchasing agent" cover, since 1933. He was to become known to the FBI as "the foxy Armenian," and in 1940 he obtained a scholarship to study at the New York Chemical Institute. He was the consummate intelligence professional, but his unscheduled departure from New York in July 1941, on the one hand, robbed the *rezidentura*, then amounting to a staff of thirteen officers supported by three technicians working from a single room on the third floor of the consulate, of a hugely competent organizer, while, on the other, ensuring that in Moscow, as General Fitin's deputy, ENORMOZ was directed with impressive skill.

Ovakimyan's arrest was to be a turning point for the NKVD, and was the result of a chain of international events that can be traced back to the Woolwich Arsenal case in England in 1938 when Percy Glading, a well-known CPGB activist, was convicted of extracting secret blueprints from sympathetic employees of the huge military facility in southeast London. Glading and two co-conspirators were imprisoned, and MI5 wound up what was then regarded as a highly successful investigation into a Communist plot that had been penetrated by a resourceful agent, Olga Gray. Guided by her

MI5 case officer, Maxwell Knight, she had ingratiated herself with the CPGB leadership, rented the Kensington safe-house used by Glading's spy ring, carried secret messages for the Comintern to India and exposed a clandestine wireless transmitter in Wimbledon, which regularly exchanged signals with Moscow. Disastrously, not all the clues from the case were pursued sufficiently vigorously by MI5, and two important agents, Edith Suschitzsky and Melita Sirnis, who were connected to Glading, survived undetected and later were to acquire some prominence, the former becoming the celebrated photographer Mrs. Tudor-Hart, and Kim Philby's recruiter, codenamed EDITH, while the latter as Melita Norwood, codenamed TINA, was a contributor to ENORMOZ in London.

Several other loose ends remained, including the identities and whereabouts of Glading's foreign contacts, among them Willy Brandes, ostensibly a salesman for the Phantome Red Cosmetic Company and the Charak Furniture Company of New York, who had been spotted during surveillance but had slipped out of the country before the arrests were made in January 1938. MI5 learned that Brandes had entered England in January 1937 on a Canadian passport, but inquiries with the RCMP revealed that his papers were false, and had been supported by a man using the name Arman Labis Feldman, who also was carrying a fraudulent Canadian birth certificate. When the RCMP eventually apprehended Feldman in November 1940, he revealed an extraordinary story.

Feldman's true name was Josef Wolodarsky, a Pole by birth, who had been sent on a mission to England in 1930 while working as an engineer for the Soviet Oil Trust, but had been convicted of some unspecified offense in November 1932. This misfortune had prompted his departure to Canada, where he had worked as Armand Labis Feldman, an alias under which he obtained Canadian naturalization papers, acting as a paymaster for a network of illegals in Montreal, headed by Ovakimyan. A self-styled specialist in industrial espionage, based in Neptune City, New Jersey, where he traded in stocks and ran the Round-The-World Trading Company, Wolodarsky later admitted that he had done much of his research in the New York Public Library, but the Soviets believed he was engaged in collecting intelligence on the American oil business and in 1936 authorized him to return briefly to Moscow on the *Normandie*, to collect his wife. Upon his return, Ovakimyan had introduced him to Willy Brandes, who was then using the alias William Hoffman, and when he left for London Wolodarsky was entrusted with making payments to the rest of the network, which included Robert Haberman, who operated between Mexico and the United States, and Eda Wallace (alias Leah Kriloff and Eda Otulsky), whom the FBI established had departed to Poland in April 1937 on a fraudulent American passport.

According to Wolodarsky, the members of Ovakimyan's Canadian organization were Fred Rose (later to feature prominently in the Canadian Royal Commission report on Soviet espionage), Adolph Stark and Aaron Marcovich, who both specialized in acquiring false travel documents. One of their clients had been Robert Haas, an illegal from Vienna, for whom Marcovich obtained a false Canadian passport in the name of Mark Jonas. The RCMP detained Stark and Marcovich as enemy aliens, but Jonas and his wife had disappeared to Europe in April 1937. Another client was Charles P. Atkin (*alias of* Peter New, Abraham C. Seatole, and Bastien), who was paid his expenses by Wolodarsky's Round-The-World Trading Company, which acted as a convenient front for supporting agents, of whom the most important was Simon A. Rosenberg, an industrial spy with access to engineering plans. Another key figure in the network was Abraham Glasser, described as "a fanatical Communist" then employed as a special attorney in the Anti-Trust Division of the Justice Department, who had access to lists compiled by the FBI of suspects under surveillance. He was responsible for tipping off Ovakimyan that "Feldman" had attracted the FBI's attention.

Warned by Glasser, Wolodarsky promptly emptied the NKVD bank accounts in New York and fled with his wife and small child to Montreal, where he hid successfully from the NKVD and the FBI by working in a hotel until the war, when he was detained routinely as an enemy alien. However, in the Canadian internment camp he was denounced by a fellow prisoner, resulting in a lengthy interrogation at the hands of the RCMP and the FBI. As a result, Simon Rosenberg was questioned by the FBI and made further disclosures. Rosenberg, also Polish by birth, had come to the United States in 1925 and had become a naturalized citizen in May 1930. Soon afterwards, he was given a job by Amtorg and sent to Moscow in 1931 when, according to his statement, he was blackmailed into becoming an intelligence agent under a threat to kill his sister, who was living in Kiev. He was sent back to America in 1932, with instructions given to him in the Atlas Hotel in Berlin by Ovakimyan, who paid him $1,200. Thereafter, Rosenberg had collected industrial plans, supervised first by a man named Eremin and then from 1934 by Wolodarsky, and remembered accompanying a man named Hoffman to Canada to collect his false passport, and recalled being introduced to Eda Wallace and Mark Jonas.

With this evidence, Ovakimyan and his Amtorg assistant Mikhail Chaliapin were placed under intensive surveillance by the FBI, which spotted Ovakimyan holding regular evening meetings in restaurants with Jacob Rasin, alias Jacob Golos, the president of World Tourists, Inc., a firm financed by the CPUSA. This trail led the FBI to Golos's lover, Elizabeth Bentley, and to a raid on the company that resulted in Golos and World Tourists being fined for breaching the Foreign Agents Registration Act.

The FBI's surveillance of Ovakimyan in April 1941 showed that his car and household goods were being crated for loading onto the *Annie Johnson*, a steamer chartered by Amtorg and bound for Vladivostok via the Panama Canal. Ovakimyan was arrested as he climbed into a taxi in downtown New York, but he protested, to no avail, that he had diplomatic immunity as an official of the Soviet government and was promptly charged under the Foreign Agents Registration Act. On July 23, he was allowed to leave San Francisco on the Soviet ship *Kim* in an exchange negotiated by the State Department for the release of six Americans held in Moscow.

The unwitting architect of this intelligence catastrophe was Wolodarsky, who was released after the war and allowed to settle in Vancouver, where the RCMP used him as a walking encyclopedia of Soviet espionage. Simon Rosenberg also escaped prosecution, but Abraham Glasser was suspended by the Department of Justice in June 1941 and allowed to resign quietly in October. He then found a position in the Office of Price Administration and resumed his espionage career, appearing in the VENONA traffic with the codename ROUBLE. In March 1953 Glasser, by then Professor of Law at Rutgers University, was subpoenaed by Congress to give evidence to the HUAC and was confronted with an FBI report in which Wolodarsky confirmed that he had met Glasser "between seven and ten times" in Washington and New York to pass information, "most of it related to the Spanish Civil War; and that occasionally Glasser was given four or five names to check from the Department of Justice files." Wolodarsky stated that Ovakimyan and another illegal, Nikolai Stern, had controlled Glasser. Glasser declined to answer the questions put to him.

As for Golos, he died of a heart attack in November 1943, leaving Elizabeth Bentley, who previously had acted as his courier, in control of his network for gathering information from his agents in Washington DC. After a series of heated disputes with her NKVD contacts, and fearing that she had been compromised, she approached the FBI in November 1945 and confessed her espionage to Special Agents Harold V. Kennedy, Thomas G. Spencer, and Joseph M. Kelly during interviews stretching over fourteen days.

Ovakimyan's arrest severely disrupted the NKVD's organization in New York and prevented the *rezidentura* from any early participation in ENORMOZ. Ovakimyan's temporary replacement as *rezident* until the arrival in 1942 of Vasili Zarubin was the inexperienced Pavel Pastelnyak (alias Pavel Klarin, codenamed LUKA), a forty-five-year-old former member of the NKVD Border Guards, who could barely speak English and had to depend heavily on the men he had employed at the World's Fair, among them Morris Cohen, who would eventually prove invaluable. Pastelnyak himself was conscious of the dangers, because in April 1940 he had complained to Moscow about Golos's network overreaching itself: "If something happens to them, much of what has been created will be reduced to ashes."

In contrast, the parallel GRU organization, split similarly between a legal and illegal apparatus, would respond impressively to the call from Moscow for atomic intelligence.

During the ENORMOZ period, Colonel Pavel P. Melkishev (codenamed MOLIERE), who served from 1941 to December 1945 under the alias of Pavel Mikhailov and under vice-consular cover, headed the GRU's *rezidentura* in New York. According to the GRU archives, he was in contact with Albert Einstein through Margarita Ivanovna, the wife of the Russian sculptor Sergei Timofeyevich Konenkov. They had arrived in the U.S. in the spring of 1924, under semi-official Soviet sponsorship, to organize an exhibition of Russian art and ended up staying in the country for the next twenty years. Margarita had met Einstein in 1935 when he had agreed to pose for her husband, and they had began an affair which intensified after the death of Einstein's wife Elsa. In 1942 she became secretary of the Help for Russia Committee, which gave her the opportunity to have official contacts with Einstein and Robert Oppenheimer. In August 1945 she persuaded Einstein to meet Mikhailov, and they began to meet regularly both in Einstein's cottage at Saranac Lake, and at the *rezident*'s New York apartment. In his letters to Margarita, Einstein never mentioned Mikhailov by name, but referred to him simply as "our consul," and writing of his "advice" and "recommendations." In one of his letters he wrote that, "in accordance with the program," he had paid a visit to the Consul, and appeared to acknowledge her intelligence links:

> I was only able to get back from there [New York] yesterday evening. How difficult the task is, and what big changes it will mean for you... although as time passes you may possibly come to regret your discreditable connection with the country where you were born.

Precisely what Einstein actually passed on to Melkishev is unknown but it was Melkishev who, as acting Consul General in September 1945, arranged for the Konenkovs to receive Soviet visas and return to Moscow in November. A month later he too was obliged to follow them, having been declared persona non grata.

The principal GRU illegal working on ENORMOZ was Artur Adams, codenamed ACHILLES, about whom very little has been published. His background has always been mysterious, but in fact he was born in Eskilstun in Sweden in 1885. When his father died, he was taken to Russia with his mother, a Russian Jewess. She died when Adams was ten, and the orphaned Adams was brought up by her relatives in Chudovo, near St. Petersburg. He became a Marxist when he entered a school for merchant navy engineers, and his interest in the Social Democrats escalated to active involvement in the revolutionary movement. Arrested several times for taking part in agitation and strikes, he was once beaten so severely by the police that he suffered from a bad back for the rest of his life. He was eventually sentenced to exile and jail but escaped to Finland in 1907 and traveled as a student, always active in left-wing politics, to Egypt, Italy, Argentina, Canada, and America. In 1919 he found a job as the head of the technical section in the unofficial Russian trade delegation to the U.S., known as the Martens Mission, and joined the CPUSA the following year. In 1921 he returned to Russia to work at the Leningrad Steelworks and then the AMO assembly plant, later to become the automotive manufacturer ZIL. In 1925 he joined the management of the Aviation Trust and was posted back to the U.S. in 1927 to gain experience in the manufacture of large cars. According to his GRU file, he undertook an unspecified intelligence role during this visit, and went back to America in 1932 to negotiate the purchase of Curtis-Wright fighter aircraft.

Adams's first illegal mission occurred in May 1938 when he returned to the U.S. through Buffalo as a Canadian radio engineer, accompanied by his wife Dorothea and assisted by Samuel Novak, a Communist sympathizer and owner of a radio manufacturing business in New York whom he had met in 1932. Novak vouched for Adams to the immigration authorities and booked him into the Peter Cooper Hotel as a chemicals salesman, a cover that justified him traveling throughout the country. Using some old connections, he then managed to set himself up as a self-employed engineer, providing services to a broad range of businesses, a useful cover. He also created, with a Canadian partner, Technological Laboratories, which operated from the offices in New York of the Electronics Corporation of America and Keynote Recordings.

Adams reported in 1940 that papers on research into uranium were no longer being published in American scientific journals, and his first contact with scientists working on the Manhattan Project came after a routine meeting with one of his agents, Clarence Hiskey, codenamed AESCULAPUS, a chemist then working at the University of Chicago.

On January 22, 1944, Hiskey told Adams that one of his friends, a left-wing scientist, had access to secret papers relating to the manufacture of the atomic bomb. Adams immediately passed this on to the Center and asked for permission to recruit him, but Moscow delayed in replying. Adams took the initiative and met the scientist at the end of January 1944. This turned out to be John H. Chapin, a chemist trained at Cornell and the University of Illinois, who had joined the Manhattan Project from du Pont. At a meeting with Adams on February 23, 1944, Chapin handed over about a thousand pages of documents, as well as samples of uranium and beryllium. Adams transmitted a summary of the papers to Moscow, describing them as reports on the development of the new weapon, directives on particular topics, reports from various sections of the laboratory, diagrams of experimental installations, specifications of the materials used, a description of methods used to produce metals of high purity, and also reports on the application of molecular physics, chemistry and metallurgy to the needs of the atomic project. All the original documents were subsequently sent to Moscow by courier. Adams addressed them personally to Ilyichev with a covering letter:

> I do not know how much you may have heard about the fact that the Americans are putting immense efforts into the problem of utilizing uranium energy (I am not sure what the actual Russian for uranium is!) for military purposes. I can report that this work has reached the stage where production technology has been developed for a new element, plutonium, which is bound to play a major role in the present War. Only physicists of the caliber of our Academician Joffe will be able to understand the material I have sent you. The following will demonstrate the level of attention being given to the problem in the US:
>
> A secret fund of nearly a billion dollars at the personal disposal of the President of the US has been almost used up on research and on work to create the production technology for manufacturing the elements named above. Six world-class scientists, Fermi, Allison,

> Compton, Urey, and Oppenheimer among them (most being Nobel Prize winners) are heading the atomic project.
>
> Thousands of technicians and engineers are employed on the work. Hundreds of highly qualified doctors are studying the effects of radiation on the human body. Dedicated laboratories have been set up for this work at Columbia University and the University of Chicago. A special commission of high-ranking officers and scientists is in charge of the project. My source told me the weapon being designed is a projectile whose radiation and shock wave will wipe out every living thing for hundreds of miles. He does not wish to see such a weapon launched against our country. The plan is to destroy Japan completely but there can be no guarantee that once they have such a weapon at their disposal our allies will not try to exert influence on us too. None of the scientists engaged on the work know of any countermeasures.[1]

At their next meeting, Chapin gave Adams another 2,500 pages of secret material, which was photographed, and in subsequent encounters between May and August 1944 he handed over 1,500 more documents. However, when Adams attempted to pay Chapin, the chemist took fright and reported a slightly misleading version of the approach to the FBI, in which he asserted that his first encounter with Adams had occurred in September 1944. The FBI placed Adams under surveillance and he was seen meeting Mikhailov, thus confirming his credentials as a GRU illegal. Adams, who had been so highly regarded by the GRU that he was even authorized to recruit agents without its prior clearance, was effectively eliminated from ENORMOZ and eventually, after a year of rather overt FBI surveillance, exfiltrated. He attempted to leave the country on a Soviet ship from Portland, Oregon, in February 1945, but returned to spend a further year as a recluse in a New York hotel before making a second successful escape bid. Chapin later joined the M. W. Kellogg Company to work on a classified Air Corps contract, and was to give evidence to Congress that incriminated both Hiskey and Adams.

To cope with the increased workload, the XY *rezidentura* in New York expanded to include three unidentified staff officers, codenamed LAVR, KURT and GLAN, as well as a former White Russian cavalry officer, Sergei N. Kurnakov, who had emigrated to the United States after the revolution, via Yugoslavia and Paris, converted to Communism during the Depression, and then operated under journalistic cover in New York, communicating to Moscow with the codename BEK. Ostensibly, Kurnakov worked as a military analyst for the *Daily Worker* and *New Masses*, but by the time the FBI realized his role in ENORMOZ, he had returned to Moscow. An item published in the *Daily Worker* on July 19, 1949, reported him in Moscow two weeks earlier, not long before he died. If Kurnakov had been in the U.S., he would have been interviewed by the FBI, which was left to guess at which cryptonyms applied to which Soviets. Trying to match the unidentified codenames was assisted by physical surveillance, although even when, for example, Mikhail Chaliapin was flagged as an intelligence professional, attached to the Consulate-General in New York, it was still not possible to confirm him as one of the *rezidentura*'s three unknown staff officers. Indeed, Amtorg took the main burden of providing cover for the technical staff, as recalled by a GRU defector, Colonel Ismail Akhmedov:

> The NKVD insisted on 60 percent of the technical intelligence agents in Amtorg on the grounds that they were responsible for economic as well as scientific intelligence. However, we did not really fare so badly. The agents allotted to the Red Navy in New York came only from GRU, and we had some of the wives of our operatives recruited, too. That left us with more than the minority of 40 percent of the agents proposed by the NKVD.[2]

The NKVD's ENORMOZ operations extended to California, but secrecy handicapped the FBI's grasp of what precisely was happening. It was during the course of a disjointed conversation on April 10, 1943, with an unknown Russian, later identified as the New York *rezident* Vasili Zubilin, who had arrived in the U.S. to take up his post under third secretary cover at the end of December 1941, and who had called at Steve Nelson's home in Oakland, that Special Agent William Branigan discovered that the NKVD *apparat* in East Bay was preoccupied with recruiting agents inside the Allied atomic weapon development project. From the transcript of the recording it was clear that Nelson was Zubilin's subordinate, and was acting as an intermediary, financing an extensive spy-ring. Until that moment, Hoover had no idea that the Manhattan Project even existed, and although Zubilin was to be placed thereafter under blanket surveillance up until his departure from New York on August 28, 1944, he was unable to persuade the White House that the Soviets were engaged in wholesale espionage against their ally. As for Steve Nelson, he was convicted under the Smith Act in July 1952 of plotting to overthrow the U.S. government, and sentenced to twenty years' imprisonment. The conviction was overturned on appeal in 1957, and he died in December 1993.

It was only after Zubilin's departure that his significance, and that of his wife, was recognized, largely through the evidence of Boris Morros, a Hollywood film producer who had originally known Zubilin as Edward Herbert, "a thick-set man with powerful shoulders. He had red hair and, despite the heavy accent...spoke French, English and German fairly well." However, it was his wife, a "frail, pretty, middle-aged woman with an aristocratic manner" who often appeared to Morros to be in charge:

> I often heard of other Communist women talking of Elizabeth Zubilin as though she was a sort of Red Joan of Arc, a saint whose faith in the Soviet was pure and bottomless. They also had great respect for her intellect and judgment. Often I heard these wives of other spies say, while in the midst of a dispute over some matter of strategy, "Well, what did she say about it?" or "Let's ask Liza," or "Don't argue, Helen said so!" as though Madame Zubilin had the last word. She was generally acknowledged to be the real brain behind whatever shrewd moves her blustering husband made.[3]

In retrospect, it is amazing that the Zubilins could have fallen under suspicion in Moscow and been investigated as traitors who had sold out to the FBI, especially as their penetration of the Manhattan Project was so comprehensive. Vasili Zubilin had become a Chekist in 1920, and five years later he was operating undercover in China. In 1926 he was appointed *rezident* in Finland, and then operated as the illegal *rezident* in Berlin, where he married Elizaveta Gorskaya. Between 1929 and 1933 they worked together in France, and then returned to Germany until 1937. Before his departure for New York in October 1941, as a *rezident* aged only forty-seven, but with the personal authority of an audience with Stalin, Zubilin had returned briefly to China to reestablish contact with one of his German agents, a man who had been appointed an adviser to Chiang Kai-Chek. Although officially accredited to the embassy in Washington DC, the Zubilins kept an apartment in New York and sent their son Piotr to the Soviet school in Manhattan.

Morros, who first approached the FBI in June 1947, was of no great assistance, except retrospectively, regarding Soviet espionage in the United States (although three spies were imprisoned on his evidence), but during the ten years he acted as a double agent he was able to offer some clues to Zubilin's atomic sources. He knew, for example, of a "husband-and-wife spy team" who "had been working for some years close to Los Alamos and various other atomic energy installations." The man was a nuclear physicist, but his identity remained a mystery. According to Morros, Zubilin had been accused by a subordinate of stealing $80,000—money that was supposed to have been passed "to a certain professor."[4]

During the Second World War there is only one recorded example of the FBI targeting an identified Soviet intelligence officer through the deployment of double agents. Andrei I. Schevchenko, ostensibly an aeronautical engineer attached to the Soviet Purchasing Commission in Buffalo since June 1942, made three recruitments: Loren G. Haas, a Bell Aircraft engineer; his colleague, Leona O. Franey, a clerk in the Bell library; and her husband Joseph, a repairman employed by the Hooker Electrochemical Company. Codenamed ARSENIJ, Schevchenko was supervising the Soviet purchase of Bell P-39 Air Cobra fighters, and was supplied with supposedly classified material by his agents which, in fact, had been prepared by the FBI. Subsequently, when the relevant VENONA texts were studied, the FBI recognized Leona Franey as the source codenamed ZERO, and saw that Schevchenko had also been running an undiscovered agent, codenamed STAMP, in the Republic

Aviation Corporation. As Hooker was engaged in Manhattan Project contracts, Joseph Franey and Schevchenko became the only case of the FBI running, albeit unwittingly, a double agent against the Soviets during the Second World War.

For its part, the FBI was slow to grasp the scale of Soviet espionage conducted on the West Coast, but much of the blame must go to the military authorities, who were reluctant to share secrets with the FBI, or even tell J. Edgar Hoover the purpose of Los Alamos.

Chapter VI

Theodore Hall and Klaus Fuchs

There was never from about two weeks from the time I took charge of the Project any illusion on my part but that Russia was our enemy.

General Leslie Groves

The discovery by Meredith Gardner in December 1946 of a list of seventeen atomic scientists in the Soviet BRIDE traffic was the first firm evidence that someone other than Allan Nunn May had been betraying details of the weapons development program to the Soviets. Nunn May, of course, had been confronted in London with evidence that had originated with Igor Gouzenko, and in May 1946 had been sentenced to ten years' imprisonment. The son of a brass door handle manufacturer who had lost his business in Birmingham in the depression, Nunn May had been a Communist since he was sixteen and was completely uncooperative with his interrogators, refusing to name anyone else involved in the Canadian spy ring. As for his movements, he had arrived in Montreal in 1943, and in January the following year had visited the Met Lab in Chicago, accompanied by a dozen other CNRC scientists. He returned in April for two weeks, and was back again at the Argonne Laboratory at the end of August for a three-day conference to discuss the Argonne pile and the planned Montreal pile. His third and final trip to the U.S. took place at the end of September 1944, but a proposed month-long stay in the spring of 1945 was vetoed by General Groves on the grounds that it was against policy for a single individual to learn too much from different areas of research.

When the BRIDE material first became available, the FBI had only limited resources to devote to the challenge of Soviet espionage. The Espionage Section of D. M.—"Mickey" Ladd's Domestic Intelligence Division—was a relatively small organization headed by Pat Coyne and consisting of a handful of specialists, but was about to lose Bill Sullivan to the newly created CIA. Sullivan's departure from headquarters, after a confrontation with J. Edgar Hoover, was a significant blow because he had taken charge of the Elizabeth Bentley case and had pursued the more than eighty leads she had gathered during her regular, fortnightly visits to Washington DC as a courier for her lover Jacob Golos, collecting dozens of rolls of film from Nathan G. Silvermaster of the Farm Security Administration. According to Bentley, Silvermaster and his wife Helen were at the heart of an extensive spy ring that ran agents inside numerous U.S. Government departments. The basement of their home was run as a clandestine photographic laboratory, processing pictures of classified information.

Until the BRIDE material became available in increasing quantities, the FBI's knowledge of Soviet espionage had been limited to the statements made by those compromised by Gaik Ovakimyan; allegations made by a disillusioned Communist, Hede Massing, who claimed to SA Hugh Finzel that she had recruited two State Department officials, Noel Field and Laurance Duggan; and the usual routine surveillance on suspected Amtorg and consular officials. Some research into the background of the Comintern had been conducted in New York by two young Special Agents, Emory Gregg and Robert Lamphere, who were both to move up to Washington to concentrate with Lish Whitson on BRIDE, the source that would provide corroboration for many of the allegations made by Bentley and Massing, confirm existing suspicions about Soviet personnel and provide new leads regarding penetration of the Manhattan Project.

The evidence in fifty-one BRIDE texts (later codenamed VENONA and amounting to some 2,200 texts) of a comprehensive hemorrhage of atomic secrets from the Manhattan Project centered on several suspects, the first of whom was Klaus Fuchs. At the time his name was passed to the Security Service in London, Fuchs was head of the Theoretical Physics Division at the Atomic Energy Research Establishment at Harwell, located on an abandoned airfield near Didcot in Oxfordshire. The problem for MI5 was the absence of any evidence to suggest he was currently an active spy, and he could not be confronted directly with the BRIDE material for fear of compromising the source. Just as MI5 was contemplating the most appropriate method of approaching Fuchs, the latter fortuitously visited Harwell's security officer, Henry Arnold, to disclose that his father had accepted a post at Leipzig University in the Soviet zone in Germany. This coincidence gave MI5 the pretext to send its interrogator, Jim Skardon, to interview Fuchs, and their three lengthy, ostensibly informal conversations resulted in the physicist's tentative, partial admission that he had been in touch with the Soviets during the war. The result of this breakthrough was an invitation to submit to several more interviews in London, where Fuchs was arrested on February 2, 1950. On March 1 he was sentenced to the maximum term of fourteen years' imprisonment for breaching the Official Secrets Act.

The other, early major spy in the BRIDE traffic was Theodore Hall, first implicated in a text dated November 12, 1944, which described the young physicist's encounter with his Soviet contact, Sergei N. Kurnakov, a former White Russian cavalry officer who had emigrated to the U.S., converted to Communism and then operated under journalistic cover in New York:

> BEK [Sergei Kurnakov] visited Theodore HALL, 19 years old, the son of a furrier. He is a graduate of Harvard University. As a talented physicist he was taken on for government work. He was a GYMNAST [member of the Young Communist League] and conducted work in the Steel Founders' Union. According to BEK's account, HALL has an exceptionally keen mind and a broad outlook, and is politically developed. At the present time HALL is in charge of a group at CAMP-2 (SANTA-FE) [Los Alamos]. HALL handed over to BEK a report about the CAMP and named the key personnel employed on ENORMOZ. He decided to do this on the advice of his colleague Saville SAKS, a GYMNAST living in TYRE [New York]. SAKS's mother is a COMPATRIOT [Communist] and works for RUSSIAN WAR RELIEF. With the aim of hastening a meeting with a competent person, HALL on the following day sent a copy of the report by SAKS to the PLANT [Soviet Consulate]. ALEKSEI [Anatoli Yakovlev] received SAKS. HALL had to leave for CAMP-2 in two days' time. He was compelled to make a decision quickly. Jointly with MAJ [Stepan Apresyan] he gave BEK consent to feel out HALL, to assure him that everything was in order and to arrange liaison with him. HALL left his photograph and came to an understanding with BEK about a place for meeting him. BEK met SAKS [1 group garbled] our automobile. We consider it expedient to maintain liaison with HALL. [1 group unidentified] through SAKS and not to bring in anybody else. MAY has no objection to this. We shall send the details by post.

Nor was this the only material on Hall, for there was further VENONA material in 1945, including this text dated January 23 from New York, which introduced OLD as Saville S. Sax, Hall's roommate at Harvard, and the hitherto unknown role of Bernard Schuster, a well-known figure in the Communist Party (and run by Konstantin Chugunov of the New York *rezidentura*) who evidently knew Sax. The telegram also revealed some tension between Sax's initial handler, Sergei N. Kurnakov, and Anatoli A. Yatskov (alias Yakovlev), who replaced him and had been sent to New York to work under the *rezident*, Leonid Kvasnikov.

> Your Nos. 316 and 121. The checking of OLD [Saville Sax] and YOUNG [Theodore Hall] we entrusted to ECHO [Bernard Schuster] a month ago, the result of the check we have not yet had. We are checking OLD's mother [Mrs. Bluma Sax] also.
> BECK [Sergei Kurnakov] is extremely displeased over the handing over of OLD to ALEKSEI (Anatoli Yakovlev]. He gives a favorable report of him. ALEKSEI has met OLD twice but cannot yet give a final judgment. YOUNG has been seen by no-one except BECK. On the 8th January YOUNG sent a letter but never made arrangements for calling to a meeting. He has been called up into the army and left to work in the Camp [Los Alamos].
> OLD intends to renew his studies at Harvard University at the end of January.

Evidently, Kurnakov had been irritated by the way Yatskov had taken over what he had probably regarded as his own recruits, and the frustration of the more experienced officer is understandable. Before his arrival in New York, via San Pedro, California, where he had landed from the SS *Ecuador* on February 4, 1941, Yatskov had received only three months of tuition in English, and he says he "left for America in fear and trembling. It's a good thing my first appointment was to act as a receptionist for American citizens. By constantly associating with them I was able to pick up the language more quickly. But not as quickly as I wanted. TWAIN [Semyon Semyonov] helped me in this difficult task." In fact, Yatskov was intended to replace Semyonov, and was to supervise Morris and Lona Cohen until his own recall home in December 1946 aboard the SS *America*.

It is likely that Kurnakov personally had chosen the codenames YOUNG and OLD, although Sax was only a year older than Hall. Nevertheless, individual case officers had the discretion to choose codenames, and often picked one that helped them remember the person concerned. With Sax and Hall having turned up together, it is easy to imagine that Kurnakov might have selected a codename to distinguish between the two, and may have felt proprietorial responsibility for them. In any event, Kurnakov was overruled, and Hall became Yatskov's star agent.

Another VENONA text, dated May 26 from Leonid Kvasnikov, showed the type of information Hall had disclosed:

> Reference your 3367. YOUNG's material contains:
>
> 3. A list of places where work on ENORMOZ is being carried out: 1. HANFORD, State of WASHINGTON, production of 49. 2. State of NEW JERSEY, production of 25 by the diffusion method. Director UREY. 3. BERKELEY, State of CALIFORNIA, production of 25 by the electromagnetic method. Director LAWRENCE. 4. NEW CONSTRUCTION, administrative center for ENORMOZ; also production of 25 by the spectrographic method, Director COMPTON. 5. CHICAGO, ARGONNE Laboratories – nuclear research. At present work there has almost ceased. Director COMPTON. 6. The RESERVATION, the main practical research work on ENORMOZ. Director VEKSEL. 7. Camp [2 groups unrecovered] base in the area of CARLSBAD, State of NEW MEXICO, the place for the practical testing of the ENORMOZ bomb. 8. MONTREAL, CANADA – theoretical research.
>
> (b) a brief description of the four methods of production of 25—the diffusion, thermal diffusion, electromagnetic and spectrographic methods.
>
> The material has not been fully worked over. We shall let you know the contents of the rest later.

Kvasnikov was better versed in the details of nuclear physics than his immediate subordinates, Anatoli A. Yatskov and Aleksandr S. Feklisov, who were not technically qualified. Two months later, on July 5, 1945, Yatskov was rebuked in Moscow by General Fitin, codenamed VIKTOR, for his performance in handling the atomic spies, citing some episode involving YOUNG:

> Your No. 613. The incident involving GRAUBER should be regarded as a compromise of YOUNG. The cause of this is ALEKSEI's [Yakovlev's] completely unsatisfactory work with the agents on ENORMOZ. His work with [9 groups unrecovered] for this reason

> we consider it of the utmost importance to ensure supervision so that the COUNTRY [23 groups unrecoverable] we once more [3 groups unrecovered] attention to [2 groups unrecovered] our instructions. For the future [4 groups unrecovered]: immediately inform us by telegraph about each meeting with the agents of ENORMOZ. In the next post [3 groups unrecovered] on this same question to send the most precise reports on meetings [14 groups unrecovered] every meeting with permanent staff [14 groups unrecovered] from all these areas. You [18 groups unrecovered] to seek safe flats in the areas of the camps. This question you must [17 groups unrecovered] our workers on the development [35 groups unrecovered] GRAUBER case meetings of our operational worker with YOUNG you must [4 groups unrecovered]. VIKTOR

As Kurnakov had correctly described, Hall was the son of a Russian furrier who had escaped the pogroms and settled in the Washington Heights district of New York. A brilliant student, he was educated at the City College of New York and in 1940 had entered Queens College, having been turned down by Columbia University on the grounds of his youth. Two years later, at age sixteen, he transferred to Harvard to study physics and advanced mathematics, and came under the spell of his roommate, the leftist Saville Sax, whose Russian-born mother Bluma ran a Russian War Relief branch. In October 1943 Hall was interviewed for a post at Los Alamos, and in January 1944 began work on the Manhattan Project. However, during his first leave, in October 1944, he met Sax in New York and together they dropped by the Amtorg office at 238 West 28th Street where they met Sergei Kurnakov, then working under journalistic cover. This encounter was described in the VENONA text dated November 12, 1944. By January the following year, the *rezidentura* still had not heard back from Bernard Schuster about Hall's credentials as a Communist, and a dispute had arisen between Kurnakov, who had handled Hall and Sax when they turned up unexpectedly, and Yatskov, who is described as having already held two further meetings with Hall, but nevertheless had remained undecided about him.

Kurnakov arranged for Sax to act as a courier for Hall, and a rendezvous was arranged in Albuquerque for December 1944. At this meeting, which Hall later described, he received a Russian questionnaire and in exchange gave Sax a two-page account of the atomic bomb's implosion principle.

What remains unexplained is the VENONA text of July 5, 1945, referring to the GRAUBER incident, which evidently had been mishandled by Yatskov. The implication is that GRAUBER was a separate spy within the ENORMOZ network, but somehow, through Yatskov's mismanagement, had led to a compromise in which GRAUBER had learned that Hall was also an active spy. The question then arises about the identity of GRAUBER. There is one immediate candidate: Dr. Roy Glauber, who had roomed with Hall, had been his close friend and had recommended him for employment at Los Alamos. A further clue is provided by Vladimir Chikov, a retired KGB officer who was granted access to the FCD [First Chief Directorate] archives and reproduced an important message sent from the Washington DC *rezidentura* to Moscow on August 2, 1948:

> LUIS [Morris Cohen] has met YOUNG. He has persuaded him to break contact with the Progressive organization and concentrate on science. Important information obtained on YOUNG's new contacts. They have declared their wish to transmit data on ENORMOZ, subject to two conditions. YOUNG must be their only contact and their names must not be known to officers of ARTEMIS [Soviet intelligence].

This text, released before the Russian authorities knew that VENONA was to be declassified, shows Hall in contact with Morris Cohen at a time when the physicist was studying for his Ph.D. at the University of Chicago and was also getting involved in politics. Clearly, Cohen had advised Hall to curtail his extracurricular activities, and encouraged him to cultivate his two new contacts.

Further evidence about Hall's network was provided in 1992 by the KGB defector Vasili Mitrokhin, who noted that its membership included ADEN, SERB, and SILVER, but does not put a date on their recruitment. It is quite possible that two of the three may have been YOUNG's new sources, as reported in August 1948, but there is no certainty. Neither ADEN nor SILVER appear in any of the VENONA texts, but SERB shows up four times, albeit in a slightly different context, and occasionally with his other codename, RELAY. On July 11, 1944, a VENONA text indicated that he did not live in New York, and could only temporarily remove documents from his workplace:

> With a view to reducing the time required for the receipt and handing back of RELAY's materials we consider it would be a good thing to make it his job to photograph his own materials and bring to TYRE [New York] only undeveloped films.

Moscow seems to have wanted to entrust RELAY with the supervision of other agents, as demonstrated by a VENONA cable dated July 4, 1944, from Apresyan in New York, and evidently tried to appoint him as "group leader" for Enos R. Wicher, codenamed KEEN, a scientist then working in the Wave Propagation Group at Columbia University's Division of War Research, and an as yet unidentified spy, FISHERMAN. A Russian immigrant by background, Wicher had been a CPUSA organizer under the alias "Bill Rain" in Wisconsin, and both his wife, Maria Wicher (codenamed DAShA), and his stepdaughter, Flora Wovschin (codenamed ZORA), were Soviet spies. Although VENONA shed no light on the information this family trio was supplying, Wovschin worked in the State Department where she was instrumental in recruiting her colleagues Judith Coplon (codenamed SIMA) and Marion Davis (codenamed LOU).

The impression that RELAY/SERB was a significant figure is supported by the same VENONA text, which also appears to accept Moscow's proposal that he should control two unknown agents, FISHERMAN and NYNA, and sheds further light on his personal and physical circumstances:

> [73 groups unrecoverable] moreover FISHERMAN and NYNA will be handed over to RELAY who has been introduced to CALISTRA-

> TUS [Aleksandr Feklisov]. Concerning MASTERCRAFTSMAN see our No. 483. Your proposal to make RELAY group leader for FISHERMAN, MASTERCRAFTSMAN [4 groups unrecovered] is impracticable. RELAY is disabled and has an artificial leg. Frequent trips are difficult for him. He has an artificial leg. He lives in the PHILADELPHIA area.[1]

Unexplained, unfortunately, is Moscow's reason for suggesting that RELAY should take charge of MASTERCRAFTSMAN, who was Charles B. Sheppard, a radio engineer working for the Hazeltine Electronics Corporation of Little Neck, New York. However, the two clues to RELAY's identity—that he was disabled and lived in Philadelphia—were to be significant. On the basis that RELAY was an atomic source, a deduction stemming from his involvement with the two key ENORMOZ controllers on the East Coast—Semyonov and Feklisov—attention focused on potential suspects, and it was noted that Philip Morrison lived with his parents in Philadelphia in 1943, and wore a caliper on a leg weakened by childhood polio.

The same message goes on to allocate various agents to a list of *rezidentura* handlers, and there may be a hint here that Semyon Semyonov was to run RELAY, although the relevant text is bracketed by unbroken code groups which makes the context uncertain:

> TWAIN [Semyon Semyonov] controls the following PROBATIONERS [agents] [9 groups unrecovered], RELAY [17 groups unrecovered]

As Semyonov is closely associated with atomic espionage, this could imply that RELAY was in the same category, and another VENONA text, dated January 11, 1945, from Leonid Kvasnikov (ANTON), seems to support this proposition, first through Kvasnikov's authorship and, second, through the content, connecting RELAY/SERB to the Cohens, and at the very least implies that he knew Morris was an NKVD agent:

> SERB has advised that VOLUNTEER has died at the front in Europe. The last meeting with LESLEY [Lona Cohen] was had by

> TWAIN [Semyon Semyonov] about six months ago. Do you consider it desirable to establish liaison with LESLEY to render her assistance and activate her in the future as a go-between [1 group unrecovered] special conspirative apartment?

This short message reflects curiously on SERB, who evidently was under the mistaken impression that Morris Cohen had been killed fighting on the Western Front. In fact, Cohen had been called up for the military draft in July 1942 and had been posted to the 241st Service Battalion of the Quartermaster's Corps at Dawson Creek in northern Canada. Almost two years later he was transferred to England and landed at Normandy on D+6. At the time SERB mistakenly reported his death to Kvasnikov, Cohen's rear echelon unit had been caught up in the Battle of the Bulge in Belgium, but he had survived the surprise Nazi offensive. So how could SERB have got this news so wrong, and why had his wife not been reactivated since Semyonov's recall to Moscow in September 1944?

A graduate in electrical engineering from the Leningrad Institute of Chemical Engineering, Semyonov had scarcely been in the NKVD a year when, in 1938, he had been sent to study at the Massachusetts Institute of Technology. In 1940 he was assigned a cover position at Amtorg in New York, but in reality was acting as handler for Morris Cohen, a Soviet agent since his recruitment during the Spanish Civil War. Morris had obtained a degree in English at Mississippi State College. When Morris had married the fiery Lona Petka in July 1941, she too was drawn into Sam Semyonov's network, which concentrated on the collection of technical intelligence. Semyonov's departure in 1944 had been prompted by intensive FBI surveillance, making his work difficult. As for Lona, she was living alone in a one-room apartment at 178 East 71st Street and commuting to work at the Aircraft Screw Products Company in Long Island City, Queens, where she had acquired a reputation as a union troublemaker following an industrial accident in which her hair got caught in a machine. There is some evidence in VENONA that she was acting as a courier for Semyonov between her husband's call-up and her handler's departure, maybe servicing letters from a mail-drop sent by William Weisband, codenamed

LINK, but why she was abandoned for six months remains a mystery. The VENONA text, dated August 30, 1944, refers to information received by VOLUNTEER's wife "from LINK through his brother." Clearly, Kvasnikov thought she could be used to run a safe house, and needed Moscow's permission to reestablish contact with her. The connection with Weisband's brother is intriguing, for Weisband himself was a significant Soviet spy, not least because he joined the BRIDE project in the Armed Forces Security Agency as a linguist fluent in Russian, Arabic, German and French, and reported on the cryptographers' progress. According to his prewar girlfriend, Patricia Baumann (later Mrs. Robert F. Callicott), he had been active as a spy before the war when she had accompanied him to empty dead letter drops. Weisband married another member of the AFSA, twenty years his junior, and was to be imprisoned in November 1950, having been convicted of contempt during grand jury proceedings in California. He died of a heart attack in Washington DC in May 1967.

At the end of the war Saville Sax returned to Harvard. He was replaced as Hall's courier by Lona Cohen, who maintained irregular contact with him until March 16, 1951, when Hall was visited at the Institute for Radiobiology and Biophysics at the University of Chicago by two FBI special agents. During a three-hour interview Hall denied any involvement with espionage, but refused the FBI permission to search his home. At a second interview, two days later, Hall declined to answer any further questions, and soon afterwards he took up a research post at Memorial Sloan-Kettering in New York. Sax, who had given up running a copy shop and was then driving a taxi in Chicago, was also interviewed by the FBI on March 16, but denied espionage, claiming that his occasional visits to the Soviet Consulate in New York had been in connection with relatives still living in the Soviet Union, and his single trip to New Mexico, to consult his trusted friend Ted Hall about another university course, had been taken after he had dropped out of Harvard. Sax denied ever having received a list of atomic scientists from Hall, and consented to a search of his home, which revealed nothing incriminating.

In 1953 Hall broke off all contact with the Soviets and eleven years later he was offered a twelve-month contract at the Cavendish Laboratory at Cambridge University. At the end of the year, instead of returning to the United States where his friend Sax had died, Hall remained at the university, and lived in the town with his wife Joan and their daughter until his death in 1999. Taken together, the VENONA texts amount to as comprehensive an indictment of Hall's espionage as could be asked for, but the necessity to protect the source's integrity meant that Hall was allowed his liberty. All he was prepared to say before his death was that "in 1944 I was nineteen years old—immature, inexperienced and not too sure of myself."

> I recognize that I could easily have been wrong in my judgment of what was necessary, and that I was indeed mistaken about some things, in particular my view of the nature of the Soviet state. The world has moved on since then, and certainly so have I.[2]

After his death in December 1999 in England, his wife confirmed that Hall had indeed spied for the Soviets, and expressed her support for him.

The question that remains vis-à-vis Hall is the nature of his relationship with the Cohens and the extent of their organization, which became known as "the volunteers." Unlike the network headed by Julius Rosenberg, which was often remunerated, the Cohens took no payment. Furthermore, it seems to have operated largely after the war, or certainly after Morris Cohen had been released from his military service with the U.S. Army in Europe in November 1945 (with a ten percent disability compensation for snow blindness). The KGB's official history has certainly acknowledged its role, claiming that "the Volunteer group…was able to guarantee the transmittal to the Center of super secret information concerning the development of the American atomic bomb." Hall remains the key source of the Volunteer Group, and it would seem that Lona Cohen left her job at Aircraft Screw Products in early 1945 to work as a full-time courier, and made at least two visits to Albuquerque to collect information from him. One took place in 1943 and, according to Vladimir Chikov, she made two further trips in 1945.

As for her husband, he was "put on ice," like all the other current agents during the Gouzenko episode in September 1945 and was not to be reactivated until July 1947 during a trip to Paris for a reunion with Semyon Semyonov and Anatoli Yatskov, who had both been transferred to the Paris *rezidentura.* Thus Morris Cohen, the steadfast Communist, both of whose parents were active CPUSA members in New York, enjoyed two periods of espionage in the United States, the first prior to his call-up in July 1942, and the second between his reactivation in 1947 and his flight to Mexico in July 1950. It is difficult to assess what he achieved during the first period, which began with his recruitment in Barcelona and upon his return to New York encompassed security duties at the New York World Fair, shared with Zelmond Franklin and Milton Wolff, the commander of the Veterans of the Abraham Lincoln Division. During the latter period, when Cohen received an M.A. from Columbia University in 1947 and a Teacher's Certificate from Columbia in 1949, the Volunteers were supervised by an illegal, William Fisher (alias Emil Goldfus and Colonel Rudolf Abel), who arrived in New York from Canada in November 1948. He in turn was controlled by a member of the local *rezidentura*, Yuri S. Sokolov, codenamed CLAUDE, a former security guard at the Yalta conference in overall change of scientific and technical intelligence operations. But where did their information come from? According to Chikov, the Volunteers at that time consisted of RAY and FRANK, but the post-Gouzenko isolation had taken its toll. "RAY had lost his job at a firm where he had picked up information on radar and underwater sonar technology. FRANK had collected 19 rolls of film on guided missiles, but as time went by and contact was not renewed, he decided to destroy them, fearing to keep such incriminating materials."

Hall recommended two other scientists for recruitment as members of the Volunteers Group. These were probably ADEN and SILVER, the pair of spies disclosed by Mitrokhin, but who were they? One clue comes from Morris Cohen who said in a television interview in Moscow that when he was obliged to flee to Mexico, he handed the control of three of his agents to Fisher, two being in California and the third in New York. Furthermore, according to Chikov, the New York source was a former OSS officer, now in the CIA, and the other pair was "a married couple working at the Hanford Engineer Works" who were in touch with OLD. Research by Humphrey Laes suggests that this couple may have been Robert and Charlotte Serber (see Chapter VIII). The FBI certainly took a close interest in the disappearance of the Cohens, to the point that they arranged for Morris to be notified through his parents that if he failed to turn up for a medical examination in August 1957, he would forfeit his disability payments. Morris did not attend, and his monthly checks were stopped.

The other major atomic spy to be identified by VENONA is Klaus Fuchs, who was the source codenamed REST (and, after a change in cryptonyms in October 1944, CHARLES). Seen in their correct chronology, the VENONA material pointing to Fuchs as a spy is compelling, but at the time of the FBI's investigation only fragments of texts were available, and the hunt was on for a spy who had been out of touch for some time, had met a contact codenamed ARNO, and had a sister codenamed ANT. FBI Special Agents Robert Lamphere and Ernest van Loon narrowed the search for the culprit to a scientist who had worked both in New York and Los Alamos, had traveled to Chicago, was scheduled to go to England and had a sister living somewhere in the United States.

The fact that Klaus Fuchs had joined Birmingham University's atomic research team on May 28, 1941, and had studied in Leipzig under Werner Heisenberg, Professor of Theoretical Physics between 1927 and 1941, dovetailed neatly with the fragments extracted from a GRU telegram.

The investigation of Fuchs's travel in the United States culminated in October 1949 when van Loon showed that the scientist had made the visit to Chicago mentioned in VENONA, and to his sister and brother-in-law, Kristel and Robert Heineman, who lived in Cambridge, Massachusetts, with their three children. According to the Fuchs personal security file, he had been absent from Los

Alamos between February 11–25, 1945, in Cambridge, Massachusetts, and November 20–December 8, 1945, to visit Montreal and then take a vacation in Albuquerque and Mexico City. In parallel, Special Agent J. Jerome Maxwell of the FBI's El Paso office conducted an intense investigation of Rudolf Peierls, and after interviewing Ralph Smith, the Assistant Director for Classification and Security at the laboratory, he reported that "both Fuchs and Peierls had almost unlimited access to highly classified information while at Los Alamos."

Kristel, evidently, was ANT, so all that remained was the identification of Fuchs's cut-out, codenamed GOOSE and then ARNO. This was eventually achieved when Fuchs, after his conviction, confirmed that surveillance footage filmed secretly by the FBI of Harry Gold was the person he had known as "Raymond," his contact in New York.

Since Fuchs had initially declined to incriminate his Soviet contacts, Commander Len Burt of Scotland Yard's Special Branch enlisted the help of Rudolf Peierls in an attempt to extract this vital information. Peierls had traveled up to London as soon as he had heard of Fuchs's arrest and had offered to find him a lawyer on the false assumption that Fuchs had undergone some kind of breakdown and fabricated a tale of espionage. Fuchs had been planning to adopt his nephew, and at first Peierls reasoned that no spy would contemplate endangering a child. However, after the first meeting with his colleague while in on remand in Brixton prison, he was obliged to alter his view, and later to acknowledge that he too must have come under investigation.

> In the course of tracing the source of the leaks from Los Alamos, the evidence indicated at one stage that a theoretician in the British group was responsible, which pointed to Fuchs and me. I must therefore have been under great suspicion for a time, but at no stage was I made to feel it.

In fact, the VENONA molehunt was not limited to a British theoretician, but simply someone who fit the description that appeared in the NKVD's intercepted texts. When sufficient clues were decrypted, the field was narrowed to Fuchs and the identification was passed to Arthur Martin, the GCHQ liaison officer attached to MI5.

Fuchs's initial confession to Len Burt was to become a source of tremendous friction between MI5 and the FBI because the British prosecuting authorities refused to allow J. Edgar Hoover to dispatch a team of interrogators to London to find out more about "Raymond" until the trial was over, and the period allowed for any appeal had lapsed. Hoover could not understand these legal niceties and strongly resented what he regarded as obstruction into an ongoing investigation, especially when Lish Whitson returned from an unannounced visit to London empty-handed. The uproar that followed at the FBI headquarters cost Howard Fletcher, the Assistant Director for the Domestic Intelligence Division, his job; an infuriated Hoover replaced him with Alan Belmont. Even worse, the Fuchs case was to cause turmoil within the Security Service because the internal post-mortem revealed that the Fuchs personal file contained an explicit recommendation, made in writing years earlier, that he ought to be investigated as a possible Communist spy. The proposal, which was ignored, was based on a prewar denunciation of Fuchs as a Communist when he had first come to Britain, the discovery of his name in a Gestapo file in Kiel, captured at the end of the war, again identifying him as having been a Communist since 1934, and the fact that his details appeared in an address book containing 436 individual entries recovered from the home of Israel Halperin, one of the spies exposed in Canada by Gouzenko and detained in 1946.

This curious, latter link had come about because Halperin apparently had tried to ease the plight of German Communists held as enemy aliens in Sherbrooke Camp, near Quebec, in 1940, after they had been transported across the Atlantic and detained with authentic Nazis. Subsequent inquiries established that Halperin's contact with Fuchs had been limited to mailing him magazines during the short period he was in Canada, but there could have been a more sinister explanation, and in any event it served to demonstrate that the detainee's political sympathies were widely known to everyone except MI5. Relations between MI5 and the FBI deteriorated even further when Fuchs mentioned that in 1941, following his return to England from internment in Canada, he had emphasized his anti-Nazi credentials by declaring, at his hearing before the Aliens Review Board, that he was a Communist. Lamphere, for one, found it hard to understand why MI5 had not shared this in formation with the FBI at the outset, when the time-consuming investigation into REST/CHARLES initially had focused on two other possible candidates.

The Director of MI5's B Division, Sir Dick White, sheepishly admitted to the Director-General, Sir Percy Sillitoe, that the suggestion that Fuchs be investigated had been overlooked, and thus placed him in a dilemma when the Prime Minister, Clement Attlee, in response to growing public criticism of MI5's handling of the case, demanded to know whether there really had been a lapse in security. Reluctantly, but under pressure from a triumvirate consisting of his Deputy Director-General Guy Liddell, Dick White, and Roger Hollis, Sillitoe lied to Attlee, who in turn assured the House of Commons on March 6, 1950:

> I do not think there is anything that can cast the slightest slur on the Security Service. Indeed, I think they acted promptly and effectively as soon as there was any line they could follow up.

Upon reflection, Sillitoe was furious that he had been browbeaten into misleading the Prime Minister. Against the advice of his personal assistant Russell Lee, on whom he relied heavily (and who was to ghost his memoirs, *Cloak Without Dagger*), he gathered the whole of MI5's B Division in the staff canteen on the top floor of Leconfield House and announced that he would never be put into the position of lying to the Prime Minister to protect the senior management from the consequences of their blunders. Aghast at this semi-public, humiliating rebuke, White canvassed friends about resigning, but was persuaded that his career was safe because Sillitoe was close to retirement.

After Fuchs had acknowledged meeting "Raymond" a total of nine times, twice in Santa Fe, and twice in Boston, and the rest in various New York City boroughs, the Swiss-born chemist confessed under interrogation to having received material from Fuchs. Gold made a lengthy statement in which he admitted having spied since 1935, initially supplying industrial information before graduating to atomic data. In December 1950 he was sentenced to thirty years' imprisonment, five more than the prosecution had recommended.

Fuchs's own confession, in a six-and-a-half-page statement delivered to Bob Lamphere and Hugh Clegg (of the FBI's Inspection Division) at Wormwood Scrubs, on a visit organized by the FBI's "Legal Attaché" liaison officer John Cimperman, and accompanied by MI5's Jim Skardon, appeared comprehensive and neatly coincided with the VENONA information. According to the note made by Lamphere, Fuchs admitted that in his estimation he had advanced the Soviet atomic test by "several years" and recalled that during the first five meetings he had attended in New York in 1944, he had passed

> [l]onghand drafts of the 13 out of 19 "MSN" papers on the principles of gaseous diffusion and other critical principles, which he himself had written.
> General information concerning membranes used to separate substances, and the composition of the sintered nickel powder used to keep apart portions of the fissionable material.
> General information on the scope, timing, progress and experiments of the Manhattan Project.
> Information on the identity and character of all those involved in the project whom he then knew.
> Information on the development of the plant at Oak Ridge, Tennessee.

Fuchs also described the information he had given his contact in Cambridge, Massachusetts, in early 1945:

> The principles of A-bomb detonation, which method had been chosen, and why.
> The principle of the lens mold system and the dimensions of the high explosive on which it worked.
> An extensive discussion of the principle of implosion, the central

new focus developed at Los Alamos.

Details about plutonium-240 multiple-point detonation, the time and sequence of construction of the A-bomb, and the need for an initiator to set off the device.

Missing from Lamphere's notes is a crucial section dealing with Fuchs's knowledge of other spies inside the Manhattan Project. Although he denied personal knowledge of any by name, he expressed a professional opinion regarding the questions he had been asked by his early GRU contacts. These had persuaded him that "in 1942 or earlier" the Soviets had acquired information about electromagnetic separation research conducted at Berkeley. In other words, Fuchs believed another spy had been at work in San Francisco long before he had ever set foot in the United States. For the assembled molehunters, this was a revelation of the utmost gravity and one that, given Fuchs's cooperation, had to be taken seriously.

Fuchs appeared to have been almost entirely truthful in his confession, except with respect to his sister, for he was anxious not to implicate Kristel who by then had suffered a nervous breakdown and was in a mental hospital. With his brother, mother and grandmother having committed suicide, Fuchs was obviously keen not to burden Kristel further, and he denied ever having passed secrets to Raymond in her house, in contradiction to Gold's version. And although she was definitely ANT, there was no additional VENONA evidence to implicate her. As she and her husband had cooperated with the FBI, and also had identified Gold from photographs as a man who had visited them unexpectedly in July 1944 in an effort to make contact with Klaus, she featured no further in the FBI's inquiries, although her husband Robert was flagged as a member of the CPUSA prior to 1937 and attracted the FBI's attention partly because he worked for the General Electric Company, but mainly because of a visit he had made to Mexico in February 1947, allegedly to write a book and obtain a degree, barely a month after he had re-registered as a Communist.

Fuchs also belatedly admitted to having reestablished contact with the Soviets, after his return to Britain in October 1946. His new handler, Aleksandr S. Feklisov, recalled their first meeting, in the Nag's Head pub opposite the Wood Green tube station in west London on the evening of Saturday, September 27, 1947: "As arranged, Fuchs came up to the panel with photos of famous British boxers, and there was a dispute about who was the best. I, too, came up to the group where Fuchs stood. He said, 'Bruce Woodcock is the best British boxer of all time.' Naturally I responded, 'Tommy Far was much better that Bruce Woodcock.' Having exchanged these code phrases, we both left separately. Fuchs walked ahead of me. I gained on him and we started talking. I passed to him an oral request to answer six questions. I could not memorize more than six. Fuchs heard the questions and promised to have the answers ready for our next meeting. Then he handed me a rather bulky parcel and we parted. Later I learned the file contained detailed information on the plutonium production process at Windscale."[3]

Future meetings, eight in total and arranged for every two or three months, were to take place either in the Nag's Head, or in The Spotted Horse on Putney High Street. The fallback contingency plans made by Feklisov were sophisticated. If either failed to appear, they would meet at the same place exactly a week later. A further failure meant a rendezvous at the other pub a month later, and if this failed they would revert to the original pub the next week. A cross chalked on a wall near Kew Gardens station indicated a cancellation, and emergency communications could be made by a message written on the tenth page of a magazine that should be tossed into the garden of a particular house in Richmond.

Feklisov, the consummate professional, was representative of a new generation of NKVD professionals who were qualified to handle technical intelligence. He had graduated from the radio faculty of the Moscow Communications Institute in 1939 and, after a further training course, had joined the NKVD's American Department but had worked in the Ministry of Foreign Affairs under deep cover. In February 1941 he traveled to New York via Yokohama, Honolulu and San Francisco under the alias Aleksandr Fomin, to improve the New York *rezidentura*'s radio link with Moscow, but after two years masquerading as a consular trainee, he was transferred to work on ENORMOZ, and stayed for a total of five and a half years. While in New York he met and married Zina Osipova, one of a group of exchange students at Columbia University who, having been stranded by the war, was employed as a secretary by the chairman of Amtorg.

In his memoirs, *The Man Behind The Rosenbergs*, published against strong official disapproval in 2001, Feklisov described how in the summer of 1942 he had cultivated another Russian, a former Amtorg employee who had returned to the Soviet Union in November 1940, after having become friendly with a Kellex engineer codenamed MONTI. Feklisov says this was not his true codename, which does not appear in the VENONA traffic, and that he "was in charge of a team of engineers who were building chemical plants in the United States and overseas. He lived very well in a beautiful house in the Manhattan suburbs" but was handled indirectly, through a cut-out, to whom he gave "the technical blueprint of the plant at Oak Ridge." At that stage MONTI allegedly was considered by Moscow to be more important than the Rosenbergs, and therefore was given "absolute priority."

In September 1946, after five and a half years, Feklisov handed over responsibility for running Julius Rosenberg to his colleague Gavril Panchenko and returned to Moscow, but after a year on the staff, he was posted to London, as deputy *rezident* to Mikhail Shishkin (and then, after November 1947, to his replacement Boris Rodin, alias Nikolai B. Korovin, a GRU officer who had been based in New York between 1939 and 1944) to run Fuchs. He was recalled in April 1950, following Fuchs's trial, and later went to Prague as deputy chief adviser to the StB (Czech Intelligence.) In 1956 he was promoted head of the KGB's American Department, and between August 1960 and April 1964 was KGB *rezident* in Washington DC, making another reputation during the Cuban Missile Crisis as a diplomatic back-channel to the Kremlin.

Chapter VII

The Rosenberg Network

The bomb will never be dropped on people. As soon as we get it, we'll use it only to dictate terms of peace.

Ernest Lawrence to *Raymond Birge*

Confirmation of Gold's espionage represented a considerable breakthrough, partly because he was no stranger to the FBI, having been called before a grand jury in 1947 looking into Elizabeth Bentley's allegations. Bentley had claimed that her lover, Jacob Golos, had received technical, but nonclassified, information from Abraham Brothman, and when called as a witness he asserted that he had been introduced to Golos by another legitimate businessman, Harry Gold. A chemist by trade, Brothman had denied having done anything illegal and had escaped all charges, as had Gold, but four years later a VENONA cable from Apresyan dated October 1, 1944 (see page 63 above) was to shed a different light on the illicit activities of Gold and Brothman.

According to Gold, Brothman had also been involved in industrial espionage since 1935, but Gold's decision to go into partnership with him effectively ended their connection with the Soviets. Gold's principal contact had been Semyon Semyonov, but in September 1944 Anatoli Yatskov took him over as a courier for Fuchs and discovered during a meeting held in New York in late 1946 that, contrary to instructions, Gold had kept in touch with Brothman. Furious, Yatskov had berated Gold for maintaining contact with someone who had come under FBI surveillance, for it was clear that Brothman had been a marked man after he had been denounced as a Soviet source by Elizabeth Bentley. Discarded by Yatskov, Gold saw no alternative to cooperating with the FBI, and giving evidence against Abe Brothman, who received a prison sentence.

As well as supporting Bentley's testimony over Brothman, it was Gold who led the FBI to David Greenglass, the former YCL member, who in turn exposed the extent of the Soviet operation ENORMOZ. In May 1945 Yatskov had asked Gold to collect information from a source in Albuquerque when he next held a rendezvous with Fuchs in Santa Fe and had given him the contact's name and address, together with $500 and a recognition signal in the form of a torn cardboard Jell-O boxtop, which would match the pair held by the spy. Under interrogation, five years later, Gold was able to pinpoint the address on a map of Albuquerque that he had visited in June 1945, and recall that his contact's wife had been named Ruth. Although he could not remember their surname, he knew that Ruth's husband was Jewish and was a young army technician. As for his information, it had consisted of several pages of handwritten notes and sketches. By the middle of June 1950 Bob Lamphere had traced David Greenglass, a soldier previously employed at Los Alamos, in George Kistiakowsky's Group E-5, and once suspected of having stolen a tiny sample of Uranium-235, to his apartment in Rivington Street, in New York's Lower East Side. Evidence of just such a spy at Los Alamos in 1944 codenamed CALIBER had been revealed in a VENONA text from Kvasnikov dated November 14, 1944:

> WASP has agreed to cooperate with us in drawing in BUMBLE-BEE (henceforth CALIBER—see your no. 5258) with a view to ENORMOZ. On summons from CALIBER she is leaving on 22 November for the Camp-2 area. CALIBER will have a week's leave. Before WASP's departure LIBERAL will carry out two briefing meetings.

That CALIBER enjoyed good access to Los Alamos was revealed in a telegram from Leonid Kvasnikov dated December 16, 1944, in which he reported the results of WASP's visit to CALIBER, although there is still no clue that he is her husband:

> WASP has returned from a trip to see CALIBER. CALIBER expressed his readiness to help in throwing light on the work being carried out at Camp-2 [Los Alamos] and stated that he had already given thought to this question earlier. CALIBER said that the authorities of the camp were openly taking all precautionary measures to prevent information about ENORMOZ falling into Russian hands. This is causing serious discontent among the progressive workers [17 groups unrecoverable] the middle of January CALIBER will be in TYRE [New York]. LIBERAL referred to his ignorance of the problem, expresses the wish that our man should meet CALIBER and interrogate him personally. He asserts that CALIBER would be very glad of such a meeting. Do you consider such a meeting advisable? If not, I shall be obliged to draw up a questionnaire and pass it to LIBERAL. Report whether you have any questions of priority interest to us.
> CALIBER also reports: OPPENHEIM from California and KISTIAKOWSKI's (YOUNG's report mentioned the latter) are at present working at the Camp. The latter is doing research on the thermodynamic process. Advise whether you have information on these two professors.

Kvasnikov was to have more to say about CALIBER on January 8, 1945, when he reported his appearance in New York:

> CALIBER has arrived in TYRE [New York] on leave. He has confirmed his agreement to help us. In addition to the information passed

> to us through WASP he has given us a hand-written plan of the layout of Camp-2 and facts known to him about the work and the personnel. The basic task of the camp is to make the mechanism which is to serve as the detonator. Experimental work is being carried out on the construction of a tube of this kind and experiments are being tried with explosive—[13 groups unrecoverable] is still [17 groups unrecovered] gave you for [91 groups unrecovered] TYRE in six months time [32 groups unrecoverable] LIBERAL to WASP [16 groups unrecovered]. Telegraph your opinion.

A check on Greenglass's army service record by the FBI showed that he had taken some leave between December 30, 1944, and January 20, 1945, and had traveled up to New York, which coincided with CALIBER's known movements. Greenglass had dropped out of his mechanical engineering course at the Brooklyn Polytechnic Institute to work for four months at the Federal Telephone Company, before joining Peerless Laboratories on East 23rd Street as a machinist. Newly married to Ruth, he was still working there in March 1943 when he was drafted into the army and inducted at Fort Dix, before being transferred to the Aberdeen Proving Grounds in Maryland for basic training. Later he was to move to Fort Ord, California, to repair tanks, then to the Mississippi Ordnance Plant as a machinist and Oak Ridge in July before arriving finally at Los Alamos in August 1944, having omitted his membership of the YCL from his security clearance questionnaire.

After prolonged interrogation, Greenglass admitted his complicity in espionage and implicated both his wife, Ruth, and his brother-in-law, Julius Rosenberg. Although he had been told the work he was doing at Los Alamos was top secret, it had taken him more than a month to learn that the project was engaged on building an atomic bomb. Initially he had worked in the Theta Shop, making experimental equipment that could not be purchased elsewhere, and then moved on to handle uranium. In a second statement, made on June 16, 1950, the day after his first encounter with Special Agents Frutkin and Lewis, he described how, during his furlough in New York, he had borrowed a 1935 Oldsmobile and picked up Julius Rosenberg, who had introduced him to a second man who climbed in as Rosenberg left: "I drove around while the man asked me questions about a high-explosive lens which was being experimented with at Los Alamos Atom Bomb Project. I tried to describe the lens to the man while I was driving. When the man left the car about fifteen minutes later, I went home." This was sufficient to incriminate Rosenberg, who was interviewed the same day by Special Agents John A. Harrington and William F. Norton, but in his statement he insisted that "he and David did not discuss the Atom Bomb from the technical standpoint either before or after the restrictions were lifted. He said that prior to the dropping of the Atom Bomb on Hiroshima, Japan, that he did not know anything about the Atom Bomb."

In fact, the involvement of Greenglass's brother-in-law had been set out very explicitly in a VENONA text from Apresyan in New York dated September 21, 1944:

> Lately the development of new people has been in progress. LIBERAL [Julius Rosenberg] recommended the wife of his wife's brother, Ruth GREENGLASS, with a safe flat in view. She is 21 years old, a TOWNSWOMAN [American], a GYMNAST [member of the Young Communist League] since 1942. She lives on STANTON Street. LIBERAL and his wife recommend her as an intelligent and clever girl. [15 groups unrecoverable] Ruth learned that her husband was called up by the army but he was not sent to the front. He is a mechanical engineer and is now working at the ENORMOZ plant in SANTA FE, New Mexico [45 groups unrecoverable] detain VOLOK who is working on a plant on ENORMOZ. He is a COMPATRIOT [Communist]. Yesterday he learned that they dismissed him from his work. His active work in progressive organizations in the past was the cause of his dismissal.
>
> In the COMPATRIOT line LIBERAL is in touch with CHESTER. They meet once a month for the payment of dues. CHESTER is interested in whether we are satisfied with the collaboration and whether there are not any misunderstandings. He does not inquire about specific items of work. In as much as CHESTER knows about the role of the LIBERAL group we beg consent to ask CHESTER

through LIBERAL about leads from among people who are working on ENORMOZ and in other technical fields.

With David Greenglass identified as CALIBER, much of the rest of the network fell into place, with Ruth, codenamed WASP, having recruited him for her brother-in-law, LIBERAL. CHESTER, who was in regular contact with Julius to collect his Party dues, was Bernard Schuster, head of the CPUSA's Control Commission, and his appearance served to confirm the very strong link between the CPUSA and the NKVD, with Stepan Apresyan appealing to Moscow to allow Julius to seek Schuster's help in recruiting more ENORMOZ agents. The unresolved item from this significant VENONA message is the identification of VOLOK, apparently a source inside Los Alamos recently sacked because of his political background.

Once Julius had been named by Greenglass, he was arrested by the FBI at his home at Apartment GE-11, 10 Monroe Street. Although he denied all knowledge of espionage, there were good grounds for believing that he was the mysterious "Julius" whom Elizabeth Bentley recalled had lived in Knickerbocker Village and occasionally had been in touch with Jacob Golos. She had taken several telephone messages from "Julius" and once, in the autumn of 1942, had accompanied Golos to a meeting with him on a street corner on the lower east side of New York, but having remained in the car, she had only caught a glimpse of him from a distance. He "was tall, thin and wore horn-rimmed glasses," and her recollection was that "Julius" was the leader of a cell of Communist engineers upon whom Golos had relied for technical information, and who later were based in Norfolk, Virginia. Initially baffled by the Norfolk connection, it was later discovered that William Perl had worked near the town, and Morton Sobell had occasionally visited there too.

The VENONA texts were to reveal a very different story to the innocence claimed by Rosenberg. Initially codenamed ANTENNA, Julius was at the heart of a massive spy ring concentrated on technical intelligence, and the FBI was to conclude that he had been a spy since his discharge from the Army Signal Corps. On May 5, 1944, Apresyan requested Moscow:

> Please carry out a check and sanction the recruitment of Alfred SARANT, a lead of ANTENNA [Julius Rosenberg]. He is 25 years old, a Greek, an American citizen and lives in TYRE [New York City]. He completed the engineering course at Cooper Union in 1940. He worked for two years in the Signal Corps laboratory at Fort MONMOUTH. He was discharged for past union activity. He has been working for two years at Western Electric [45 groups unrecoverable] entry into the COMPATRIOT [Communist Party]. SARANT lives apart from his family. Answer without delay.

As well as drawing in members of his family (though not his elder brother David, a pharmacist, nor his twin sisters), his neighbors and many of his oldest friends, in this case Al Sarant, Rosenberg was revealed to be his network's key figure, even to the point of handling his sub-agents' data himself, as was disclosed in a telegram to Moscow dated May 22, 1944, which showed that his productivity had increased during the year, and established a direct link with Anatoli Yatskov at the Soviet Consulate:

> The work of the KhU [Economic Directorate] connected with the receipt of bulky materials is attended by great risk particularly the secret materials which were coming in during 1943 and are coming in now. The danger has increased because of the periodic surveillance of the cadre workers and the increasing surveillance of the PLANT [Soviet Consulate] to which the materials are being brought for filming. It has become impossible to bring [18 groups unrecoverable] to film at ALEKSEI's [Anatoli Yakovlev] apartment to which a portable camera had been brought earlier. It is intended in the future to practice such filming only now and then. What is your opinion? We consider it necessary to organize the filming of ANTENNA's [Julius Rosenberg] PROBATIONER's [agents] materials by ANTENNA himself. Again the question of a camera for ALEKSEI has been raised. Exceptionally secret materials are conveyed in the original or in manuscript which is more dangerous than the presence of a camera at ALEKSEI's. It is incomprehensible why one cannot do this in the course of the next half year (your No. 2031). We assume

> that it is connected with conservation and not the danger of ALEKSEI's disclosure [34 groups unrecoverable]

Apresyan subsequently addressed the problem of copying documents on June 14, 1944, by passing it to Leonid Kvasnikov, who headed the parallel *rezidentura* in New York on behalf of the 8th Department:

> Your No. 2542. ANTON's [Leonid Kvasnikov] apartment is needed for photographing the material of ANTENNA's [Julius Rosenberg] group.

Having established where the photography was to take place, Moscow was unable to supply the necessary equipment and on July 11, 1944, arranged for German cameras, which were the subject of a wartime trade ban in the U.S., to be purchased in Mexico:

> Please give instructions to the COUNTRYSIDE [Mexico] to buy two cameras and send them to TYRE [New York] by the first post. You allowed one camera for ANTENNA [Julius Rosenberg]. The second is needed for the work of the OFFICE [*rezidentura*]. The cameras find their way to the COUNTRYSIDE from Germany and cost 200 dollars. There are no cameras in TYRE. Inform us of your instructions.
>
> With a view to reducing the time required for the receipt and handing back of RELAY's materials we consider it would be a good thing to make it his job to photograph his own materials and bring to TYRE only undeveloped films. For this purpose we want to pass on to him INFORMER's [Joseph Katz] old camera. The camera [17 groups unrecoverable]

The NKVD's demand for good German cameras in New York was reflected in a VENONA text recovered from the Mexico City circuit dated September 30, 1944, in which Moscow had directed:

> Buy up quickly, and send to WASHINGTON for VADIM [Anatoli Gorsky] 10 "LEICA" cameras with a full set of lenses. Report their cost to the CENTER.

This demand is significant for it names Anatoli Gorsky, until recently the NKVD *rezident* in London, as a member of the Washington DC *rezidentura.* He had arrived in the United States on September 15, 1944, partly to supervise the handling of Donald Maclean, who had been posted to the British embassy in May, but also to take over the post of *rezident* from Vasili Zubilin, who had been recalled to face charges leveled against him by one of his disgruntled subordinates, Vasili Mironov, alias Colonel Markov. Mironov, who evidently hated Zubilin for whom he acted as secretary, had written a long letter to Stalin accusing the *rezident* of being a spy for the Japanese, and in August 1943 had authored a similar denunciation to the FBI.

A subsequent VENONA text, sent on October 22, 1944, revealed the existence of another member of LIBERAL's organization:

> Inquiring [36 groups unrecovered] [34 groups unrecoverable] was explained that he, as a specialist, received from the draft board an inquiry about where he is working and on what means he lives. [60 groups unrecoverable] …". In view of poor health [24 groups unrecovered] LIBERAL. He worked there 5 months in 1942. Contact was discontinued because of [36 groups unrecovered] COMPATRIOTS. He was a volunteer in Spain. He lives in the western part of New York State, for the past three years has not carried on active political work. LIBERAL has known him since childhood, during the past 14 years has known him in political life. He characterizes him and his wife as devoted and reliable people. The wife by profession is a dressmaker and can open a shop in the city for cover. Let us know whether you consider LENS more suitable to go to YAKOV [William Perl]. A reply for communicating to LIBERAL is necessary before 23 October. At the meeting with LIBERAL LENS expressed readiness to renew contact with us.

LENS was the network's photographer, Michael Sidorovich, once the Rosenbergs' neighbor in Knickerbocker Village, New York, a former YCL member and a veteran of the Abraham Lincoln Brigade in the Spanish Civil War, now working in a factory as a locksmith. According to David Greenglass, who identified Michael from an FBI photograph on July 17, 1950, Sidorovich's wife Ann, a dressmaker by trade, had acted as a courier for him prior to Harry Gold's adoption of that role. The FBI also learned that she was the daughter of Mikhail Tkach, a senior CPUSA functionary who edited a Ukrainian language newspaper in New York, and a suspected NKVD source within the large Ukrainian émigré community appearing in the VENONA traffic under the codename PERCH. Despite the FBI's persistent cross-examination, neither of the Sidoroviches was willing to make an incriminating admission, and in an interview on July 25, 1950, Michael denied ever having known William Perl. He also denied any recollection of David Greenglass, his classmate at Brooklyn Polytechnic. As for evidence from VENONA, there were only two other fleeting references to LENS, both from Leonid Kvasnikov, and largely administrative. On November 17, 1944, he signaled:

> In connection with the plans for the photographing of material by LIBERAL [Julius Rosenberg] and then by LENS, a shortage of cassettes is making itself felt. We cannot get them without a priority. Please order 100 cassettes for a Leica camera through the COUNTRYSIDE [Mexico] and send them to us without delay.

A month later, on December 20, 1944, there was a further telegram from New York, describing the Sidoroviches recent move to "JAKOV's town," meaning Cleveland, where William Perl (YAKOV) was then living:

> LENS and his wife have left for YAKOV's town. At the end of December LIBERAL will go there and will put LENS in touch with YAKOV. Before making the move, LENS and his wife visited he town and took an apartment, the address of which we reported in letter No. 9. LENS sold his house and spent part of the money on the move. We gave him a once for all payment of $500: I consider that [24 groups unrecoverable]

Thus both Sidoroviches were members of Rosenberg's ring. With encouragement from Moscow, he developed a large organization, but depended heavily upon his circle of Communist friends as recruits, many of whom were his contemporaries whom he had met while at the City College of New York, such as Morton Sobell, Max Elitcher, William Perl, Joel Barr, and Al Sarant. Of these five, only Max Elitcher helped the FBI, and he implicated Sobell, with whom he worked at the Reeves Instrument Company, and Rosenberg, both his former CCNY classmates. He confirmed to his FBI interrogator, John Walsh, that Julius had asked him for information for the Soviets, and said he had accompanied Sobell, who had recruited him into the CPUSA in 1939, when he had carried material from his home in Long Island to the Rosenbergs' apartment. Elitcher also disclosed the NKVD ran the existence of a previously unknown union for federal employees, which he alleged was run by the NKVD.

Sarant had studied electrical engineering at Columbia University. Between October 1942 and September 1946, the period when his codename HUGHES appears in the VENONA intercepts, he was a radar expert working for Bell Telephone Laboratories in New York on highly classified computer systems for the B-29 bomber. That some of this data, relating to the AN/APQ-7 high resolution airborne radar developed by the Massachusetts Institute of Technology, was compromised by him emerged unmistakably in part two of a long text dated December 13, 1944, from New York, which also referred to LIBERAL (Julius Rosenberg), WASP (Ruth Greenglass), CALIBER (David Greenglass), YOUNG (Theodore Hall), ARNO (Harry Gold) and METER (Joel Barr). The burden of running so many agents was becoming too much for one man, and on December 5, 1944, Apresyan warned about the danger of overworking Rosenberg:

> Expedite consent to the joint filming of their materials by both METER [Joel Barr] and HUGHES [Al Sarant] (see our letter no. 8). LIBERAL [Julius Rosenberg] has on hand eight people plus the filming of materials. The state of LIBERAL's health is nothing splendid. We are afraid of putting LIBERAL out of action with overwork.

Ten agents were obviously too much for Rosenberg to handle. Accordingly, the *rezidentura* sought to introduce two additional handlers, Aleksandr Raev and Aleksandr Feklisov, to share the workload and help handle Sarant and Joel Barr.

> Further [14 groups unrecovered] Both are COMPATRIOTS [Communists]. Both are helping us and both meet LIBERAL [Julius Rosenberg] and ARNO [Harry Gold] [3 groups unrecovered] HUGHES [Al Sarant] handed over 17 authentic drawings related to the APQ-7 (postal despatch No. 9). He can be trusted. The transfer of HUGHES to LIGHT [Aleksandr Raev] is no way out of the situation. It will be necessary to put LIGHT in touch with CALISTRATUS [Aleksandr Feklisov] in order to bring material for photography into the PLANT [Soviet Consulate]. I cannot carry material in and out of the PLANT late in the evening. I insist on bringing HUGHES and METER [Joel Barr] together, putting the latter in touch with CALISTRATUS or LIGHT and separating both from LIBERAL. In TYRE [New York] [16 groups unrecoverable] round the clock. There are no major contradictions between letters 5 and 7 about LIBERAL. They complement each other. LIBERAL's shortcomings do not mean that he will be completely useless for photography. He is gradually getting used to photography.

In 1948 Sarant had taken a post at the Cornell nuclear physics laboratory, and when interviewed by the FBI at his home in Ithaca, New York, in July 1950, he acknowledged having been a Communist and having known Julius through their union, the Federation of Architects, Engineers, Chemists, and Technicians (FAECT). Sarant was interviewed by the FBI on July 19, 1950, and denied any involvement in espionage, claiming not to have seen the Rosenbergs since 1946, but when later the same month he realized he was under FBI surveillance he drove to Tucson and crossed the border into Mexico on August 8, 1950. Thereafter the trail went cold, although he was seen to have taken an internal flight in Mexico to Guadalajara, and then later turned up in Prague. According to Aleksandr Feklisov, Sarant went into hiding in Mexico for six months before crossing the border into Guatemala and boarding a ship bound for Morocco. The rest of his journey, through Spain and Warsaw, finally brought him to Moscow to be reunited with his friend Joel Barr, who had left New York on January 1, 1948, to study at Stockholm for a year. According to an FBI request to the CIA dated November 19, 1948, Barr had intended to study at the University of Delft for a second year, and had spent two weeks in Finland in August 1948. However, in June 1950 he was in Paris, but fled to Prague through Switzerland as the FBI began arresting Harry Gold's contacts. Feklisov says that "between 1944 and 1945, Barr and Sarant gave us 9,165 pages of secret documents relating to more than one hundred programs in the planning stages."

Including Sarant, Rosenberg's network included not eight, but ten sub-agents in December 1944, and they look like Michael Sidorovich (LENS), his wife Ann (SQUIRRELL); Harry Gold (ARNO); Joel Barr (METER); William Perl (GNOME); Ruth Greenglass (WASP); David Greenglass (CALIBER); Lona Cohen (LESLEY); Morton Sobell, and an unknown source codenamed NILE.

Although never formally a Party member, Sobell had been one of Julius's classmates at the City College of New York, and had served in the U.S. Navy before gaining an electrical engineering degree. In 1941 he left the navy and joined the General Electric Company to work on classified military contracts both there and, later in 1947, at the Reeves Instrument Company in New York. He lived and worked in Schenectady between 1941 and 1947, when he was a regular visitor to the Rosenberg home on the weekends, but on June 22, 1950, when the Rosenbergs were questioned, Morton, his wife Helen and their children had taken a flight to Mexico City. When traced by the FBI, they were returned by the Mexican police on August 16, 1950, to Laredo on the Texas border, where Morton was arrested. Throughout the time Sobell was a fugitive, his mail had been intercepted by the FBI, even though he had addressed much of it to William Danziger, a friend of Julius Rosenberg's and intermediary who acted as a postdrop for the letters and redirected them. The following year, protesting his innocence, but unwilling to give sworn evidence and submit to cross-examination at his own trial, Sobell was sentenced to thirty years' imprisonment without parole. When the illegal William Fisher was arrested in 1957, the FBI recovered documents which not only revealed Sobell's codename as STONE, but showed that his wife Helen had been an active member of the network, who secretly had been given financial support by the NKVD to campaign on behalf of the Rosenbergs.

VOLUNTEER was Morris Cohen, and LESLEY was his wife Lona, who later was to achieve notoriety in England under the alias Helen Kroger (and be sentenced in March 1961 to twenty years' imprisonment). She had been recruited as a courier by her husband Morris, a veteran of the Abraham Lincoln Battalion who had attended a special NKVD spy school in Barcelona during the Spanish Civil War, after he had been wounded in the legs on October 13, 1937, at the battle of Fuente de Ebro while serving as part of a political cadre assigned to the Mackenzie-Papineau Battalion. Formerly a waiter, journalist and college football coach, and the son of immigrants from Tarashchi in the Ukraine and Vilna, Cohen had joined the CPUSA from the YCL in December 1935, but had been talent-spotted in Spain, allegedly by Alexander Orlov, who had supervised his training as a clandestine wireless operator. After his return to New York in December 1938 aboard the *Ausonia*, Morris married Lona, then a factory worker and union activist who occasionally removed items of interest to him from the manufacturing plant where she worked, and acted as a courier for Theodore Hall while he was at Los Alamos. She has recalled with pride having bribed an acquaintance in a Hartford munitions plant to steal the components for a complete prototype machine-gun for $2,000 so it could be smuggled into the *rezidentura* in a case designed for a double bass. According to Pavel Sudoplatov, "when Morris was drafted into the U.S. Army in July 1942… Anatoli Yatskov, aka Yakovlev, used Lona as a courier to pick up information. Lona's trips to New Mexico were explained as visits to a sanatorium for a tuberculosis cure."[1]

Joseph Katz, codenamed INFORMER, and X, one of those denounced to the FBI by Elizabeth Bentley who had known him as "Jack," and also named as a contact by Harry Gold, were implicated as well in the 1944 ANTENNA traffic. Katz, ostensibly a prosperous businessman who owned the Tempus Import Company, was a partner in the Meriden Dental Laboratories in Meriden, Connecticut, and a parking lot company in Manhattan. He had first come to the FBI's attention when he was spotted holding a meeting with Mikhail Chaliapin of the New York *rezidentura*, and he was later shown to have run several other agents, among them Thomas L. Black, Robert L. Menaker, and Floyd C. Miller, the latter two being relatively low-level sources directed against the Trotskyite Socialist Workers Party who were to cooperate with the FBI. Black, on the other hand, possessed far greater knowledge, having been active since recruited by Ovakimyan in 1934. From 1950 onwards he supplied valuable information to the FBI's Philadelphia Field Office, his offenses having been time-barred under the Statute of Limitations.

According to a very short VENONA text from New York dated July 22, 1944, Katz had helped run another spy, Amadeo Sabatini, a veteran of the Spanish Civil War, in San Francisco. Katz had been put in touch with him by the local *rezidentura*, which Grigori Kasparov was later to head:

> INFORMER [Joseph Katz] can leave for the West for a meeting with NICK [Amadeo Sabatini]. We can ask GIFT [Grigori Kasparov] for the address. We await your [1 group unrecovered]

When the FBI researched Katz's background they discovered he had been born Joseph Hlat in Lithuania in 1912, and had changed his name legally in New York in 1928. He had acquired U.S. citizenship when his father had been naturalized in 1925, and he had married Bessie Bogorad in Los Angeles in 1936. Their daughter Paula Jo had been born in New York in January 1941, but when the FBI attempted to trace Katz in December 1950 they learned that he had moved to the Hotel Luece in Paris in 1948, but as soon as the DST (French Security Service) expressed an interest in him he disappeared, eventually turning up in Haifa, where he was interviewed, but denied any knowledge of espionage. Nevertheless, the FBI maintained technical surveillance on his wife and her family in West Haven, Connecticut, at least until January 1953, in the hope of luring him back to America.

Although the FBI failed to repatriate Katz, Menaker and Miller gave useful collateral information that helped identify members of various *rezidenturas*, and shed light on Gold's contribution to ENORMOZ. When Menaker realized he had come under surveillance, he approached an FBI retiree, Thomas M. McDade, and arranged to surrender himself in New York on February 6, 1951. Under interrogation he admitted having been recruited in 1937 and named one of his controllers as Gregor L. Rabinovich, who had spent nine years in the United States from 1930 as representative of the Soviet Red Cross. Menaker's ostensible employment while he operated as a Soviet agent was with the Midland Export Corporation, which led the FBI to its director, Michael Burd, who turned out to be another Soviet agent.[2] He also identified his friend Floyd Miller as his recruit, and he surrendered voluntarily three days later. As well as corroborating much of Menaker's story, Miller acknowledged that he had joined the Socialist Workers Party (SWP) under the name Michael Cort and had traveled to Mexico under instructions to befriend Trotsky's widow.

Another name in the 1944 VENONA traffic concerning ANTENNA was that of Max Elitcher, who was to be confirmed as a vital member of Rosenberg's network, although his recruitment was not signaled until a telegram from Apresyan dated July 26, 1944:

> In July ANTENNA was sent by the firm for ten days to work in CARTHAGE [Washington DC]. There he visited his school friend Max ELITCHER, who works in the Bureau of Standards as head of the fire control section for warships (which mount guns) of over five-inch CALIBER. He has access to extremely valuable materials on guns.
>
> Five years ago Max ELITCHER graduated from the Electro-Technical Department of the City College of NEW YORK. He has a Master of Science degree. Since finishing college he has been working at the Bureau of Standards. He is a COMPATRIOT [Communist]. He entered the COMPATRIOT's organization [Party] after finishing his studies.
>
> By ANTENNA he is characterized as a loyal, reliable, level-headed and able man. Married, his wife is a COMPATRIOT. She is a psy-

The Soviet Atomic Bomb. Operation ENORMOZ allowed Soviet scientists to successfully detonate an atomic device at least two years before Western analysts anticipated they would be able to do so.

Kim Philby. In 1945 Philby alerted his NKVD handler to the information compromised by the defector Igor Gouzenko. Later, in Washington DC, Philby monitored the progress of the MI5 and FBI molehunts.

John Cairncross. Arguably the first Soviet atomic spy in England, Cairncross supplied a copy of the MAUD report to his Soviet contact in September 1940.

Donald Maclean. Codenamed HOMER, Maclean was only identified as a Soviet spy in May 1951, and was warned by the Labour minister, John Strachey MP, that he was under MI5 surveillance.

Guy Burgess. Anxious to protect Donald Maclean from a hostile interrogation by MI5, Burgess escorted him across the Channel, but by failing to return to London he compromised Kim Philby and Anthony Blunt.

Whittaker Chambers. Amongst the testimony given by Chambers to the FBI was information about an NKVD network in California, headed by Isaac Folkoff, who was later to be a key link with the CPUSA.

Elizabeth Bentley. Her hundred-page statements to the FBI in November 1945 identified dozens of NKVD agents whose codenames later emerged in the VENONA intercepts, although she was never allowed to know her allegations had been verified from the secret source.

Anthony Blunt. The NKVD's star spy inside the wartime Security Service, Blunt reassured the Soviets that MI5 was not maintaining a watch on the *rezidentura* in London, thereby allowing them to concentrate on atomic targets.

Kitty Harris. Donald Maclean's NKVD contact in London and Paris, and apparently publicly compromised by the GRU defector Walter Krivitsky, she was sent to Mexico and America to manage spies who had penetrated Los Alamos.

Allan Nunn May. Although convicted of espionage in 1946, Dr. May even refused in his deathbed confession in December 2002 to reveal who had recruited him as a Soviet spy, and when.

Bruno Pontecorvo. Although never definitely confirmed as the atomic spy codenamed QUANTUM, Pontecorvo admitted before his death in Russia that he had passed information to the Soviets while he had worked on the Manhattan Project.

Rudolf Peierls. Considered a strong espionage suspect by the FBI, and tainted by his long friendship with the Communist physicist G. E. Brown, Peierls was refused a security clearance in 1957, which effectively ended his career as a research scientist, but did not stop him from receiving a knighthood eleven years later.

Klaus Fuchs. Having confessed to his role as a Soviet spy, Fuchs cooperated enthusiastically with MI5 and ruined the careers of two of his colleagues whom he denounced as security risks.

Jim Skardon *(left)* and **Henry Arnold.** A former wartime MI5 officer, Henry Arnold was an experienced counterintelligence expert, whereas Jim Skardon, from the Metropolitan Police, had gained a not entirely justifiable reputation as an expert interrogator. Skardon extracted a confession from Klaus Fuchs, but never knew the compromising information about him came from VENONA, which was inadmissible as evidence in any criminal prosecution.

Clement Attlee. As Prime Minister in 1950 Attlee was assured by MI5's Director-General, Sir Percy Sillitoe, that the investigation into Klaus Fuchs had been conducted efficiently, although a glance in his file would have revealed that Courtney Young had minuted five years earlier that Fuchs was probably a spy and deserved immediate attention. The recommendation had been ignored for four years until VENONA had identified Fuchs as the source of a leak from Los Alamos.

Pavel Fitin. Codenamed VIKTOR in the VENONA traffic, Lieutenant General Fitin was head of the NKVD's foreign intelligence branch and personally supervised Operation ENORMOZ.

Vasili Zarubin. The NKVD *rezident* in Washington DC, Zarubin and his wife were experienced officers who had operated in Europe until their assignment to the United States. He was withdrawn in December 1944 after being denounced by a subordinate.

Grigori Kheifets. The NKVD *rezident* in San Francisco until August 1944, Kheifets came under intensive FBI surveillance, which proved his reliance on the CPUSA membership.

Aleksandr Feklisov. A key member of the wartime New York *rezidentura*, Feklisov was sent to London to supervise Klaus Fuchs, and eventually broke ranks to write his memoirs.

Leonid Kvasnikov. A graduate of the Institute of Chemical Engineering, Kvasnikov was placed in charge of the NKVD's industrial espionage in 1939, and became a key figure in ENORMOZ.

Anatoli Yatskov. While in New York he adopted the alias of Anatoli Yakovlev, and handled Theodore Hall and Saville Sax. A true professional, Yatskov was horrified when he discovered Harry Gold had been associating with suspects who had been interrogated by the FBI.

Gaik Ovakimyan. A veteran undercover operator, Ovakimyan was expelled from New York in July 1941 after a decade of successful recruitments. Upon his return to Moscow he was promoted head of the NKVD's Third Department of the First Chief Directorate.

Semyon Semyonov. An inexperienced member of the New York *rezidentura*, Semyonov posed as a student at MIT and tried to persuade his contact Harry Gold to take some basic security precautions.

Harry Gold. An industrial spy long before the NKVD used him as an intermediary in an ENORMOZ spy-ring, Gold would be compromised by his contact Klaus Fuchs, and imprisoned.

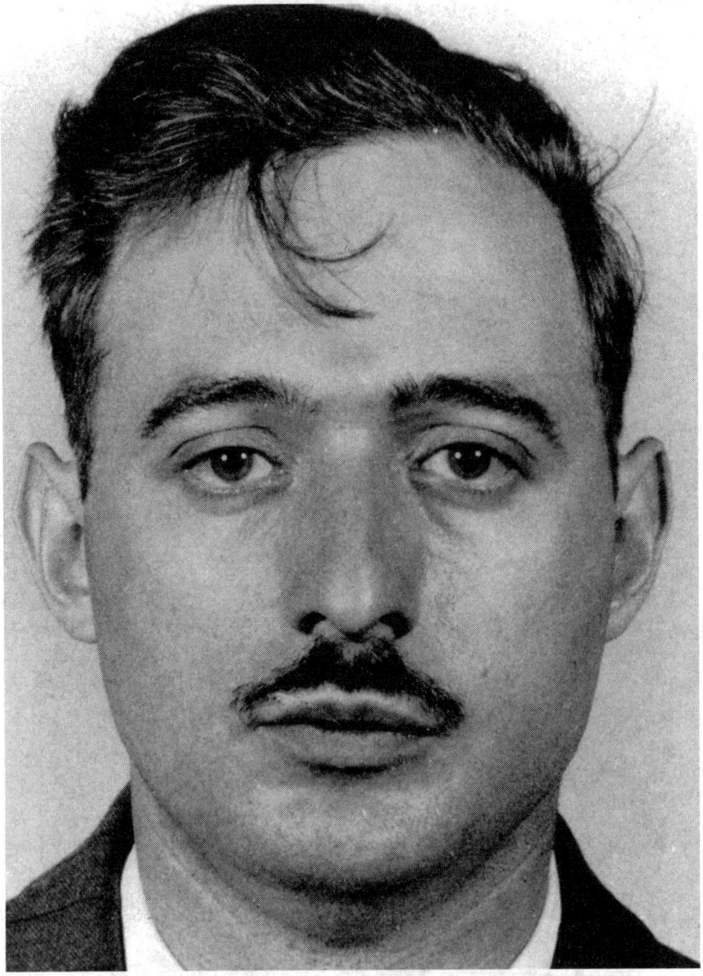

Julius Rosenberg. An enthusiastic CPUSA member, Julius recruited many of his CCNY classmates, but failed to exercise any compartmentation, thereby allowing the FBI to easily round up his network.

David Greenglass. A technician at Los Alamos, David Greenglass named his sister Ethel as his recruiter and helped the FBI identify all the members of the Rosenberg spy-ring. He was released from prison in November 1960.

Joel Barr. Incriminated as a member of the Rosenberg spy-ring, and identified in the VENONA traffic as METER and SCOUT, Barr fled New York for Stockholm in January 1948 and was never interrogated by the FBI.

Ruth Greenglass. Codenamed WASP, she was never charged with any offenses, although her husband David was imprisoned for nine years.

Judith Coplon. Well-placed in the Justice Department to tip off the NKVD to suspects coming under FBI surveillance, her conviction for espionage was quashed on appeal, although the VENONA traffic identified her as a spy, codenamed SIMA.

William Perl. An expert on supersonic flight and jet propulsion, Perl appeared in the VENONA traffic codenamed GNOME and YAKOV. In July 1950 he was imprisoned for five years when he lied to the FBI about never having known Morton Sobell or the Rosenbergs.

Margaret Browder. The sister of the CPUSA's General-Secretary, Earl Browder, Margaret was an experienced NKVD "illegal," who was trained as a wireless operator in Moscow and undertook undercover assignments in Mexico and France. Her brother was always anxious that her exposure might compromise the Party.

Joseph Katz. Photographed in 1941, Katz was an important prewar and wartime NKVD recruiter and organizer who appeared in the VENONA traffic code-named DOUGLAS, INFORMER, and X. When the FBI identified him, he fled to Paris in 1953 and refused to answer any questions about his Soviet espionage.

Bertha Schuman. Born Bertha Kipnes, she was one of many NKVD suspects believed by the FBI to have participated in atomic espionage. This photo, taken in 1935, was distributed to surveillance teams to assist in the recognition of targets.

Morris Weisbord. The director of the Midland Export Company, Moishe Weisbord, alias Michael Weisbord, alias Michael Burd, provided commercial cover for the NKVD in New York, and ostensible employment for other agents.

Morton Sobell *(left)* and **Julius and Ethel Rosenberg, 1951.** Years after his release from prison Morton Sobell protested that his identification by NSA analysts as the spy codenamed RELAY was incorrect, and he was ultimately proved right.

> chiatrist by profession, she works at the War Department.
> Max ELITCHER is an excellent amateur photographer and has all the necessary equipment for taking photographs.
> Please check ELITCHER and communicate your consent to his clearance.

A childhood friend of Morton Sobell, Elitcher had graduated as an electrical engineer from the City College of New York in 1938, where he had studied alongside Julius Rosenberg and Morton Sobell, and had joined the U.S. Navy. In 1948 the Office of Naval Intelligence had investigated Elitcher as a possible Communist, prompting him to buy a house next to Sobell in Queens, New York, and join his friend at the Reeves Instrument Company. When the FBI interviewed him in July 1950, he admitted having been approached by both Sobell and the Rosenbergs, but denied having passed any classified documents to either. Instead, he agreed to give evidence against them, and appeared as a prosecution witness at their trial in March 1951. Although the FBI had some doubts about the extent to which Elitcher had refused to help Morton and Julius, there was no further VENONA material to incriminate him, and the single text in which he was mentioned by Apresyan gave no indication that he had subsequently become an active member of the network.

On September 2, 1944, Moscow changed many of the cryptonyms assigned to the New York *rezidentura* as a security precaution and listed a total of twenty-two in a VENONA text, among them ANTENNA who became LIBERAL. Another was William Perl, codenamed GNOME, a member of Rosenberg's ring who was transformed into YAKOV, but on September 14 Apresyan was still referring to him as GNOME:

> Until recently GNOME was paid only the expenses connected with his coming to TYRE [New York]. Judging by an appraisal of the material received and the last [1 group garbled] sent to us GNOME deserves remuneration for material no less valuable than that given by the rest of the members of the LIBERAL group who were given a bonus by you. Please agree to paying him 500 dollars.

On September 20, Moscow gave Apresyan permission to pay Perl, still referring to him as GNOME:

> Your No. 736. We agree to paying GNOME five hundred dollars [12 groups unrecovered] September on trips to TYRE [New York] [2 groups unrecovered], and [211 groups unrecoverable]

Perl had shared a room at Colombia University with Al Sarant, and had studied with Elitcher, Barr, Sobell and Julius Rosenberg at the City College of New York. An expert on supersonic flight and jet propulsion, he was supervising a team of fifteen scientists working on a research project at the National Advisory Committee on Aeronautics, at Cleveland, Ohio, when he was interviewed by the FBI in July 1950. Perl denied knowing Sobell and Rosenberg; for this lie he was sentenced to five years' imprisonment on a perjury charge in 1950, but the FBI remained convinced that he had been responsible for the leakage of several classified files on the subject of advanced jet propulsion that David Greenglass mentioned as having reached Julius Rosenberg, and was a key figure in his spy ring. While at Columbia University in 1946 and 1947, Perl had occupied an apartment at 65 Morton Street in Greenwich Village, rented in Al Sarant's name, it had been occupied by Joel Barr's former girlfriend, Vivian Glassman, and was used as a photographic studio by Rosenberg. On July 23, 1950, she had visited Perl and, while sitting on a couch, had written him a series of notes so as to avoid being overheard. In them she identified herself as a friend of Julius Rosenberg and offered him money, asking him to flee to Mexico. Perl had dated Vivian's sister Eleanor, so he knew who she was, and clearly was connected to the Sidoroviches, with whom he was seen in Cleveland negotiating the purchase of a car. Anxious about what he suspected was heavy FBI surveillance and maybe an attempt to entrap him, Perl rejected Vivian's proposal and told his lawyer to inform Special Agents John A. Harrington and John B. O'Donoghue about the incident. In the absence of any other evidence, or the damning request for payment to GNOME in September 1944, Perl was convicted of perjury in May 1953 and sentenced to five years' imprisonment for having lied about not knowing Rosenberg and Sobell.

The FBI's investigation of Vivian Glassman revealed that she too had been an important spy, and had been classmates at CCNY with Sobell, Perl, Elitcher, Barr, Rosenberg, and Sidorovich. A mathematician by training, she had been employed by the U.S. Army Signal Corps from May 1942, and had worked on sensitive projects in the General Development Laboratory at Long Branch, with her sister Eleanor, and at Fort Monmouth in New Jersey where she "had access to material of a secret and confidential nature."

On November 14, 1944, a VENONA message from Kvasnikov introduced yet another member of the Rosenberg ring, Joel Barr, codenamed METER:

> LIBERAL has safely carried through the contracting of HUGHES [Al Sarant]. HUGHES is a good friend of METER [Joel Barr]. We propose to pair them off and get them to photograph their own materials having given a camera for this purpose. HUGHES is a good photographer, has a large darkroom and all the equipment but he does not have a Leica. LIBERAL will receive the films from METER for passing on. Direction of the PROBATIONERS [agents] will be continued through LIBERAL, this will ease the load on him. Details about the contracting are in letter No. 8.

Barr had much in common with others in Rosenberg's network. He had studied electrical engineering with Sobell and Elitcher, graduating in 1938. He had worked alongside Al Sarant in the Army Signal Corps laboratory at Fort Monmouth until his discharge in 1942 because of his political activities on behalf of the Communist Party, and then had found a job as a radar specialist with Western Electric, designing systems for the B-29 bomber. In 1946 he had switched to Sperry Gyroscope, with a reference signed by Al Sarant, but had left a year later when his security clearance had been declined. By the time the FBI linked him to the source codenamed METER, Barr had been living in Paris since January 1948, but he promptly disappeared and moved to Finland, well beyond its reach. The NKVD had obviously cultivated Barr as a spy in November 1944, but there was no further VENONA evidence apart from a single reference in the text dated December 5, 1944 (see Chapter VI), which certainly implies that Barr and Sarant (METER and HUGHES) were highly productive.

There can be no doubt of either Rosenberg's industry, for he was managing two apartments in Manhattan, at 65 Morton Street and at 131 East 7th Street, as photographic studios, nor of his ideological commitment. As Moscow was always keen to reward effort, a telegram on March 6, 1945, refers to a financial inducement, and mentioned another source, codenamed NIL, who has not been identified.

> [66 groups unrecovered] decision was made about awarding the sources as a bonus the following sums: to LIBERAL 1,000 dollars, NIL [58 groups unrecoverable] either the purchase of valuable gifts for the PROBATIONERS [agents] or payment to them of money on the basis of well thought out cover stories. [28 groups unrecovered]

As the FBI researched the links between LIBERAL's organization and started building the legal case against the Rosenbergs, doubt was expressed about the wisdom of charging Ethel, because the proof against her, apart from testimony from Ruth Greenglass, was contained in a VENONA text dated November 27, 1944, from Kvasnikov:

> Your 5356. Information on LIBERAL's wife. Surname that of her husband, first name ETHEL, 29 years old. Married five years. Finished secondary school. A COMPATRIOT [Communist] since 1938. Sufficiently well developed politically. Knows about her husband's work and the role of METER [Joel Barr] and NIL. In view of delicate health does not work. Is characterized positively and as a devoted person.

The text was of particular importance because the search for LIBERAL, formerly ANTENNA, and married to ETHEL, had been underway since August 1947 when Meredith Gardner had identified the pair of spies in his first "Special Analysis Report." Cryptographically, the word ETHEL had been a special challenge, for Gardner had broken the spell-code for "E" and "L," but initially had been baffled by a single value for "THE," for there is no definite article in Russian. However, he deduced that the NKVD must have anticipated enciphering masses of English text, and therefore had attributed a codegroup to THE, which is, after all, the most common word in the language.

The damning sentence about Ethel's knowledge of her husband's work was enough to persuade those privy to VENONA, but who had doubted her involvement, that she had played a role in Julius's organization. After her arrest she proved rather more resilient that Julius, but the evidence which condemned her to the electric chair was strictly limited to what was admissible in court. According to those familiar with the FBI's recordings of their private conversations, Julius expressed an interest in cooperating with the Bureau, but was talked out of his weakness by Ethel. The FBI's final attempt to save Julius by establishing a specialist team in Sing Sing during the execution, standing by in the hope he would agree to make a statement naming "names in upstate New York" at the last moment, was thwarted by the prison governor's decision to execute him first so as to prevent Ethel from enduring the harrowing experience of walking past his cell to the execution chamber.

CHAPTER VIII

THE PERS MYSTERY

I am sure that at the end of the world—in the last millisecond of the earth's existence—the last man will see what we saw.

George Kistiakowsky

Once convictions had been obtained against Julius, Ethel, Harry Gold, and the Greenglasses, the FBI concentrated on the various loose ends that remained unresolved at the end of a lengthy analysis of the confessions, the clues contained in Elizabeth Bentley's testimony and the evidence from VENONA. Principal among the mysteries were the identities of the sources in America codenamed QUANTUM, ERIE, HURON, and PERS. The first of only three references to QUANTUM had occurred in one of the earliest ENORMOZ texts, a telegram dated June 21, 1943, noting that on June 14 QUANTUM had arranged to visit the Soviet embassy in Washington DC, presumably asking to see the ambassador, and had been introduced to Maxim Litvinov's deputy,

Andrei Gromyko, who then held counselor rank, and had promptly passed him on to EGOR from the *rezidentura.* At that time, shortly before the arrival of Vasili Zubilin, Washington was regarded merely a sub-*rezidentura* of New York, not usually in direct communication with Moscow. QUANTUM's purpose was to explain that he had already sold some information to Semyon Semyonov in New York, and to sell some more:

> On 14 June a meeting took place with QUANTUM in CARTHAGE [Washington DC]. By arrangement he was received by GRANDFATHER's deputy [Andrei Gromyko] who after a short conversation with him handed him over to EGOR in whose presence [20 groups unrecovered] with TWAIN [Semyon Semyonov] QUANTUM declared that he is convinced of the value of the materials and therefore expects from us similar recompense for his labor – in the form of a financial reward [18 groups unrecovered] his attitude on this question. He was told that the question [38 groups unrecoverable] QUANTUM was given $300.

Although little can be deduced about EGOR (whose name only appeared in one other VENONA message, the context of which confirmed he was a member of the embassy's relatively tiny *rezidentura* and most likely was either Vasili D. Mironov or Vasili G. Dorogov), it is reasonable to suppose that the meeting took place by prior arrangement, and that therefore QUANTUM, by seeing a diplomat of Gromyko's status, was a personage of some importance. The next VENONA text to refer to QUANTUM, dated June 22–23, 1943, displayed considerable technical knowledge:

> Information from QUANTUM. Translated from the English. The basic idea for a method of separation of ENORMOZ consists in repeated [1 group unrecovered] distillation by sublimation (vaporisation from a crystal state) and rapid condensation of vapors. With the specified components and degree of vaporization of chemically [1 group unrecovered] identical molecules (but different in mass) is inversely proportional to the square root of the mass and directly proportional to the partial vapor pressure sustained by a molecule

> without condensation. On the other hand the partial vapor pressure of such molecules, in accordance with quantum mechanics, is inversely proportional to the cube of the square root of the mass. Consequently the speeds at which two isotopic molecules [7 groups unrecovered] will be proportional to the square [19 groups unrecovered]

This message, which included a series of technical algebraic calculations, was followed on August 27, 1943, by the following fragment from New York, which introduced another cryptonym, SOLID:

> About his affairs and [43 groups unrecovered] for SOLID and No. 534 of 22 June reported information from QUANTUM on ENORMOZ.

This text suggested there was another ENORMOZ spy, perhaps in touch with SOLID, and maybe based at either the Kellex plant or the Substitute Alloy Material (SAM) Laboratory at Columbia where the separation work was pioneered. As for QUANTUM's identity, the strong suggestion is that he was Bruno Pontecorvo, who reportedly was in Washington DC on the day of QUANTUM's visit to the Soviet embassy. The circumstantial evidence is that QUANTUM declared that he had been in contact with Semyon Semyonov who, according to Vladimir Chikov, is known to have been Pontecorvo's handler. The problem is that Chikov gave Pontecorvo's codename as CASPAR, but the former KGB officer was not averse to changing and crafting new codenames for agents, and listed those whom he said had been inside the Manhattan Project: YOUNG (Ted Hall), CHARLES (Klaus Fuchs), CALIBER (David Greenglass), METHOD, IDEA and CASPAR. These six, according to Chikov, were supported by an equal number of couriers or contacts, of which he identified only LESLEY (Lona Cohen), RAYMOND (Harry Gold) and OLD (Saville Sax). METHOD and IDEA, says Chikov, "cannot be revealed" and there must be considerable doubt about the authenticity of these codenames as they do not appear in any VENONA text nor anywhere else in the public domain.

As for SMART, ERIE and HURON, they seemed to be connected to Harry Gold, according to a VENONA text from Stepan Apresyan dated June 27, 1944:

> Your No. 2700. [19 groups unrecovered] and canalization. Connected with us in the KhU Line [Economic Directorate] [1 group unrecovered] is SMART. We propose to transfer ERIE and HURON to him. We request your sanction. To transfer these PROBATIONERS [agents] to GOOSE [Harry Gold] [6 groups unrecovered] GOOSE. [14 groups unrecovered] receive constant [1 groups unidentified]. He is wondering why the monthly payment of 100 dollars was discontinued [15 groups unrecovered] with him.

This left the FBI wondering about SMART, ERIE and HURON, calculating that SMART was more likely an intermediary than an actual handler from the *rezidentura*. His codename appeared in only five other VENONA texts, all on the New York to Moscow circuit in 1944, with a short one from Stepan Apresyan, dated September 6, giving details of the arrangements for an imminent arrival of an (unidentified) agent codenamed SENOR from Denmark, then still under Nazi occupation, and the recent departure of SEAMAN:

> SENOR is in Copenhagen. We shall be able to arrange a password for a meeting with SMART only after SENOR's arrival—after 18 September. SEAMAN since departing for GENEVA has not reported anything to us. He is possible at sea. We shall arrange a password for a meeting with him on his first visit to TYRE [New York].

This, like the other texts, only served to demonstrate that SMART was considered one of Apresyan's subordinates, but did little to advance his identification. Twelve days later, on September 18, 1944, Apresyan sent another, largely administrative message to Moscow, complaining about the impact of hostile surveillance on Leonid Kvasnikov, and then going on to mention SMART again, in the context of other XY case officers, and to link him to BERG:

> By telegrams: Your number 2962 could not be carried out because of surveillance on TWAIN [Semyon Semyonov]. [1 group unrecovered] BERG, who was in liaison with SMART, was without liaison with us; this was evident from the [1 group unrecovered] on the occasion of handing over TWAIN's liaison. There has been a report on SEAMAN's absence (see also our number 701). Your number 3554. The money was received by MAKSIM [Vasili Zarubin]. ANTON [Leonid Kvasnikov] has nothing to do with this matter. Your telegram number 3338. Refer to our numbers 550 and 711 [28 groups] unrecoverable] and passing on your directive was entrusted to ECHO [Bernard Schuster]. The task was passed on through X [Joseph Katz] The task is being protracted by reason of the subsequent absence from TYRE [New York] of X on a trip to the West, ECHO on leave, at present PHLOX [Rose Olsen] is absent, has left with her husband for RAMSAY's area. ECHO cannot meet PHLOX until her return in only about three weeks' time.

Obviously, Apresyan is reporting to Moscow on delays that have occurred in recent communications, but the reference to BERG being in liaison with SMART reinforces the impression that, like Roz Childs, Bernard Schuster and Joseph Katz, he was a trusted intermediary with responsibility for running his own agents, albeit under the authority of the *rezident.* The final VENONA text to mention SMART was sent by Apresyan on September 27, 1944, giving instructions to the Center in Moscow on how SMART should be met by a NEIGHBOR, meaning a GRU officer. The clandestine nature of the rendezvous demonstrates convincingly that SMART was definitely not a member of the *rezidentura*, for otherwise the meeting could have been conducted quite safely in the Consulate or Amtorg's offices:

> [65 groups unrecoverable] [4 groups unrecovered] month of October. The time of the meeting 6 o'clock in the evening. SMART will have on a white shirt, dark blue tie, a hat on his head. He will be holding in his hand a newspaper the New York Post. The NEIGHBOR should inquire: "Where is the stadium?" SMART will point to

the South and reply: "Down this way." After this the NEIGHBOR should call him by the name "ELLIOT."

Thus SMART is established as an NKVD agent and an intermediary, but little else is known about him. Unfortunately, Harry Gold was unable to shed any light on either SMART or the other two agents, and to have pressed him harder would have jeopardized VENONA. One possible clue to their identities is to be found in a pair of administrative circulars, dated September 2 and October 5, 1944, in which Apresyan announced to Moscow a fairly comprehensive change in codenames. The first dealt with a total of twenty-two agents:

> In accordance with our telegram no. 403 we are advising you of the new cover-names:- CAVALRYMAN – BECK [Sergei Kurnakov], THRUSH – AKHMED, CLEMENCE – LEE, ABRAM – CZECH [Jack Soble], TULIP – KANT [Mark Zborowski], AIDA- KLO [Esther Trabach Rand], OSPREY – BLOCK, RELAY – SERB, ANTENNA – LIBERAL [Julius Rosenberg], GNOME – YAKOV [William Perl], SCOUT – METER [Joel Barr], TU… – NIL, VOGEL – PERS, ODESSITE – GROWTH. All these cover-names were selected by you with a view to economy of means. Among the new cover-names introduced by you there were disadvantageous ones which we propose to replace as follows: STELLA – EMILYA, DONALD – PILOT [William Ullman], LAWYER – RICHARD [Harry Dexter White], DOUGLAS – X [Joseph Katz], SHERWOOD – PRINCE [Laurance Duggan], [1 group unrecovered] T – ZONE, MIRANDA – ART [Helen Koral], SENOR – BERG. All these cover-names are economical from the point of view of encoding. Please confirm. Continuation will follow later.

The continuation came a month later, dealing with a further twenty-five sources:

> Further to our 700. Herewith are changes in covernames:
> GOOSE – ARNO [Harry Gold], L – BEER, CONSTRUCTOR – EXPERT [Abraham Brothman], ERIE – [1 group unrecovered],

> HURON – ERNEST, BLACK – PETER [Thomas L. Black], EMULSION – SIGNAL, BROTHER – THOMAS, FIN – FERRO [Aleksandr N. Petroff], ZERO – ERIC [Leona O. Franey], SPLINE – NOISE [deleted], STAMP – ARMOR [deleted], REST – CHARLES [Klaus Fuchs], SOLID – KINSMAN, EXPRESS MESSENGER – JEAN [Ricardo Setaro], PLUCKY – KURT, OSPREY – KEEN, JUPITER – ODD FELLOW, HUDSON – JOHN, FAKIR – ARNOLD, RAY – KARL [Ricardo Setaro], JEANNETTE – CUPID, LONG – DAVIS, TALENT – HENRY [William M. Malisoff], OLA – JEANNE [Christina Krotkova]. Please confirm. Continuation later. No. 798.

While there was to be a vital clue in the change of HURON's codename to ERNEST, ERIE is more difficult, as the unrecovered group is most likely either GEORGES or LEADER. Curiously, four days after this directive, Apresyan was still using HURON's original codename:

> [23 groups unrecovered] I request your consent in principle to the use for this purpose of BLACK [Thomas Black] who has no work at present. We will negotiate with BLACK upon receipt of your answer. RAY will be in liaison with BLACK should BLACK be transferred [16 groups unrecoverable] BLACK HURON [6 groups unrecovered]
>
> Reference your No. 563. We object to the transfer of MARGARITA to BLACK in view of the undesirability [22 groups unrecovered]
>
> 2. A report with all the technical details of the COUNTRY's (America] robots [guided weapons] and their [3 groups unrecovered] robots. The COUNTRY's robots are fitted with I-16 engines, information about which was sent to you. Also other reports.
>
> We have received from METER [Joel Barr] a 730A valve, which is of particular interest. Technical details of this valve were sent in number 71 [7 groups unrecovered]. Confirm receipt of the materials by diplomatic post.

This appears to link HURON to Harry Gold's original recruiter, Thomas Black, though not necessarily to RAY and MARGARITA, whose identities have been deleted by the National Security Agency on privacy grounds in the VENONA footnotes. Equally tantalizing are the other unidentified codenames that simply do not appear in other VENONA texts. That, combined with the indication that there was a further continuation, gives an idea of the sheer volume of agents run by the New York *rezidentura* in 1944. For those sleuths convinced the NKVD sometimes hid a clue in the codename, attention focused on PERS, one of the most fascinating atomic spies, known initially as VOGEL, and referred to on February 11, 1944, in a very fragmented text from New York:

> Herewith a report on the work of ENORMOZ [163 groups unrecovered] 800 pounds for the neutralization of weak [305 groups unrecoverable]

On 16 June Pavel Fedosimov made another intriguing reference to VOGEL in a telegram to Moscow:

> By the same post were dispatched the secret plans of the layout of the ENORMOZ plant received from VOGEL.

Apart from one routine administrative message, dated September 2, 1944, confirming that VOGEL was henceforth to be known as PERS, there was only one further, highly fragmented text, dated December 13, 1944, from New York which, though far from conclusive, confirmed his vantage-point inside ENORMOZ:

> [45 groups unrecovered] PERS. [7 groups unrecovered] Camp-1. Our proposal [24 groups unrecovered] not to give any more on ENORMOZ.
> 2. To leave WASP [Ruth Greenglass] and CALIBER [David Greenglass] in contact with LIBERAL [Julius Rosenberg] until [3 groups unrecovered] work.
> 3.YOUNG [51 groups unrecoverable]

While PERS has been identified mistakenly as a spy codenamed PERCY, the footnotes show that PERS was considered for PER-

SIAN by the VENONA analysts. He has also been linked to PERSIUS, allegedly a crucial atomic source handled by illegals reporting to Anatoli Yatskov, although the two are probably quite different persons. As to who this important spy might be, believed to have been based at the huge, purpose-built Oak Ridge site, there have been several candidates, but some NSA analysts latched onto the possibility of a clue in the codename VOGEL, which is German and not Russian, to his true identity. Among the German émigrés working on the Manhattan Project was Sir Rudolf Peierls, who virtually adopted Klaus Fuchs as a son. Peierls, who was himself born in Berlin and naturalized in February 1940, knew Fuchs "had been politically active as a member of a socialist student group (which was essentially communist),"[1] had brought him into the British research team, and had arranged his security clearance in May 1941. Fuchs went to live with the Peierls as a lodger in Birmingham, traveled to America with Peierls on the *Andes* in November 1943, and even went on a motoring holiday with them to Mexico in December 1945 when the British contingent completed its work at Los Alamos.

Peierls was to attract much attention from MI5 and the FBI, not least because he had married a Russian physicist, Eugenia Kannegiesser, whom he had met while on a visit to Odessa in the summer of 1930. They were married in Leningrad in March 1931, and to their surprise no obstacles were placed on her emigration abroad or on her acquisition of German citizenship. This was unusual, considering the sensitive nature of her work and her family circumstances: her sister Nina was a biologist and her widowed mother had married a writer. Coincidentally, Peierls's older brother Alfred had also married a Russian, a woman who had been working for the Soviet Trade Delegation in Berlin when they met in a minor road accident. Alfred was an expert on electric condensers and, after he fled Germany in 1935, managed a condenser factory in London until his internment in the Isle of Man, along with his wife, as an enemy alien.

Rudolf Peierls, with his strong Russian connections, was initially considered a likely suspect by MI5, especially as he had worked at Kellex upon his arrival in New York, before the British party moved to Los Alamos in August 1944, but the search in England for a leak was abandoned as soon as Fuchs confessed. However, in America the FBI continued to pursue both Peierls and his wife, and developed a large dossier on the couple. In it are reports from the CIA that Peierls had confided in a friend that he had once joined a Communist Party front in Switzerland, and that his wife had been a member of the German Communist Party (KPD). Indeed, scrutiny of the KPD's records, captured after the war, confirmed a reference to "Comrade Kannegiesser." The FBI noted that Eugenia had worked as a nurse at the Queen Elizabeth Hospital in Birmingham between 1939 and 1941, and then had joined General Electric as a planning engineer. In America she had applied for a job at Los Alamos. However, of greater concern was MI5's revelation that Peierls had received his original security clearance through the intervention of John Strachey MP, who was himself an espionage suspect. A former minister of food, and then Secretary of State for War for the last year of the Attlee administration, Strachey was a confirmed Marxist, and had been recorded holding an "open code" telephone conversation with Donald Maclean shortly before the latter's defection in 1951. According to a CIA report dated February 1952, Strachey had also "been responsible for having the surveillance on Bruno Pontecorvo lifted, which reportedly made possible Pontecorvo's escape to Russia" in 1950.

The FBI reinvestigated Peierls and his wife in March 1956 when he applied to join the Brookhaven National Laboratory on Long Island, New York. On that occasion it was reported that Eugenia "had admitted to being a Communist and had been publicly opposed to Britain's participation in World War II until the USSR entered the war." Actually Peierls did not go to Brookhaven, although he did visit in 1966 when his son was on the staff. His attendance at other American conferences was approved by the AEC, but only on the condition that "he would have no additional access to classified information other than he already had."

None of this amounted to evidence of espionage on the part of Peierls, but his associations were certainly considered suspicious, despite MI5's assertion that no "sinister implications" could be drawn from his friendship with Fuchs. However, as well as having been Fuchs's confidante and colleague, he had been close to the American physicist G. E. Brown. Brown had lived with Peierls in 1950 and 1951, at the beginning of a career at the University of Birmingham that was to last until 1961, when he moved to the Niels Bohr Institute in Copenhagen. Originally from South Dakota, Brown had been educated at the University of Wisconsin until 1946 and then had spent four years at Yale under Gregory Breit, and had established a reputation as a Communist. According to his passport application, Brown acknowledged having joined the CPUSA at Yale in January 1948 and, while in Birmingham, had associated with CPGB members.

The FBI reported that in 1951 Peierls was vice president of the Council of the Association of Atomic Scientists, then considered to be a Communist front (although MI5 denied this), and in August 1947 had petitioned the Home Secretary for the release of Allan Nunn May. The FBI's inquiries culminated in a permanent removal of Peierls's security clearance by MI5 in 1957 and soon afterwards he resigned his consultancy post at the Atomic Energy Research Establishment at Harwell, but neither setback prevented him from receiving a knighthood in the 1968 New Year's honors.

Whatever the truth, the mystery of VOGEL/PERS remains unresolved, although the true identity of another spy, codenamed TINA, has been decrypted. According to an almost complete text from Moscow addressed to the London *rezidentura* and dated September 16, 1945, there was yet another source with access to ENORMOZ papers:

> We agree with your proposal about working with TINA. At the next meeting tell her that her documentary material on ENORMOZ is of great interest and represents a valuable contribution to the development of the work in this field. Telegraph [1 group unrecovered]. In the [1 group unrecovered] which have arisen, instruct her not to discuss her work with us with her husband and not to say anything to him about the nature of the documentary material which is being obtained by her.

In 1964 MI5 determined that TINA was Mrs. Melita Norwood, an active CPGB member and a secretary employed in London by the British Ferrous Metals Association, a branch of the Manhattan Project working on metallurgical research. Of Lithuanian background, Melita Sirnis had been noted as a CPGB member at the end of the war; her security clearance was suspended in 1950 when positive vetting was introduced.

The case officer Anatoli Yatskov, who maintained before his death in March 1993 that "perhaps less than half"[2] his network had been uncovered by the FBI, claimed that PERS was an abbreviation for PERSIUS, a source whom he believed to be alive in 1992, and whose identity required protection. Although PERS's identity remains a tantalizing enigma, the NSA's censorship suggests that HURON's real name was discovered, whereas very little seems to be known about either him or ERIE. Nevertheless, just the codenames suggest a Chicago link, bearing in mind the NKVD preference for obscure connections between the sources and their cryptonyms. The Soviets were also adept at using illegals, such as Gaik Ovakimyan, as recruiters and handlers, and not all of the most experienced agents with a knowledge of operations in the West had perished in Stalin's bloody purges.

A Comintern agent of long-standing who had entered the country through Buffalo on a Canadian passport in May 1938, together with his wife Dorothea, Adams had acted as an intermediary for Pavel Mikhailov of the New York *rezidentura*, and had set up a business, Technological Laboratories, with a Canadian partner which operated from the City offices of the Electronics Corporation of America and Keynote Recordings. His previous visas had been issued in 1927, when he had represented AMO, the first Soviet car manufacturer, and then in 1932, ostensibly on a mission to buy Curtis-Wright aircraft. Badly crippled, apparently as a result of beatings inflicted in Russia in the turmoil of 1905, he had visited the U.S. on several occasions as a Soviet trade official, and was often seen at the Soviet Consulate, but it was his interest in atomic scientists as a suspected GRU officer that led to intensive CIC surveillance.

Adams attempted to leave the country from Portland, Oregon, in February 1945 on a Soviet ship, but returned to spend a further year as a recluse in a New York hotel before finally disappearing without trace. A GRU defector, Colonel Ismail Akhmedov, testified in October 1953 that Adams was an

> illegal agent, or illegal *rezident*, correctly speaking, of the Fourth Section… He was head of the network, having his contact with legal network through cutout… Adams was born in some Scandinavian country, Sweden or Norway. He was an old Bolshevik working for the Comintern. He was a friend of Lenin and an engineer. He came to the United States several times during the late 1920s and '30s, ostensibly for business purposes. Now, somewhere in the late '30s, according to his file, he was sent illegally to the US… He was sent through Canada by a false passport and when I was Chief of the Fourth Section Adams was operating in the United States, having contact with Amtorg foreign chief engineer Korovin.[3]

Hiskey's link with Adams, with whom he was spotted on several occasions, was cut when the scientist was called up for military service, posted to the Quartermaster Corps and sent to a remote arctic base near Mineral Springs in Alaska where he sorted winter underwear. During a posting to Whitehorse in the Yukon, he was the subject of a clandestine search, and he was found to have

> had in his effects a personal notebook which contained notes that he had made while working on the atomic bomb project at Chicago, Illinois, relative to the development of several components of the bomb.

After he protested about the waste of his talent, Hiskey was transferred to an army installation in Hawaii manufacturing soap for troops in the Pacific. He was discharged in May 1946 and began teaching analytical chemistry at the Brooklyn Polytechnic Institute in Brooklyn, New York. In 1950, having refused to testify about Adams before Congress, he was indicted for contempt, but the charge was dismissed in April 1951. Considering Hiskey's connection with Adams, and his own access to Manhattan Project secrets, he must be considered a likely candidate for RAMSEY. Certainly his relationship with Adams was highly suspicious, as the FBI later discovered after the war from two witnesses, John H. Chapin and Edward T. Manning. Dr. Chapin, who knew Hiskey as a colleague at Columbia, had studied chemistry at Cornell and the University of Illinois, and was recruited into the Manhattan Project from DuPont. When Hiskey was drafted he asked Chapin to meet Adams, and in September 1944 the two men discussed in Chicago how the scientist could help the Soviets. When Adams offered Chapin money for classified data, the chemist took fright and eventually reported the approach to the FBI. Similarly, Manning, who worked as a technician on the metallurgical project at Columbia and Chicago, had been introduced to Adams by Hiskey, but when they met in New York they must have been under surveillance for he was suspended. In January 1945 he was drafted into the army and had one final meeting with Adams who declared that it was still not too late for him to supply details from his former work. Manning angrily blamed Adams for wrecking his career, and later reported his encounter to the FBI. The combined testimony of Chapin, who later joined the M. W. Kellogg Company to work on a classified Air Corps contract, and Manning, appeared to confirm that Adams was an active Soviet spy, and incriminated Hiskey.

Pavel Mikhailov's role in ENORMOZ appears to have been that of a coordinator for the GRU. A VENONA text from New York addressed to Moscow, dated August 12, 1943, shows him to have extended his interests into Canada, judging from his instruction to a member of the Ottawa *rezidentura*, Sergei Kudriavtsev, codenamed LION:

> FRED [Fred Rose], our man in LESOVIA [Canada], has been elected to the LESOVIAN parliament. His personal opportunities [1 group garbled] undoubtedly are improving, but warn LION [Sergei Kudriavtsev] about increasing caution to the maximum.
> 2. In SACRAMENTO, California, in Radiation Laboratories, large-scale experimental work is being conducted for the War Department. Working there is a progressive professor LAWRENCE, whom one can approach through the KORPORANT [Communist] [Paul G.] PINSKY – one of the directors [24 groups unrecoverable]

Curiously, Lawrence's name was deleted from the VENONA text declassified by the NSA, but his link with Pinsky must have been of considerable significance for the FBI because in 1943 the latter was a Communist who was then the research director of the Congress of Industrial Organizations (CIO) in California and head of the local FAECT branch. Born in Harbin, Manchuria, Pinsky had emigrated to California in 1931 and studied at Berkeley under Ernest Lawrence but dropped out in 1935 and, after being fired from the Del Monte Company for union activism, became a statistician at the Pacific Coast Labor Union. Pinsky remained a union organizer until he left the CPUSA in 1949, had Louise Bransten work for him as a researcher, and knew such figures at Berkeley as Robert Oppenheimer, George Eltenton, Steve Nelson, and Piotr Ivanov.

As for Fred Rose MP, who had been born Fred Rosenberg to Russian parents in Lublin, Poland, he had emigrated to Canada at the age of thirteen, been elected as a Communist in August 1943 and his NKVD activities were to be exposed two years later by the defector Igor Gouzenko. According to an entry in Zabotin's notebook, stolen by Gouzenko, Rose had been an NKVD spy since 1924, and had volunteered his services again to Major Sokolov in May or June 1942. His offer had been referred to Pavel Mikhailov, the GRU *rezident* in New York, who had authorized his reactivation. Both Rose and his mistress Freda Linton were vital links between the GRU *rezident*, Colonel Zabotin, and a large network, which included Kay Willsher of the British High Commission. Freda Linton, who had been born Fritzie Lipchitz in Montreal of Polish parents, and had recently worked for the Film Board of Canada, apparently had acted as a go-between for Professor Boyer, an academic from McGill University who had researched the development of high explosives, about whom we will hear much more.

The reference to the "progressive professor" Lawrence is mildly incriminating, knowing that the NKVD rarely passed up an opportunity to make an approach to a target individual regarded as sympathetic to the CPUSA. Of course, this VENONA text does not amount to evidence that he was ever recruited, either by Pinsky or anyone else, but clearly the issue is of some sensitivity as his name was excised by the NSA on the dubious grounds that it was covered by the Privacy Act, although it must have been known by the NSA that Lawrence, one of the most famous physicists of his generation who won a Nobel Prize, had died in August 1958. The telegram is strange because the Radiation Laboratory was at Berkeley, not at Sacramento.

A further VENONA text, from Moscow addressed to Leonid Kvasnikov in New York dated March 21, 1945, contains more important clues about ENORMOZ:

> 1. In our Nos. 5823 of 9 December 1944, 309 of 17 January 1945 and 606 of 1 February 1945 instructions were given to send HURON to Chicago to reestablish contact with VEKSEL. Carry these out as soon as possible. HURON should also make use of his stay in CHICAGO to renew his acquaintance with Goldsmith, who is known to you and who is taking part in the work on ENORMOZ.
> 2. [15 groups unrecovered] – the well-known physicist Gregory BREIT, an emigrant from RUSSIA. According to available information BREIT is taking part in the work on ENORMOZ.
> 3. [4 groups unrecovered] 759 of 8 February 1945 [2 groups unrecovered] with RAMSEY.
> 3. By the next mail report on the carrying out of the instructions in our No. 416 of 25 January 1945 concerning the collection through PETER [Thomas L. Black] and the other agent network of information on the structure and activities of the Bureau of Standards.

This VENONA text is important because it emphasizes the need for HURON to make contact with VEKSEL, apparently the fourth such request. It is also significant for the mention of Thomas Black, codenamed PETER, a chemist employed by Organics in New York between 1944 and 1949, who reported to Joseph Katz. Black was interviewed by the FBI in June 1950 and admitted having collected information for Gaik Ovakimyan since 1934, but was not charged with espionage. HURON, of course, was to become ERNEST, and this highlights some confusion over these two spies, compounded by the footnotes of a VENONA text from San Francisco dated November 27, 1945, in which ERNEST is stated to have been "known as ERIE" in a previous telegram from New York sent on February 20, 1945. On that date Kvasnikov was instructed to "leave the covername HURON unchanged; ERIE amend to ERNEST." In fact, of course, ERIE had become GEORGES on October 5, 1944, just as HURON had already been transformed into ERNEST.

> Part I At the second meeting with WOLF [Andrei R. Orlov] [10 groups unrecovered] about the production of high octane gasoline which includes a diagram of the production process [18 groups unrecovered] [10 groups unrecovered] in the near future [32 groups unrecovered] the TOWNSMEN [Americans] [80 groups unrecovered] [49 groups unrecoverable]
>
> Part II After this Professor SMYTH was forbidden to print [4 groups unrecovered] laboratory. ERNEST has [17 groups unrecovered]. In the book there is no information about the quantity of uranium being crushed but he confirms this information in conversations with the people connected with [6 groups unrecovered] at his place and can turn it over to us at any time. In the book there is a complete description of the process with a diagram and all necessary materials are enumerated. Two weeks ago ERNEST received a letter from D. who said that he had not written because of lack of time. WOLF permitted ERNEST to meet the people with whom Professor SMYTH collaborated. Among them are the engineer Morris PERELMAN and Professor [67 groups unrecovered] dictionary.

As this text was transmitted on November 27, 1945, the letter received by ERNEST two weeks earlier would suggest a date of about November 13, and imply that the letter's author, D, was some kind of source for ERNEST.

Professor Henry D. Smyth's official history of the bomb project, *Atomic Energy for Military Purposes*, had been published some months before this text had been sent by an unknown member of the San Francisco *rezidentura*, but it did show that HURON/ERNEST had been run by Andrei P. Orlov, who operated under Soviet Government Purchasing Commission cover, and was connected to Morris

Perelman, an engineer at Los Alamos. As for the source "D," it is likely that this is an abbreviation for his full codename, which most probably appears in one of the unrecovered groups. There is also a strong implication that ERNEST was in a position to gain access to the classified portion of Smyth's book "at any time."

There remains, regrettably, unresolved conflict over ERIE and HURON. On October 5 HURON became ERNEST and ERIE became GEORGES. Then, four months later, Kvasnikov in New York is told that HURON's codename is still valid. The question is whether Orlov in California was handling HURON/ERNEST or ERIE/ERNEST. One explanation is that someone in Moscow belatedly realized that using ERNEST as the codename for someone who really was called Ernest was inherently insecure.

Although VENONA texts frequently referred to sources by the real names, the Soviets demonstrating their full confidence in the integrity of their cipher system, it seems unlikely from the context that Grigory Breit could have been a spy. Of Russian origin, as mentioned in the VENONA text, Breit had taught theoretical physics at Yale, lived in South Dakota and was the co-author of the Breit-Wigner formula. While at Los Alamos, Breit, who had lodged with Rudolf Peierls, held the title Director of Rapid Rupture, and had joined with Leo Szilard to argue against the openness advocated by Fermi. Appalled by the authorities' reluctance to impose greater security restrictions on their research, Breit resigned in 1943 and went to work on a U.S. Navy project, where he was already well established by the date of Moscow's telegram to Kvasnikov on March 21. Fluent in Danish, Russian, and German, Breit married a German girl in 1952 and in 1960 took up a teaching post in Copenhagen.

Since there is no mention in the published text of "Goldsmith," nor of anyone else working on ENORMOZ, it is safe to assume that this is the deletion made in connection with HURON, and perhaps is a reference to Hyman Goldsmith, a respected physicist of Austrian origin who trained at the City College of New York and worked at the Brookhaven Institute before he moved to Chicago to work with Fermi. Goldsmith died in an accident in Vermont in 1949, so he was never interviewed by the FBI, and there is no obvious explanation for the redaction of his name in the only VENONA text in which he is mentioned. VEKSEL, of course, had been identified previously as Dr. J. Robert Oppenheimer, and his status as the leader of the Manhattan Project explains official American reticence, although doubts about his political reliability dated back to at least June 1954 when his security clearance had been suspended by the Atomic Energy Commission.

Chapter IX

Oppenheimer and Soviet Espionage

The spy business isn't as easy as it appears in the movies.

Robert Serber

J. Robert Oppenheimer had been accused by William L. Borden, formerly the secretary to the Joint Committee of Congress on Atomic Energy, of being "an espionage agent operating under a Soviet directive," listing two dozen items of "derogatory information," and in consequence the AEC passed the issue to the Personnel Security Board which held a hearing to review the physicist's clearance. Borden's allegations were really treated as charges by the PSB and Oppenheimer engaged a lawyer to answer them, and was able to have witnesses cross-examined. The resulting high drama saw a detailed scrutiny of all the available evidence against Oppenheimer, and the disclosure that he had been the Soviet spy at Berkeley mentioned by Fuchs who had betrayed details of the electromagnetic separation method "in 1942 or earlier." Apart from the Chevalier episode, in which Oppenheimer admitted he had been "an idiot," the charges concentrated on his friendships and associations with Communists. Indeed, Borden asserted that Oppenheimer "had no close friends except Communists."

Although Oppenheimer denied ever having been either an overt or underground Party member, the PSB took a week to examine the accumulated evidence in private, which was not made public (but consisted of transcripts of FBI recordings and telephone taps), and concluded that "during the period 1942–45, Dr. Hannah Peters, Bernadette Doyle, Steve Nelson, Jack Manley, and Katrina Sandow made statements indicating that Dr. Oppenheimer was then a member of the Communist Party." All had been senior CPUSA officials and the subject of intensive technical surveillance by the FBI which had accumulated hours of conversation between, for example, Hannah Peters, who was the organizer of the Professional Section of the Alameda County Party, and her Party comrades. However, the PSB rejected the charge that Paul Pinsky and David Adelson had made the same statements about Oppenheimer. This suggests that the PSB read the FBI's transcripts but could not find such statements attributable to these particular two CPUSA figures. So what is the truth of Oppenheimer's alleged membership of the Party? He said he had attended a couple of social gatherings, one held at Louise Bransten's home "after the end of 1940," that had been addressed by William Schneiderman of the CPUSA, who had "attempted, not with success as far as we were concerned, to explain what the communist line was all about" and supported numerous Communist fronts "but no one ever asked me to join the Communist Party." Instead, he regarded himself between late 1936 and 1942 as a fellow traveler, defined as "someone who accepted part of the public program of the Communist Party, who was willing to work with and associate with Communists, but who was not a member of the Party."

When questioned by the FBI in 1946, Oppenheimer said that he had undergone a change of mind at the time of the Molotov-Ribbentrop Pact in 1939, and in another interview in September 1950 he had elaborated further, stating that he had lost whatever interest he had and had become "fed up with the whole thing" at the time of the break between Germany and Russia in 1941. Not surprisingly, these assertions did not impress the FBI which knew he had continued to make monthly contributions to the CPUSA of $150 until April 1942. Furthermore, while the events of 1939 had tested the commitment of many Party members, Hitler's invasion of the Soviet Union in June 1941 had achieved precisely the opposite impact. If Oppenheimer had wanted ideological grounds to abandon the Party, they were certainly apparent in 1939, but rather less so two years later.

While there is no empirical proof that Oppenheimer even joined the Party formally, he acknowledged having subscribed to its west coast newspaper, *People's World*, having contributed money to the Party, given his name to numerous front organizations, pamphlets and petitions, supported a strike fund sponsored by the Party and attended Party meetings. Certainly, according to a recording made in December 1942 by the FBI's microphones hidden in the Alameda County CPUSA branch office, both Hannah Peters and Bernadette Doyle believed he was a Party member, but could not play any active role "because of his employment on a special project."

The security authorities' doubts about Oppenheimer had been manifest, and Captain Horace Calvert, the District Security Officer, had submitted an adverse recommendation, so his original security clearance had only been granted on the basis that Groves had ordered it, on July 20, 1942, "without delay irrespective of any information you have regarding Mr. Oppenheimer." When challenged by the PSB about this decision in 1954, Lansdale denied that "our conclusions as to clearance were necessarily dictated by indispensability. I wish to emphasize it for myself. I reached the conclusion that he was loyal and ought to be cleared." However, Boris Pash had been wholly opposed to a clearance, and previously had reported:

> In view of the fact this office believes that subject still is or may be connected with the Communist Party, and because of the known interest of the Communist Party in the Project, together with the interest of the USSR in it, the following possibilities are submitted for your consideration: A. All indications on the part of Communist

> Party members who have expressed themselves with regard to the subject lead this office to believe that the Communist Party is making a definite effort to officially divorce the subject's affiliation with the Party, and subject himself is not indicating in any way interest in the Party. However, if subject's affiliation with the Party is definite and he is a member of the Party, there is a possibility of his developing a scientific work to a certain extent, then turning it over to the Party without submitting any phase of it to the US Government.[1]

Pash's second possibility, which he considered less likely, was that Oppenheimer would pass the information through an intermediary, although he did not name the principal candidates. Oppenheimer's alleged suspect associations with senior CPUSA figures included Clarence Hiskey, Joseph Weinberg, Steve Nelson, Isaac Folkoff, Jack Manley, Bernadette Doyle, Kenneth May, Katrina Sandow, Thomas Addis, and Rudy Lambert. Among this group, Oppenheimer denied knowing Hiskey, Manley, and Sandow, but admitted he had met Dr. Addis and Rudy Lambert through his support for the Spanish republicans. A distinguished medical scientist, Addis had introduced him to Folkoff, a CPUSA official responsible for collecting money for "the Loyalist cause." He "saw a little of Kenneth May," knew Weinberg only "as a graduate student," and recalled that Steve Nelson "came a few times to visit with his family." As for Bernadette Doyle, he doubted that he had met her "although I recognize her name." She was, of course, Alameda County's Party organizational secretary, and the fact that Oppenheimer was friendly with Nelson is significant, even though he claimed that neither he nor his wife had seen him since "1941 or 1942" and testified that he had nothing in common with Nelson "except an affection for my wife."[2] So was Steve Nelson a spy?

Born in Chaglich, Yugoslavia, where he had been active in radical politics, Nelson had landed in New York illegally in June 1920, accompanied by his mother and two sisters and pretending to be Joseph Fleischinger, an American citizen who was actually married to his mother's sister. The impersonation was discovered and deportation proceedings were initiated, but then abandoned two years later, thus allowing him to become a naturalized American citizen in Detroit in November 1928. It was under his true name, Stephan Mesarosh, that in 1930 he had used Golos's firm World Tourists, Inc. to travel to Moscow where he attended a course at the Lenin School between September 1931 and May 1933. After his graduation he had undertaken a secret mission in Central Europe, and was spotted in Shanghai where he was associated with Arthur Ewert, a veteran Comintern agent. Nelson returned to the U.S. in 1933, having renewed his U.S. passport in Austria in July, to organize CPUSA industrial branches in Pittsburgh, Chicago, and Cleveland, and served as a political commissar in the Abraham Lincoln Battalion during the Spanish Civil War. In February 1937, while still in Spain, he obtained another U.S. passport in the name of Joseph Fleischinger (even though he twice misspelled the surname on the application form).

Nelson's experience in Spain bears all the hallmarks of a recruited Soviet spy, and his successor as political commissar in the International Brigade, the Englishman Douglas Springhall, was himself arrested and imprisoned for espionage in London in June 1943. Indeed, Nelson was to be closely linked to Vasili Zubilin, who visited his Oakland home, and to Piotr Ivanov of the San Francisco *rezidentura.* The question of whether his relationship with the Oppenheimers was entirely innocent is one that is open to doubt, but there is some evidence that he did once make a direct approach to Robert for information. The FBI microphone hidden in Nelson's home picked up a conversation held on March 23, 1943 with Joseph Weinberg in which Nelson mentioned that Oppenheimer had turned him down.[3] Whatever the truth, the physicist was, by his own admission, in close contact with him, with Khiefets's mistress Louise Bransten, Isaac Folkoff and, of course, Haakon Chevalier.

Accused of having discussed atomic secrets with people he knew to be CPUSA officials, Oppenheimer made a categoric denial and stated, "I never discussed anything of my secret work or anything about the atomic bomb with Steve Nelson." He also rejected the assertion that he had helped Lomanitz, Friedman, and Weinberg join the Manhattan Project, but he protested that none had worked at Los Alamos and that he "had nothing to do with the employment of Friedman and Weinberg by the Radiation Laboratory; I had no responsibility for the hiring of anyone there." He did acknowledge asking "for the transfer of David Bohm to Los Alamos" and supporting "the suggestion of the personnel director" that David Hawkins move to Los Alamos, but denied he knew at the time that either had been Communists. Furthermore, he pointed out that all his recommendations were routinely dependent upon a security clearance, which, in Bohm's case, had not been forthcoming. Peer de Silva, in charge of security at Los Alamos, had been unimpressed, and had reported to Colonel Pash that "in the opinion of this officer Oppenheimer must either be incredibly naïve and almost childlike in his sense of reality, or he himself is extremely clever and disloyal." De Silva concluded, on September 2, 1943, that "Oppenheimer is playing a key part in the attempt of the Soviet Union to secure, by espionage, highly secret information which is vital to the Soviet Union." At this stage de Silva had no hard evidence against Oppenheimer, but Lansdale later admitted that "we continued to the best of our ability to investigate him. We kept him under surveillance whenever he left the project. We opened his mail. We did all sorts of nasty things that we do or we did on the project."

On September 6, 1943, Pash, on the basis of de Silva's memorandum, reported to Lansdale that "this office is still of the opinion that Oppenheimer is not fully to be trusted and that his loyalty to a Nation is divided. It is believed that the only undivided loyalty that he can have is to science and it is strongly felt that if in his position the Soviet government could offer more for the advancement of his scientific cause he would select that government as the one to which he would express his loyalty."

The classified evidence examined by the PSB, which has never been made public (although the transcripts of the witness evidence ran for a thousand pages), was based on FBI and CIC surveillance reports and intercept transcripts, collectively known as CINRAD, for "Communists in the Radiation Laboratory." Later this would be absorbed into a larger generic case, COMRAP—"Communist apparatus." What the three-man panel did not see was the VENONA material, which would have added a further significant dimension to its deliberations. Whereas the FBI files were damning about Hiskey, Weinberg, and Nelson, VENONA demonstrated that William Schneiderman, the Russian-born head of the CPUSA in California (and incidentally the official representative to the Comintern in 1934 and 1935) was a spy codenamed NAT, and that Isaac Folkoff had appeared in the traffic as UNCLE.

Folkoff was a founding member of the CPUSA, the proprietor of the Model Embroidery and Pleating Company in San Francisco and, according to an early FBI report dated April 1922, had been a close friend of Nathan Silvermaster, who was later to run a wartime spy ring in Washington DC. As well as having been the financial director of the CPUSA between 1937 and 1941, Folkoff was identified by Whittaker Chambers as the person to whom he had delivered $10,000 in 1935 on behalf of the NKVD. Among Folkoff's sub-agents was James W. Miller from the Office of Censorship, codenamed VAGUE, who kept the *rezidentura* informed about mail intercepts and the monitoring of Russian money transfers. VENONA also mentioned several other Party apparatchiks, such as Paul Pinsky and Rudy Lambert, and thereby showed the extent of Soviet interest in ENORMOZ and, most relevantly, proved the scale of the overlap between the NKVD and the CPUSA.

Even without the benefit of VENONA, the PSB reached some devastating conclusions, finding that twenty-three of the twenty-four instances of "derogatory information" had been substantiated, including that Oppenheimer indeed had been a guest at a Party meeting held at his brother's house on January 1, 1947, that had also been attended by Paul Pinsky and David Adelson, in direct contradiction to his own testimony. Furthermore, in spite of his repeated denials to the FBI on September 5, 1946, and in 1950, the PSB ruled that Oppenheimer's own home had been used for "a closed meeting of the professional section of the Communist Party of Alameda County, California, which was held in the latter part of July or early August 1941." On this latter point the evidence against Oppenheimer looked dubious, and depended upon an FBI "special consultant," Paul Crouch, who had testified against more than fifty fellow CPUSA members since 1950 when he and his wife had become semi-professional witnesses for the FBI. The Crouches had been vague about the precise date of the meeting, held "in July or early August 1941" but Oppenheimer had been able to demonstrate that he had been at his ranch in New Mexico on the most likely date, July 23, 1941, had left Berkeley a few days after July 4, and had not returned until after the first week of August. In support, Hans Bethe remembered having visited the Oppenheimers at their ranch on July 24.

The scientific community was divided over Oppenheimer, with witnesses appearing before the PSB for both sides. Lawrence, who intended to give evidence against Oppenheimer, curiously left Berkeley but only reached Oak Ridge and withdrew, pleading a collapse in his health caused by an attack of colitis. Some believed that his illness was one of convenience, for he telephoned his colleague Luis Alvarez at Berkeley and demanded he refuse to appear for Oppenheimer. After some soul-searching, Alvarez defied Lawrence and testified. Another witness, General Groves, conceded that he "would not clear Dr. Oppenheimer today if I was a member of the Commission," a judgment that may have helped to seal the scientist's fate, for the PSB informed the AEC that, by a majority verdict, they had decided that reinstatement of Oppenheimer's clearance would not be clearly consistent with the security interests of the United States.

Oppenheimer, who died in February 1967, was always a controversial figure, not least because his younger brother Frank, his sister-in-law Jackenette, his wife Kitty, and his mistress Jean Tatlock (who committed suicide in January 1944) were all CPUSA members, although only Frank's name appears in a VENONA text, from VAVILOV in San Francisco dated November 13, 1945:

> Part I A trustworthy dockworker [Jerome Michael] CALLAGHAN has advised that his friend, the Communist Rudolph LAMBERT [43 groups unrecoverable] Nevada, Utah and Arizona.
> Concerning Uranium deposits [4 groups unrecovered] before the publication of the communication on [48 groups unrecoverable] to us. Please advise whether we are interested in receiving further [8 groups unrecovered].Supplementary to our no. 47 the brother of Robert OPPENHEIMER – Frank [1 group unrecovered] member of [9 groups unrecovered], took part in atomic research. One must

> [1 group unrecovered] that scholars who have taken part in these pursuits are under the surveillance of the American counterintelligence.
> Part II Robert OPPENHEIMER and the Ernst LAWRENCE mentioned in our number 435 (two of the chief scientific leaders on the atomic bomb) [53 groups unrecovered]. VAVILOV.

Evidently, Rudolph C. Lambert, a senior member of the CPUSA's Northern California District, had relayed some information about atomic research, but the message is too fragmented to understand the NKVD's interest in the Oppenheimer brothers. Could Frank, who collaborated closely with Ernest Lawrence on the electromagnetic separation method, have been the Soviet source at Berkeley mentioned by Fuchs? Certainly the text is relevant to his brother Robert who later said that "our association never became close" when he was challenged by the 1954 Personnel Security Board for having associated with such a well-known CPUSA functionary as Lambert. He admitted to having met him half a dozen times, and to having had lunch with him and another CPUSA official, Isaac Folkoff, once or twice, to discuss his financial contributions to the Party.

The precise nature of Robert Oppenheimer's relationship with the NKVD has long been a topic of intense interest. Although Robert was never formally a member of the Party, practically all his friends were, and as he subsequently admitted, he "probably joined every Communist front on the West Coast." Even after his marriage he continued to have a relationship with the unstable Jean Tatlock, who had remained a CPUSA member in the Bay Area, and on June 9, 1943, was spotted by CIC agents when he slipped away from Berkeley to spend the night with her, instead of catching a train to Los Alamos. Frank, who joined the Radiation Laboratory in 1941 from Stanford University (and worked at both Oak Ridge and Los Alamos), had been a member (and later chairman) of the CPUSA's Palo Alto branch since 1936, under the alias "Frank Folsom," as was Robert's wife Kitty. Her first husband, Joseph Dallet, was a CPUSA official whom she had met in December 1933 when she was still a student in Wisconsin. By February the following year she had married Dallet and was working as an unpaid volunteer in the Youngstown headquarters of the CPUSA. Dallet had subsequently signed up to fight in Spain as a member of the International Brigade, and they spent ten days together in Paris before he enlisted. She was on her way to join him, at Albacete in 1937, when news of his death had been broken to her in Paris by one of his comrades, Steve Nelson. Her second husband, whom she married in December 1938, was an English physician, Richard Harrison, who was interested in radiation and took her to Pasadena where she attended a graduate course in mycology and met Robert Oppenheimer. After eighteen months of marriage, Kitty divorced Harrison and married Oppenheimer. This was how he came into contact with Nelson, who was a senior CPUSA functionary as well as an NKVD courier for Oppenheimer's students Joseph W. Weinberg, Giovanni Rossi Lomanitz, Max B. Friedman, and David Bohm, all of whom worked at the Radiation Laboratory at Berkeley (and were later to take the Fifth Amendment when questioned about their CPUSA memberships).

The FBI's investigation, codenamed CINRAD, eventually led to the compilation of files on more than three hundred CPUSA members in Berkeley, and provided a pattern of front organizations, covert meetings and unofficial links between Party members designed to further the penetration of the Radiation Laboratory. The FBI estimated that, of the CPUSA's thirty-six districts, the largest after New York and Chicago was in California, with a total membership of some six thousand. Through the use of surveillance, wiretaps and informants, the FBI monitored such groups as the Science for Victory Committee, chaired by Weldon Dayton, which included Bernard Peters on its executive committee. In March 1944 Peters tried to get Dayton a job at the Rad Lab, but discreet steps were taken to ensure that the U.S. Navy objected to his transfer. The SVC, which had been created in 1943, was run by CPUSA members such as Al Marshak and Rose Segure and succeeded in obtaining consultancy posts for three confirmed Communists: the organic chemist David Adelson, the physiologist and pathologist Thomas Addis, and the physical chemist Frank C. Collins. The SVC was finally would up in August 1945 when its activities became virtually synonymous with the CPUSA.

Originally from New York, Weinberg had graduated from the City College and become an active member of the Young Communist League before moving to California. His wife Muriel, who had studied at the University of Wisconsin, was also a Party activist; CPUSA literature mailed to Radiation Laboratory scientists was traced to her. In March 1943 FBI surveillance on Steve Nelson's home and telephone identified Weinberg as a late night visitor who wanted to copy a formula that had been written in the handwriting of another scientist. This had been followed soon after by a covert rendezvous held by Nelson in a park with a Soviet vice consul, Piotr Ivanov, at which packages were seen to be exchanged, and then by Zubilin's visit to Nelson's home. In August Weinberg was watched by Counter-Intelligence Corps (CIC) agents George Rathman, Wagener, Murray, and Harold Zindle while he hosted a clandestine Party gathering at his apartment in Black Street, Berkeley, attended by Nelson and Lomanitz. Weinberg always denied his membership of the Party, involvement in espionage, or even knowing Steve Nelson, despite surveillance evidence showing Nelson's secretary, Bernadette Doyle, as a visitor to his home. He was indicted on four counts of contempt after he had pleaded the Fifth Amendment before the House Un-American Activities Committee. The charges were dismissed in March 1953 on the grounds that Weinberg had exercised his constitutional right, but nevertheless he lost his post at the University of Minnesota's Department of Physics. According to John Lansdale, "we proved to our satisfaction that he gave information to Steve Nelson for money."

Archive material in Moscow tells a rather different story about Weinberg, with HURON reporting that "Weinberg said that the passing of classified information involves too much risk, is dangerous and harmful. But it is possible to export to the USSR the brains that made the bomb… He knows at least one who is willing to 'fall ill,' retire from the project and then go over to the USSR." According to the file, HURON speculated that "Weinberg must have meant Oppenheimer."

Weinberg was closely connected with another brilliant young physicist, Giovanni Rossi Lomanitz, originally from Bryan, Texas, who was an openly declared member of the CPUSA and a union organizer for the Federation of Architects, Engineers, Chemists, and Technicians (FAECT). He ran the CPUSA's Merriman branch until it was dissolved by Nelson, and specialized in recruiting atomic research staff into the union and the Party. He also established the FAECT branch in Lawrence's Radiation Laboratory, Local 25, which came under close FBI scrutiny. Surveillance reports, replete with car license numbers, filed after union meetings, showed Dr. Irving D. Fox and Bernard Peters as being on the executive committee, with Bohm and Lomanitz as active members. According to Robert R. Davis, a young computer technician who confirmed his membership in the Party between January and April 1943, when he had been transferred from Berkeley to Los Alamos, it had been Lomanitz who had recruited both him and his wife Charlotte into the CPUSA. Davis had joined D Division at Los Alamos in April 1943, on the recommendation of Ernest Lawrence, as a group leader and was editor of the Technical Series Publications.

Although Ernest Lawrence was to appoint Lomanitz as the liaison between Berkeley and Oak Ridge, the Counter-Intelligence Corps arranged for him to be drafted in the army and moved continuously from one military post to another until the end of the war to keep him out of access. Colonel Lansdale later testified, "I remember Ernest Lawrence yelled and screamed louder than anybody else about us taking Lomanitz away from him," and Oppenheimer recorded that on August 10, 1943, while on a visit to Los Alamos, Lawrence had exclaimed, "For goodness' sake, lay off Lomanitz and stop raising questions!" Having pleaded the Fifth Amendment before Congress, Lomanitz was indicted on contempt charges in December 1949, and was acquitted in June 1951, as was Bohm, who chose to move to São Paulo, Brazil, that same autumn, where his American passport was confiscated by the local U.S. consulate, returnable only if he traveled home to the States. Instead, Bohm took Brazilian nationality in November 1954 and the following year settled in Haifa, Israel. Two years later Bohm was in England. Upon the recommendation of J. D. Bernal, the Marxist head of the physics department, he was appointed Professor of Theoretical Physics at Birkbeck College, London University, where he worked until his death in October 1992.

Born in Philadelphia to immigrant parents, his father being from Hungary and his mother from Russia, Bohm had been close to Lomanitz, with whom he had roomed at Berkeley, and to both Peters and Weinberg, and had joined the CPUSA in 1941, although he dropped out after just two years. Nevertheless, he never lost his commitment to Marxism, often took part in CPUSA activities and distributed copies of Earl Browder's *Victory—And After*. For this reason Bohm's application to join Los Alamos was rejected on security grounds, Oppenheimer having described him in a security report as potentially dangerous, and he remained at Berkeley for the rest of the war, concentrating on unclassified aspects of the Manhattan Project, before joining Oppenheimer upon his return to the Radiation Laboratory in 1946.

Oppenheimer was also in touch, between 1938 and early 1942, with another CPUSA official, Isaac Folkoff, and with Piotr Ivanov, the subordinate to San Francisco *rezident* Grigori Kheifets, who was suspected by the FBI of being a GRU officer. Another of Kheifets's sources was Oppenheimer's friend, the chemist Dr. Martin Kamen, who was monitored by the FBI when the Soviets pumped him for details of the American stockpile of uranium in Chicago. Born in Canada to Russian immigrants, but educated in Chicago, Kamen had co-discovered Carbon-14 and had been credited with pioneering a method of using a cyclotron to make Iron-55. He had worked at Berkeley's Radiation Laboratory since 1936, and had been connected with several Communist front organizations, including the American-Soviet Science Society, the Joint Anti-Fascist Refugee Committee, the American League against War and Fascism, and Russian War Relief. On July 2, 1943, an FBI surveillance team attempted to eavesdrop on a dinner conversation held in Berstein's Fish Grotto in San Francisco with Kheifets and Grigori Kasparov, during which Kamen was recorded mentioning Niels Bohr, atomic piles and Santa Fe. Because of background noise in the busy restaurant, the quality of the recording was poor, but it was sufficiently incriminating for Kamen's security clearance to be suspended ten days later and his transfer to a non-sensitive post in a shipyard. When he was later confronted with the FBI's evidence, he insisted that he had met Kheifets only twice socially, and that the purpose of the dinner was simply to thank him for intervening on behalf of a Soviet official in Seattle whose leukemia needed radiation treatment. Nevertheless, the FBI regarded Kamen with deep suspicion, and for a while he too experienced difficulties with the State Department in obtaining a U.S. passport, although his reputation was fully restored in 1996 when he was awarded the prestigious Fermi Prize, worth $100,000, and the adulation of his peers. He now lives in Santa Barbara, California.

Kheifets was Jewish and an experienced intelligence officer who had acted as secretary to Lenin's widow, Nadezhda Krupskaya, and had served as deputy *rezident* in Italy before the war. While working as an illegal in Germany, he had achieved a diploma at the Jena Polytechnical Institute. He spoke fluent English, French, and German and, while in San Francisco, conducted an affair with Louise Bransten, the wealthy former wife of Bruce Minton, about whom Elizabeth Bentley had said much, crediting him with being one of Jake Golos's recruiters, and a contributor to the CPUSA's journal *New Masses*. Mrs. Bransten, the heiress to the Rosenberg dried fruit fortune, was a popular socialite and seems to have used her status to hold frequent soirées attended by NKVD personnel and targets intended for cultivation. Although Kheifets was both sophisticated and professional, he adopted the alias "Mr. Brown" to run unwittingly at least one double agent who reported to the FBI, so the local field office never harbored any doubts about his dual role. Grigori Kasparov, of course, was also a senior NKVD officer who succeeded Kheifets as *rezident* in San Francisco, when the latter was recalled to Moscow in May 1944 to participate in the investigation into the Zubilins, and was later transferred to Mexico City.

According to Pavel Sudoplatov, Kheifets had targeted the leftist physicists Enrico Fermi and his pupil Bruno Pontecorvo for recruitment long before they joined the Manhattan Project. As the NKVD's Director of Special Tasks in Moscow responsible for supervising Kheifets, Sudoplatov should have been well positioned to help identify the VENONA cryptonyms, but he has only muddied the waters by suggesting that Bruno Pontecorvo's codename was YOUNG (which was actually Ted Hall), and his claim that Fermi and Oppenheimer were both active spies, which leaves unresolved the question of how far Oppenheimer collaborated with the NKVD. Sudoplatov recalls that Elizaveta Zubilina, herself an experienced intelligence professional who had worked as an illegal in Turkey, had traveled to California to recruit sources inside the Manhattan Project, a mission for which she was ideally suited:

> She hardly appeared foreign in the United States. Her manner was so natural and sociable that she immediately made friends. Slim, with dark eyes, she had a classic Semitic beauty that attracted men, and she was one of the most successful agent recruiters, establishing her own illegal network of Jewish refugees from Poland, and recruiting one of Szilard's secretaries, who provided technical data. She spoke excellent English, German, French, Romanian, and Hebrew. Usually she looked like a sophisticated, upper-class European, but she had the ability to change her appearance like a chameleon.[4]

As well as establishing direct contact with Oppenheimer through his wife, Elizaveta cultivated another source close to his family. Her

> other mission was to check on the two Polish Jewish agents established on the West Coast as illegals by Eitingon in the early 1930s. They had remained under deep cover for more than ten years. One of these agents was a dentist with a French medical degree that the OGPU had subsidized. His code name was CHESS PLAYER. The dentist's wife became a close friend of the Oppenheimer family, and they were our clandestine contacts with Oppenheimer and his friends, contacts that went undetected by the FBI.[5]

The proposition that the notorious Leonid A. Eitingon had established an embryonic illegal network in California in the "early 1930s" deserves closer scrutiny, especially as Sudoplatov alleged that one of the agents was in contact with Oppenheimer. Eitingon was a ruthless NKVD officer who acquired an unsavory reputation as Alexander Orlov's deputy during the Spanish Civil War. While

Orlov, as *rezident*, busied himself with recruiting Morris Cohen and running Kim Philby, Eitingon was enforcing discipline on the cadres, usually at the point of a machine-gun. Eitingon was to ensure his place in intelligence history by seducing Caridad Mercader and persuading her son Ramon to assassinate Leon Trotsky in Mexico in August 1940. The plot did not go entirely to plan and Ramon was arrested, leaving Eitingon and Caridad to make their escape to Moscow, via California and China, in February 1941. According to Sudoplatov, Eitingon used his time in Los Angeles and San Francisco to make contact with the *rezident*, his old friend Grigori Kheifets, and activate his two sleeper agents. One, as we have seen, was described as a Jewish dentist, and the other was "the owner of a medium-sized retail business" and they were put to work "to become couriers in the network obtaining American atomic secrets from 1942 to 1945." While the holder of the French medical degree, codenamed CHESS PLAYER, does not coincide with any of the agents appearing in the VENONA texts, the description of Jewish retailer could fit Isaac Folkoff, codenamed UNCLE, who did own a similar business in the clothing trade in San Francisco, was active in Berkeley and was Robert Oppenheimer's occasional lunch companion.

Another participant in these events was Kitty Harris, Earl Browder's wife and a legendary NKVD illegal. Codenamed ADA, she had run Donald Maclean in London and Paris before the war, but had been compromised twice, once by a former CPUSA member, Ben Gitlow, who had named her before the Dies Congressional Committee as an NKVD agent, and then again most comprehensively by the defector Walter Krivitsky, formerly the GRU illegal *rezident* in The Hague, who had broken with Stalin in October 1937 and subsequently fled to the United States. In his book, *I Was Stalin's Agent*, he described her as "Kitty Harris, originally Katherine Harrison" and having "been connected with our secret service for some years." He also recalled that on April 29, 1937, following an introductory meeting at the Savoy Hotel in Moscow, he had dispatched her on a mission to Switzerland. She had proved "exceptionally reliable. At that time I needed a woman agent in Switzerland, and the holder of an American passport was particularly welcome."[6] Despite her notoriety, the NKVD sent her to the United States in October 1941, where she arrived from Petropavlovsk on a tanker, the SS *Donbass.* According to her declassified personal file in Moscow, Harris's safe arrival in San Francisco was signaled by Grigori Kheifets. She spent two weeks in a local hotel registered as Elizabeth Dreyfus of Chicago, recovering from the ordeal of a stormy voyage that had lasted six weeks. She then moved to Los Angeles, where she remained until November 15, 1942, when she was given a new assignment in Mexico, but in the meantime was ordered to find and activate "two agents, both pre-war Jewish immigrants from Poland." One was the owner of a small grocery store in Los Angeles, and the other was CHESS PLAYER, "a dentist whose training in France had been financed by Jakov Serebriansky, a senior NKVD officer who had instructed him to settle in San Francisco in the early 1930s." According to Harris's biographer, the KGB officer Igor Damaskin, "CHESS PLAYER's wife was a close friend of the Oppenheimer family" and the pair "played a part in organizing the effort to uncover American atomic secrets, together with the ubiquitous Naim Eitingon."[7]

While Damaskin appears to support Sudoplatov's memory of Oppenheimer, the latter's true meaning remains difficult to interpret, for he insists that the scientist cooperated fully. "In all, there were five classified reports made available by Oppenheimer describing the progress of work on the atomic bomb," he recalls, noting that "Oppenheimer, together with Fermi and Szilard, helped us place moles in Tennessee, Los Alamos, and Chicago as assistants in those three labs. In total there were four important sources of information who transmitted documents from the labs to the New York and Washington *rezidenturas* and to our illegal station, which was a drugstore in Santa Fe." While this sounds conclusive, Sudoplatov explains that not all sources were necessarily conscious agents:

> The line between valuable connections and acquaintances, and confidential relations is very shaky. In traditional espionage terminology, there is a special term, *agenturnaya razvedka,* which means that the material is received through a network of agents or case officers act-

> ing under cover. Occasionally the most valuable information comes from a contact who is not an agent in the true sense—that is, working for and paid by us—but who is still regarded in the archives as an agent source of information. Our problem was that the atomic espionage business required new approaches; we used every potential method to penetrate into a unique area of activities that was intensely guarded by the American authorities.[8]

So into which category did Oppenheimer fall? The question has to be asked because the physicist had reported Haakon Chevalier, then Professor of French at Berkeley, to Boris Pash's security office when, at a dinner party in March 1943, he had been pitched with the line that it was a moral duty to share technical data with the Russians. Born in America to French and Norwegian parents, Chevalier was a scholar who had studied at the Leningrad Institute and, when first introduced to Oppenheimer in late 1937, had established a reputation as André Malraux's translator and the author of a study of Anatole France. He had taught at the university since 1927 and was also the faculty unit organizer for the CPUSA's Alameda County branch, a post he had held since 1934. Its secret meetings, attended by such senior CPUSA figures as Rudy Lambert, had often taken place in his home. Oppenheimer had refused what he had interpreted as Chevalier's proposal, which supposedly had been made at Steve Nelson's suggestion, later declaring it to be outright treason, but he waited several months, until August 1943, to report the incident. Oppenheimer's initial statement, on August 25 in Durant Hall to Lieutenant Lyall A. Johnson, had been in the form of a suggestion that an Englishman named Eltenton was a security risk and ought to be watched. The following day Boris Pash interviewed Oppenheimer and obtained further information, which was recorded secretly and later transcribed. Included in the five-thousand-word document was Oppenheimer's reflections on security, apparently minimalizing the impact of what had happened:

> My view about this whole damn thing, of course, is that the information we are working on is probably known to all the governments that care to find out. The information about what we are doing is

> probably of no use, because it is so complicated. I don't agree that the security problem on the project is a bitter one if one means by the security problem preventing information of technical use to another country from escaping. But I do think that the intensity of our effort and our concern, uh, the international investment involved—that is, information which might alter the course of other governments.

On this second occasion Oppenheimer declined to name the intermediary who had relayed Eltenton's offer, but eventually did confide in General Groves, in his room in Los Alamos, having been ordered to do so, on December 12, 1943. This resulted in a telegram being circulated to all the Manhattan District security offices by Groves's deputy, General Kenneth Nichols:

> Haakon Chevalier to be reported by Oppenheimer to be professor at Rad Lab who made three contacts for Eltenton. Ref. EIDMMI-34. Classified secret. Oppenheimer believed Chevalier engaged in no further activity other than three original attempts.

This episode, which had taken place casually in Oppenheimer's kitchen, with just the two men present, also served to incriminate George C. Eltenton, a British-born physicist who, having graduated from Cambridge and worked in the cotton industry, had moved to Leningrad to work at the Institute of Chemical Physics and had remained there until 1938 when he went to the Shell Development Corporation laboratory at Emeryville, nine miles from Berkeley. During his encounter with Oppenheimer, Chevalier had named Eltenton, well-known as a FAECT union activist at the Radiation Laboratory, as his link to the Soviet Consulate in San Francisco, but when he was interviewed by the FBI three years later, Eltenton denied any involvement with espionage, and in 1947 returned to England. His wife Dorothea, a cousin of the Labour MP and future Attorney General Sir Hartley Shawcross (whom she did not know), was active in the Institute of Pacific Relations, had attempted to find a job with the American-Russian Institute, and was friendly with Grigori Kheifets and Piotr Ivanov. Oppenheimer's version of precisely what had happened was to vary, whereas Chevalier protested to the FBI that he had not asked his friend to betray atomic secrets, but merely had described Eltenton's purported relationship with the Soviets as a warning. Oppenheimer claimed that Chevalier had described Eltenton as someone "who had very good contacts with a man from the embassy who was attached to the consulate who was a very reliable guy—that's his story—and who had a lot of experience with microfilm work, or whatever the hell." According to Oppenheimer, Eltenton had approached "two or three physicists" at the Radiation Laboratory for secret information, including his own brother Frank. The identification of Eltenton as an NKVD recruiter, shown through surveillance to be in touch with Piotr Ivanov, led to Lansdale attending an urgent conference, called by Quinn Tamm and Lish Whitson, at the FBI's headquarters in Washington DC. According to his statement to the FBI made in May 1946, Eltenton had met Ivanov in December 1942, and had been persuaded by him that Moscow "did not feel it was getting the scientific and technical support it deserved." Eltenton said he had "convinced myself that the situation was of such a critical nature that I would be in my own mind free in conscience to approach Haakon Chevalier" and then, having done so, "with considerable reluctance we agreed that we must try and contact Oppenheimer."

> The question of the transmission of any possibly obtainable data was discussed and I informed Mr. Chevalier that Mr. Ivanov had given assurances that such data when available would be "safely" transmitted through his channels. This involved photo reproduction and subsequent transmission by means unknown to me. It is my belief that Haakon Chevalier approached Dr. Oppenheimer because a few days later the former dropped by my house and told me that there was no chance whatsoever of obtaining any data and Dr. Oppenheimer did not approve.

In Eltenton's statement, which he dictated to three FBI special agents, he recalled his mainly social contacts with Kheifets and Ivanov, and described how they had asked him about how well he knew Oppenheimer and Lawrence, and had sought his opinion about other physicists who might be suitable candidates for an academic award from the Soviet Union. A third scientist in whom Ivanov expressed interest, or so Eltenton thought he recalled, was someone named Alvarez, which resulted in an FBI investigation of Luis Alvarez, a scientist who had already been warned about a breach of the censorship rules and being indiscreet about his work at Los Alamos.

Chevalier was later refused a security clearance to work at the Office of War Information and continued to write, with a short stint as a translator at the Nurenberg trials, and finally left the U.S. in November 1950. The State Department proved reluctant to renew his American passport, so he acquired a French passport from the consulate in New York, and then took up a post as an interpreter with UNESCO in Paris, but continued to experience difficulty with the State Department over his American passport for many years. His FBI file, which includes a forty-one-page summary, is filled with reports of him attending the John Reed Club (a well-known Communist front for artists and writers) and meetings of the Alameda County branch of the CPUSA, and boasting that he was the CPUSA's organizer at the University of California.

Chevalier's only interview with the FBI took place at the California Street Field Office in San Francisco on June 26, 1946, conducted by Special Agents Fred R. Elledge and Wilbert H. Kehe, at the precise moment that George Eltenton was being interrogated by the FBI at the Oakland Field Office. This was a regular FBI technique designed to reduce the risk of witness collusion. According to Chevalier, he was questioned about having approached three different Manhattan Project scientists for information on three different occasions. However, he described his conversation with Eltenton, at the latter's home on Cragmont Avenue, Berkeley, and insisted that he had "approached no one except Oppenheimer to request information concerning the work of the radiation laboratory."

> I may have mentioned the desirability of obtaining this information for Russia with any number of people in passing. I am certain that I never made another specific proposal in this connection. I felt at that

> time and still feel that in time of war we should share any knowledge we have to further the war effort and bring it to a successful conclusion, but feel that this should be done through regular channels.

Curiously, despite the impact of Oppenheimer's allegation on his career, Chevalier remained friendly with him, and saw Robert and Kitty socially in Paris in December 1953. The Eltentons' commitment to the Soviet Union remained undiminished, and in 1947 Dorothea wrote a slim, illustrated booklet for children, *Boy From Leningrad*, extolling the virtues of Russia, which was published by the American-Russian Institute "to help give our elementary school children an understanding of their Soviet friends."[9] Upon their return to England, George was interviewed by Brigadier Ralph Bagnold of MI5 at the end of October 1947, writing a statement in response to a questionnaire a few days later, but continued to work for Shell at Thornton, becoming deputy directory of the laboratory. They lived for several years at Bromborough in Cheshire until his death in April 1991. Eight years later Dorothea published her memoirs, *Laughter in Leningrad*, and died in London in March 2001.

The Chevalier incident ultimately led in March 1954 to Oppenheimer losing his security clearance, and he was the subject of much criticism for his initial reluctance to implicate Chevalier because he regarded the only sinister role in the affair to have been played by Eltenton. So what was Chevalier's explanation? He was later to describe Oppenheimer as his "most intimate and steadfast friend" who had been circumspect about his atomic research, but had occasionally let slip a hint, such as the occasion in 1942, when he had opined, "As things now stand and given the present relation of forces, the Axis powers are almost bound to win."

> He gave me a mysterious look and at the same time his eyes twinkled. "But perhaps we can think up a few tricks," he added, almost jokingly. The he shook his head. "It may be our only chance."[10]

Chevalier, who was never directly involved in the Manhattan Project but counted many of the physicists, including Philip Morrison and Robert Serber as friends, described how, following a telephone call, he had visited Eltenton's home, "late in 1942 or early in 1943—none of us remember exactly" and had been stunned by what he had heard. Eltenton had talked of the importance of the work being undertaken by Soviet and American scientists and had asserted that their role could be decisive.

> The Soviet scientists, he said, felt that in order to make the most telling use of scientific know-how and resources of both countries for the combined war effort it was highly desirable that there be a close collaboration between the scientist of both countries, as there was in other fields. There should be exchanges of information as to strategically important research, so that each could benefit by the work being done by the other. Oppenheimer was known to be in charge of an important war project, and was also known to be very much of a left-winger. He was therefore likely to be sympathetic to the idea of closer scientific collaboration and because of his eminence could be effective in promoting it. Since I was a friend of his, the idea was that I should be asked to sound him out as to how he felt about the possibility of such collaboration. Eltenton's manner was somewhat embarrassed. He seemed not too sure of himself. Through his roundabout phrases it gradually became clear to me that what the people behind him were really interested in was the secret project Oppenheimer was working on. It took me a moment to grasp some, at least, of the major implications of what was being proposed. The thing made no sense. The fact that Eltenton was making such a proposal made no sense. The answer that I gave was of course an unqualified "No," but I did not at the moment see the full gravity of Eltenton's proposal.[11]

This version of events, taken from Chevalier's account in *Oppenheimer: The Story of a Friendship*, seems remarkably disingenuous, considering that Chevalier was a committed member of the Party, a fact omitted from his autobiography in which he described himself as "extreme left," and at that stage had been friends with the Eltentons for more than five years, having first encountered Dorothea when she had volunteered to do secretarial work for the League of American Writers in San Francisco. Chevalier claimed that he "had felt fairly convinced, by the time I left him, that Eltenton was not deeply involved in any kind of conspiracy. But what about those for whom he was acting? Whoever was behind this was not likely to give up after a first unsuccessful try. There might be other approaches, and these might cause trouble." Thus Chevalier claimed that he had decided to warn Oppenheimer.

> My chief misgiving was over mentioning Eltenton's name. I didn't want to get him into trouble. I could of course merely report the conversation without mentioning his name. But that would not be very helpful, and if the people who had approached him were involved in a serious attempt to get information, it was something that Oppie would know how to handle.

Accordingly, a short time later, while at a small dinner party given by the Oppenheimers at their home in Berkeley, Chevalier had "reported the conversation I had had with Eltenton because I thought he should know of it, and he agreed that I was right in telling him. He was visibly disturbed, we exchanged a remark or two, and that was all." The crucial difference between the two versions is that Chevalier insists he merely "reported" Eltenton, whereas in Oppenheimer's recollection Chevalier had actually taken the opportunity to make the offer for Eltenton. Furthermore, according to Eltenton, Chevalier had not only consented to make the approach to Oppenheimer, but had subsequently made a second visit to explain its failure. Strangely, Oppenheimer had offered a slightly different version to the FBI when he had been interviewed on September 5, 1946. On that occasion he "was quite positive" that Eltenton "came to his house in Berkeley, California, accompanied by Mr. Chevalier at which the incident referred to above was discussed."

Which version was true? Obviously, it was in the interests of both Chevalier and Eltenton to play down their contributions, with each passing the blame up the line, Chevalier to Eltenton, and Eltenton to Ivanov. Oppenheimer was to admit that he had fabricated some of his original tale to Johnson and Pash, including the approaches to three other scientists, in the hope of protecting his friend Chevalier, but he was to be the subject of considerable criticism for having delayed for so long in supplying his name to Groves, and was to pay a heavy price for his prevarication. Furthermore, there was a curious, never resolved contradiction about whether he had been pitched by Chevalier alone, or with Eltenton present. Chevalier was bitter about the entire experience:

> The tempest that his fabrication had stirred up in the vast network of the intelligence agencies had been so formidable, the strain to which they had been put so great, that the truth would have been hard, perhaps impossible, for them to take. How could he explain what he had done? How could he justify having created such a mountain out if such a molehill? So he gave my name, and in so doing attached it to his fabrication. He had three months and seventeen days since August 25th to work out an escape from the predicament he had got himself into. What he came up with was something that left his own reputation unscathed, but that gravely compromised a close friend.

Superficially, Chevalier's indignation is entirely understandable, but when he wrote this in 1965 he had not seen what George Eltenton had told the FBI, which served to corroborate Oppenheimer's memory, even though the two men did discuss their simultaneous interviews soon after they had taken place. In short, this in turn serves to further undermine Chevalier's credibility.

Precisely when VENONA played a part in the Oppenheimer investigation is difficult to determine, but the FBI certainly considered him a possible suspect in the hunt for the accomplice who was believed to have collaborated with Klaus Fuchs. Based on the Fuchs interrogation conducted in London after his conviction, the FBI and the AEC realized that the spy had not acted alone, and Fuchs confirmed that the Russians had run an agent in Berkeley who had told them about electromagnetic separation research in 1942, or even earlier. Could Oppenheimer have been that spy? The FBI certainly thought so and compiled an impressive list of reasons for continuing their inquiries: his commitment to the Party had been sufficiently strong to survive the two crises, the Molotov-

Ribbentrop pact and the invasion of Finland, that tested the most hardened supporters; he recruited Communists into the Berkeley atomic project, and even brought in non-technical CPUSA members to Los Alamos; his open financial support for the Party only dried up in May 1942, the month following his employment by the government; and his application for a security clearance. In addition, there was his contact with known NKVD agents, and his opposition to postwar weapon development, which led to him calling for the Los Alamos laboratory to be disbanded. However, despite the weighty circumstantial evidence, and Oppenheimer's own lamentable performance while under cross-examination during his AEC security review, the case against him remained inconclusive, for there was nothing incriminating in the VENONA texts, but is this enough to conclude he was a conscious source? Sudoplatov certainly believed he was, and even alleged that Oppenheimer had been instrumental in obtaining Fuchs's transfer to Los Alamos, an intervention that he might not necessarily have been aware of. Slightly improbably, Sudoplatov suggests that, as the son of German immigrants, Oppenheimer expressed a preference for German refugees with a history of opposing fascism.[12]

There is indeed a circumstantial case to be made against Oppenheimer, based upon his unconcealed association with Communist officials, such as Folkoff, Schneiderman, and Nelson, who also happened to be spies, but there are also some convincing indications that he never deliberately compromised classified information. There is the conversation recorded by the FBI between Steve Nelson and Joseph Weinberg in which Nelson mentioned that his approach to Oppenheimer had been unsuccessful. In addition, there is the further approach made by Chevalier, on behalf of George Eltenton. If Oppenheimer had been a fellow conspirator, why had he ever mentioned the issue in the first place? Much of the criticism he later endured over this episode concerned his delay in reporting it, and then seeking to protect Chevalier's role. In the end, of course, he did admit Chevalier's name, and the FBI interviewed all concerned. But was this evidence of Oppenheimer's active involvement in espionage, or merely an attempt to engage him in espionage? Considering Nelson's previous failure, the latter explanation looks more plausible. That, of course, is not to deny that Oppenheimer was undoubtedly an important NKVD target, and there is plenty of evidence to show that he was a focus of attention. Accordingly, there seems some room for doubt about the degree to which Oppenheimer actively cooperated with the NKVD, although Sudoplatov is less ambiguous about others, and clearly identifies George Gamow as a source coerced by Elizaveta Zubilina who

> approached Gamow through his wife, Rho, who was also a physicist. She and her husband were vulnerable because of their concern for relatives in the Soviet Union. Gamow taught physics at George Washington University in Washington DC, and instituted the annual Washington Conference on Theoretical Physics, which brought together the best physicists to discuss the latest developments at small meetings. We were able to take advantage of the network of colleagues that Gamow had established. Using implied threats against Gamow's relatives in Moscow, Elizaveta Zarubina pressured him into cooperating with us. In exchange for safety and material support for his relatives, Gamow provided the names of left-wing scientists who might be recruited to supply secret information. On some occasions Gamow had essential data in his house for several days, in violation of security regulations. Scientists on the bomb project asked him for his comments on the data, which he then verbally repeated to our illegals by arrangement with Zarubina.

The disclosure that Gamow was a coerced spy was remarkable, for hitherto no suspicion had been attached to him, even though in his 1970 autobiography, *My World Line*, he mentions having served in a non-combat role as an artillery lieutenant-colonel in the Red Army.[13] His distinguished scientific career had begun in his native Leningrad, and he had achieved recognition within the quite small international community of nuclear physicists for his explanation of alpha decay, described by his friend Sir Rudolf Peierls as "one of the early successes of quantum mechanics." This comment naturally suggests a possible identity for the mysterious QUANTUM who visited the Soviet embassy in Washington on June 14, 1943, although it would seem likely that Gamow would have communicated in his native language with his Soviet contact. In any event, Gamow, who never visited Los Alamos, made no admission before his death of alcohol-related liver disease in August 1968. According to the VENONA text dated June 22/23, 1944, QUANTUM's message had been translated from English.

The line of communication between the New York *rezidentura* and Los Alamos was via a system of couriers, among them Harry Gold and Lona Cohen, and this was the method adopted to exchange messages with Klaus Fuchs and Ted Hall, but what of the others? Sudoplatov reveals another parallel link to the Center via Mexico. Apparently a veteran agent, Joseph Grigulevich, who had fought in the Spanish Civil War, had been assigned a support role in the assassination of Trotsky, which required him to establish a commercial cover in New Mexico.

> Like his father, who ran a pharmacy in Argentina, Grigulevich was a druggist by profession, so he had opened a drugstore in Santa Fe. When he was recalled in 1941 he had transferred the ownership to one of his agents, and this had been the link to a "mole" who worked with Fermi and Pontecorvo. The mole in Tennessee was connected with the illegal station at the Santa Fe drugstore, from which material was sent by courier to Mexico. These unidentified young moles, along with the Los Alamos mole, were junior scientists or administrators who copied vital documents to which they were allowed access by Oppenheimer, Fermi, and Szilard, who were knowingly part of the scheme.[14]

The brilliant, dashing and popular experimental physicist Bruno Pontecorvo was unquestionably a Communist, as was most of his family, his cousin being Emilio Sereni, a Communist senator in Rome, his brother a successful movie director, and his brother-in-law, Duccio Tabet, a member of the Agricultural Staff of the Italian Communist Party. Despite these links, General Groves had authorized him to stay at Chalk River in 1946, but after the defection of Klaus Fuchs, Sir John Cockcroft had told him that his security clearance at Harwell, where he had worked since 1948, would be withdrawn, and he ought to take up the post of professor of physics at Liverpool University. Instead, Pontecorvo had most dramatically demonstrated his political commitment by defecting with his Swedish wife Marianne and three sons to Russia via Finland in September 1950. His route also indicated some use of Soviet tradecraft, for he only purchased his airline tickets at the last moment in Rome with cash, while on vacation, leaving his parents waiting at Chamonix where he had planned to join them for a skiing weekend. Instead, the Pontecorvos flew to Copenhagen, caught a ferry to Stockholm and then flew to Helsinki where they were seen being met at the airport by a limousine.

There was never any evidence that Pontecorvo had been in contact with the Soviets during the six years he had spent working on the heavy-water pile at Chalk River between 1943 and 1948, nor afterwards at Harwell. Previously, he had trained in Rome under Fermi, then from 1935 in Paris alongside Hans von Halban and Lev Kowarski at Joliot-Curie's Radium Institute and then the Collège de France, but had left in July 1940. Sudoplatov alleges that Pontecorvo had been cultivated in Rome before the war by Grigori Kheifets, and then contacted by Lev Vasilevsky, the Mexico City *rezident* working under diplomatic cover, in January 1943:

> At the end of January 1943 we received through Semyonov a full report on the first nuclear chain reaction from Bruno Pontecorvo, describing Enrico Fermi's experiment in Chicago on December 2, 1942.[15]

Quite how Pontecorvo might have gained access to this highly classified breakthrough is unexplained, because at the time he was working for an oil survey company in Oklahoma, having arrived in New York as a refugee on August 20, 1942, from Lisbon aboard the SS *Quanza*, and he was not invited to join the British contingent to the Manhattan Project in Montreal until after its arrival in January 1943. Nevertheless, Sudoplatov is emphatic that Vasilevsky "was the first intelligence officer to approach Pontecorvo directly in 1943." According to the FBI, Vasilevsky had moved from Mexico City to New York in December 1944 and then arrived in San Francisco on January 5, to sail for home six days later. He was later purged because of his Jewish origins and died in 1979.

Pontecorvo made no reference to these events when he held a press conference in Moscow on March 4, 1955, but before he died in 1993, at the Soviet nuclear research center at Dubna, outside Moscow, he gave an interview to a Russian journalist in which he acknowledged his wartime espionage and confirmed that he had defected because he feared his arrest was imminent. After his disappearance in 1950, the FBI conducted an intensive investigation to see if it had overlooked any evidence of his espionage, and found that its original file, having been originated in November 1942 during a routine, random search of Pontecorvo's apartment in Tulsa on a warrant describing him as a suspected enemy alien, was very thin. The search showed only a collection of books on communism, and a few dust jackets bearing swastikas, but nothing incriminating. However, by the end of the FBI inquiries in 1950, his dossier had grown to 1,011 pages.

Sudoplatov's proposition that Enrico Fermi, the Italian Nobel prizewinner responsible for the world's first controlled nuclear chain reaction and the Hungarian Leo Szilard were also spies, has been the subject of much criticism. So who was HURON, and did he succeed in making contact with VEKSEL and "Goldsmith"? An AFSA report dated August 30, 1947, on the subject of NKVD tradecraft and sloppy security procedures relating to the selection of cryptonyms, mentions that the choice of the Great Lakes as covernames was no coincidence, and that "ERIE gave the clue for the identification of HURON." So who was he? The AFSA analysts had obviously found a connection between the two Great Lakes Erie and Huron and the spy's true name, which immediately makes Dr. Ernest O. Lawrence a strong possibility. Lawrence, a brilliant experimental physicist of Norwegian stock from a small prairie town near Huron in South Dakota, had been educated at the universities of South Dakota, Minnesota, Chicago, and Yale. His father was the president of a teacher's college in Springfield, South Dakota, and both he and his brother John, a physician, devoted their lives to the study of the atom. When in 1938 their mother Gunda was diagnosed with cancer of the pelvis and given three months to live, Ernest and John arranged for her completely secret and unorthodox treatment at Berkeley with a bombardment of neutrons from a cyclotron. The cancer disappeared and she lived for another eighteen years.

At Berkeley Lawrence was a good friend of Oppenheimer, and although they were thought by many not to share the same politics, Lawrence exercised considerable political influence over the younger man, especially in 1930 when, on long walks together across San Francisco Bay, he had explained about the Stock Exchange crash the previous year, an event that Oppie, who at that time read no newspapers or magazines and did not possess a radio, had no knowledge of. In January 1941 Lawrence named his fourth child Robert, after Oppenheimer, and even agreed as a favor to employ Frank in the Radiation Laboratory after he had had been dismissed from Stanford for radical political activity. Indeed, Lawrence had been responsible in the first place for bringing Robert into the Manhattan Project.

In October 1944 HURON's codename changed to ERNEST, itself something of an indiscretion, as the St. Lawrence is the waterway connecting the two Canadian lakes. Lawrence was, after all, the "progressive professor" referred to in the VENONA text dated August 12, 1943, who was described as approachable through Paul Pinsky. Certainly, the Soviets regarded Lawrence as "progressive," for on the very date of the Washington VENONA text he had visited the Soviet embassy to be awarded a certificate by the ambassador to mark his election to the prestigious Soviet Academy of Sciences, an honor that he was particularly proud of, and one that, as he liked to remark, entitled him to free travel on public transport in Moscow. The impressive, Morocco-bound document resembled a passport and gave the holder permission to enter the Soviet Union at any time. When, in May 1954, Lawrence was reinvestigated by the FBI, he was asked about this honor, and the scientist observed that he had sought and received the permission of General Groves before he had traveled to Washington DC. The FBI found no evidence of his espionage, but questioned him about his 1946 membership in the American-Russian Institute for Cultural Relations, a front organization described by the California Committee on Un-American Activities in 1948 as "a direct agent of the Soviet Union, engaged in traitorous activities."

The exposure of HURON/ERNEST as Ernest Lawrence, the director of the Berkeley Radiation Laboratory, who was known to the MED as "Mr. E. Lawson," throws much of the rest of the ENORMOZ effort into sharp relief and maybe offers an explanation for his appointment of Rossi Lomanitz, his hostile reaction when Lomanitz was drafted into the army to terminate his access to secrets, and Colonel Lansdale's recollection that "we had more trouble with Ernest Lawrence about personnel than any four other people put together." It is also curious that the charge that Oppenheimer had helped find jobs for Max B. Friedman and Joseph Weinberg would have been rather more appropriate if it had been directed at Lawrence, who headed the Radiation Laboratory. Indeed, it was Lawrence's Rad Lab that contained a FAECT branch and the one authenticated Communist cell within the Manhattan Project, the one attended by Robert Davis, was occasionally addressed by Steve Nelson, and had a membership that included Bohm, Friedman, Lomanitz, and Weinberg.

There were other oddities about Lawrence. For example, when in 1949 his own former subordinate, Martin Kamen, decided to sue the Chicago *Tribune* for identifying him as "Scientist X," the man who had lost his security clearance for being indiscreet in an San Francisco restaurant by dining with two Soviet "diplomats," Lawrence declined to appear as a witness unless he received immunity from cross-examination, a legal impossibility. Another of Lawrence's old friends, the Englishman Wilfred Mann, who had spent two years at Berkeley before the war on a research fellowship, was cultivated by the KGB to the point that he was run as a double agent by the CIA's Counterintelligence Staff.

There are altogether just three VENONA texts disclosing aspects of HURON's activities, but there is no evidence to show when he had been recruited, and nothing to link him to the source described by Klaus Fuchs as having passed the Soviets details of the electromagnetic separation research in 1942 or earlier. However, by June 1944 he was definitely in harness, as Stepan Apresyan (while he was still in New York, before his transfer in March 1945 to San Francisco as *rezident*) had asked Moscow's permission to let him be handled by SMART, and in December 1944, and again in January,

February, and March 1945 he was being directed to Chicago to see VEKSEL and renew his relationship with Hyman Goldsmith. The fact that Moscow had sent no less than four messages to San Francisco insisting HURON go to Chicago "as soon as possible" might suggest that HURON may have been of such seniority and stature that he was not obviously and immediately subordinate to the NKVD's discipline. It might also imply that HURON was not entirely free to travel to Chicago from California as easily as the NKVD believed or hoped, and this is undoubtedly appropriate for someone in Lawrence's crucial position at Berkeley. Equally, Lawrence was certainly able to pass a complete copy of Professor Smyth's secret report "at any time."

Clearly, HURON was someone of stature, for the people named with whom he was in contact were Hyman Goldsmith, VEKSEL (maybe Oppenheimer but more likely Fermi), Morris Perelman and Henry Smyth. All three were at the most senior levels within the Manhattan Project, and it follows that HURON was likely to be their equal or at least close to their level.

As to who was responsible for handling HURON, it would seem that after a debate about whether SMART or Harry Gold was the more appropriate, Stepan Apresyan settled on Andrei Orlov, codenamed WOLF, ostensibly employed as a senior inspector by the Soviet Government Purchasing Commission in San Francisco. Despite being only twenty-eight and very inexperienced, never having been abroad before, Apresyan appears to have enjoyed a meteoric rise within the NKVD's *rezidenturas* in the United States, first in New York as Zubilin's subordinate until late in 1943 when Zubilin was transferred to Washington DC. Apresyan was a gifted linguist, speaking more than a dozen languages, including Arabic and Turkish, and was said to be able to achieve fluency in a new tongue in a matter of two or three months. However, he demonstrated appalling nerves in the field, possibly because of his personal knowledge of the consequences of failure. His elder brother, a People's Commissar in one of the Soviet Central Asian republics, had been arrested and shot during the purges.

When Apresyan, codenamed MAY, was appointed *rezident*, he busied himself with the running of Klaus Fuchs and Harry Gold until March 1945, when he was succeeded by his deputy, the TASS correspondent Roland Abbiate, alias Vladimir S. Pravdin, and was made *rezident* in San Francisco under vice-consular cover. Throughout his clandestine career in the United States, Apresyan was assisted by his wife Aleksandra Grigorevna, who appears in a couple of VENONA texts with the codenames ZOYA, EL and ELIZA.

The post of San Francisco *rezident* previously had been held by Grigori Kheifets until August 1944 when he left for Vladivostok in the aftermath of the Mironov affair, and then Grigori P. Kasparov, codenamed GIFT, until his departure early in January 1945 for Mexico City, when FILIPP filled in temporarily as acting *rezident* pending Apresyan's arrival. It may be significant that Apresyan, with his considerable knowledge of ENORMOZ agents, was sent to California in 1945. One reason may have been the internal squabbles that had beset the New York *rezidentura*, with his deputy Roland Abbiate, who had worked in Europe before the war as an illegal, constantly sniping about his poor performance. In contrast to Apresyan, Abbiate had proved himself a reliable Chekist under the most adverse conditions, having worked in Paris under the alias François Rossi, ostensibly a journalist from Monaco, and having traveled to Switzerland in 1938 to carry out the murder of Ignace Reiss, the legendary illegal who had been sentenced to death in the purges, but had disappeared instead of answering a summons to return to Moscow. Abbiate had used his (purported) fiancé, Gertrude Schildbach, an aging German actress and Communist trusted by Reiss, to lure him from his refuge in the tiny Valais village of Finhaut in the Swiss Alps to Lausanne, where his bullet-riddled body was found by the side of a quiet street off the Chamblandes road on September 4, 1937. The Swiss police issued an arrest warrant for François Rossi, alias Py, only to discover he was already wanted in the United States, but when he turned up in New York two years later as Vladimir Pravdin, a correspondent for TASS, accompanied by his wife Olga who worked for Amtorg, his past went undiscovered.

Abbiate's participation in Reiss's murder was confirmed by Renata Steiner, a Swiss Communist who had rented the vehicle used to abduct the victim minutes after he had dined with Schildbach at a Chamblandes restaurant. She confessed that, while on a stroll after the meal, Reiss had been forced into a car and shot at point-blank range by Abbiate and another NKVD agent, Etienne Martignat. Steiner had been traced when the rental car was found abandoned in Geneva, and her confession served to implicate Schildbach, Martignat, an employee of the Soviet Trade Mission in Paris named Lydia Grozovskaya (who was arrested by the French police on a Swiss extradition warrant but disappeared while on bail), and Abbiate. The crime had all the hallmarks of a carefully planned assassination, as was later confirmed by Reiss's friend Walter Krivitsky, after the latter's defection.

Abbiate was an impressive, sophisticated operator and handled some high-level sources, among them Isadore Stone of *The Nation*, who was also the Washington correspondent for *PM*. Abbiate ran his own network, and the FBI spent considerable resources identifying his agent codenamed IDE, who turned out to be a Boston-born journalist, Samuel Krafsur, the deputy TASS bureau chief in Washington DC who had fought with the Lincoln Battalion in Spain. Another of Abbiate's recruits, before he returned to Moscow in March 1946, was Josef Berger, an extraordinarily well-connected journalist employed by the Department of Justice as a speechwriter for the Attorney General, Francis Biddle, and later secretary to the chairman of the Democratic National Convention. Abbiate's wife, Olga B. Pravdina, was identified by Elizabeth Bentley as a substitute Soviet contact whom she met "about five or six times over a four month period" in early 1942 and knew as MARGARET.

Apresyan's choice of Orlov, who was also the Party organizer, is also interesting as the latter holds the unusual distinction of appearing in the VENONA traffic no less than forty-five times, which makes it easier to chart some of his clandestine career. He first appears in Seattle in the "Fifth Line," the branch responsible for handling counterintelligence issues arising from NKVD agents aboard Soviet ships. The Fifth Line maintained what amounted to a sub-*rezidentura* with representatives in the ports of Seattle, Portland, Los Angeles and San Francisco, and much of the traffic concerns incidents of desertion from ship's crews. Some simply failed to return after being allowed liberty ashore, others seem to have been enticed by a White Russian émigré organization in Seattle that, according to a VENONA text from San Francisco on July 17, 1945, Orlov penetrated with an agent codenamed SUKhUMSKIY:

> IN SEATTLE with the help of the agent SUKhUMSKIY [Boris M. Boguslavsky] we have succeeded in penetrating the organization of the priest DANIL'ChIK. By this manoeuvre we have pinpointed the existence of a widely-ramified White Guard organization in SEATTLE working on our seamen in [1 group recovered] with the police and intelligence organs. Our agentura has gotten the organization's passwords for meeting, and the agent SUKhUMSKIY has succeeded in seeing, in the apartments of the organization, many of our traitors. All detailed information on this matter and our proposals have been sent to you with MUKhIN. Telegraph your decision on them.

As Party organizer, Orlov was unquestionably a senior figure within the hierarchy of the San Francisco *rezidentura*, as is indicated by two episodes. In March 1945 Orlov visited the Consul General, Andrei Vasiliev, in the hospital and found him in deep conversation with the consulate's chief cipher clerk, Vasili Fedoseev, apparently discussing the content of highly confidential messages. Shocked at the indiscretion, Orlov questioned Vasiliev's wife and Fedoseev to learn this was not an isolated event, and reported both men to Moscow. When Vasiliev had recovered from his illness, Moscow ordered him to Washington DC to take up a post as first secretary at the embassy, but he pleaded with Orlov, as Party organizer, to intervene and have the transfer rescinded. For the Consul General to ask the ostensibly junior Orlov, who was not even a diplomat, to intercede and exercise his influence on his behalf is quite remarkable. The other noteworthy incident occurred in March 1946 when Orlov was connected in some way with Lieutenant Nikolai G. Redin, codenamed VLADISLAV, formerly a Fifth Line officer in Seattle. Redin was arrested in Portland, possibly in circumstances that compromised Orlov, and was expelled from the United States, thus prompting a request on April 27 from the consulate for Orlov to be switched to New York:

> In the light of recent events I would recommend first sending WOLF [Andrei Orlov] away to work in New York and then home from there, If he leaves direct from here it will seem suspicious to THE HUT [FBI]. Inform us of your permission.

The implication of this message is that Orlov's departure for home from San Francisco would be likely to attract the FBI's attention, and this was considered highly undesirable. This a curious reaction, because once Orlov had returned he would not have to endure the FBI's surveillance, so the focus must be on the danger for someone else left behind, and one possible explanation is that the NKVD was anxious to avoid jeopardizing one of Orlov's agents. It may be that the NKVD suspected that Orlov had been spotted meeting a particular source whom it feared might be compromised, and the expedient of sending Orlov to the east coast was intended to enhance his cover and thereby protect the agent. This may in part also be the reason why a Fifth Line officer, with no known experience in Line XY, was assigned an ENORMOZ case. Whatever the explanation, it was unusual, and clearly involved Orlov's role as a professional intelligence officer, and therefore raises questions about his agents.

As for running agents, the VENONA texts only offer fragmentary glimpses of Orlov's activities, but in April 1944 the *rezident* in San Francisco, Grigori Kheifets, referred to him as being in touch with an unknown woman, codenamed MAP, and a local CPUSA official, Isaac Folkoff, codenamed UNCLE. In another message Stepan Apresyan also gave his approval to Orlov running these two sources, as apparently he himself was unable to do so, although he had established contact with MAP's "institution," according to his VENONA text dated April 3, 1945.

In January 1946 Apresyan sought Moscow's permission for Orlov to supervise the work of Nikolai E. Yezhov, codenamed ZhAROV, the *rezidentura*'s disorganized cipher clerk, who had replaced I. I. Fedoseev in June 1945. From the limited clues that can be gleaned from half a dozen very fragmented VENONA texts, it seems that Yezhov was suspected of having discarded cipher documents in the consulate's waste paper, an egregious breach of security at a time when there was great concern, following Gouzenko's defection in Ottawa, about the security of *referenturas* and the escalating level of FBI surveillance. Certainly another cipher officer, Aleksandr P. Saprykin, was in San Francisco by February 1 to recommend new security procedures for the uncooperative Yezhov. Apparently Yezhov had refused to accept the NKVD's authority, saying he had no connection with the organization, and when reproached by a member of the *rezidentura* codenamed GRANDSON, had complained to the Vice Consul, Viktor Afanasiev. Whatever the exact background, the *rezident* clearly was confident that Orlov was someone whom he could trust to exercise some effective discipline over the careless clerk.

There is a further clue to Orlov's status in a VENONA text dated September 23, 1944, in which Moscow authorized Orlov's maintenance allowance for the last quarter of 1944 at $133 a month, which was considerably more than his other two colleagues in the Fifth Line. Another strong clue to HURON/ERNEST being located in California is the fact that a VENONA text referring to him, dated November 27, 1945, was sent from the San Francisco *rezidentura.*

It may be argued that the change of codename from HURON to ERNEST did nothing to improve Lawrence's security, but the reality is that NKVD personnel were, by modern standards, appallingly insecure in their selection of codenames. In the VENONA traffic there are numerous examples of agents being assigned wholly inappropriate, virtually transparent and certainly indiscreet, cryptonyms, for example, Alfred Slack as AL, Morris Cohen, the radio operator, as ANTENNA, and Sergei Kurnakov, the former Czarist officer as CAVALRYMAN. Even YOUNG, for the nineteen-year-old Ted Hall, was unwise, though rather less so than the choice of BLACK for Thomas Black! Partial anagrams and inside jokes abounded, an example being Boris Morros's designation as FROST, which is *moroz* in Russian, and the most fundamental rule, that cryptonyms and true names should never appear in the same text, was often breached by very inexperienced case officers sent from Moscow by an organization that had been denuded of staff with any practical knowledge of basic, universal tradecraft.

Ethel and Julius Rosenberg died in the electric chair at Sing Sing in June 1953; Harry Gold was released from prison in May 1966, after serving fifteen years, and died of heart failure in Philadelphia six years later. Al Sarant changed his name to Saros and became a senior research scientist, founding the Zelenograd microelectronics center in Leningrad to develop computer designs for Soviet submarines and anti-aircraft systems, and died while on a visit to Moscow in March 1979. In 1991 Carol Dayton, by whom Sarant had four children, returned to the U.S. with her youngest daughter. She had previously been married to Weldon B. Dayton, a physicist employed by the U.S. Navy, who was also a well-known CPUSA activist, and Al Sarant's next-door neighbor in Ithaca, New York. Joel Barr, who married in the Soviet Union but for twenty years failed to tell his Czech wife, Vera Bergova, or his four children of his past, adopted the identity of a South African, Josef V. Berg, but eventually returned to New York in 1992 on a Soviet passport, resumed his American citizenship and died in Moscow in August 1998. Lona Cohen, who had been released from a prison sentence in England as part of a spy swap in 1969, died in Moscow in 1993; her husband Morris survived another two years and died in July 1995. In November 1950 Abe Brothman and Miriam Moscowitz received two years each for perjury; Ben Smilg, named by Gold as a member of his network, was acquitted, and Fred Heller was not charged on the grounds that he did not have access to classified information. Michael Sidorovich died in 1962. David Greenglass was released from prison in November 1960 and, according to his account given to Sam Roberts in *The Brother*, is now uncertain whether he really did see his sister type documents for Julius Rosenberg, or if he ever saw a console table in their apartment that had been converted to be used as a photographic stand, as he had deposed fifty years earlier.

In retrospect, it seems astonishing that the FBI was so slow to react to the threat to the Manhattan Project, but it must be remembered that the program was so secret that not even J. Edgar Hoover had any idea of its existence until April 10, 1943, when he became aware of it... from the Soviets! This remarkable state of affairs came about through the FBI's clandestine surveillance on the home in Oakland, California, of Steve Nelson, the CPUSA functionary who supervised the East Bay branch, which covered the Berkeley campus. The FBI was slow to grasp the grand scale of Soviet espionage, and by the time it was ready to take the threat seriously, it was almost too late and some important suspects, such as Al Sarant and the Cohens, slipped away unimpeded.

As for Morrison, who had been a member of the YCL at the age of eighteen before his full CPUSA membership in the Berkeley branch, he had joined the Metallurgical Laboratory as a group leader in late 1942, and had remained in Chicago until 1944 when he joined DuPont to work on the construction of new facilities at Hanford. However, instead of moving to the state of Washington, he was assigned by military intelligence to a study of German atomic research. Once this had been completed in late 1944, he was transferred to Los Alamos where he participated in the first bomb test before flying to the Mariana Islands in the Pacific as a member of the weapon assembly team. He was also one of a group of scientists who visited Hiroshima and Nagasaki, and later returned to Los Alamos and remained there until the early autumn of 1946 when he returned to academic life. However, he failed to disclose his CPUSA membership until May 1953, when he was called to give evidence to the Senate Internal Security Subcommittee, and even at that late date was a leader of a CPUSA front, the American Peace Crusade. Morrison was cross-examined by the Committee about his contacts with Marcel Scherer, a prominent CPUSA organizer, with whom he was photographed at a meeting by the *Daily Worker* in June 1951, and challenged about an article that he had written in November 1949 for *Soviet Russia Today* in which he had celebrated the Soviet atomic test. "No thinking person can continue to believe that the secret of the atom is a political issue. Naturally, secrets will remain, here—in the USSR—everywhere. That is the nature of the world today. But secrets and secret-keeping will be relegated to the security agencies where they belong, as quiet accessories of an armed world. They must not be allowed to fix the policy and the opinion of nations."

Both Morrison and his wife Emily had been members of the American Student Union, a CPUSA front disbanded in 1942, and the CPUSA-dominated American Federation of Teachers. A friend of Haakon Chevalier, and always politically active, Morrison's parents were of Polish Jewish extraction, and when he was chairman of the Wallace for President Committee at Ithaca, he complained about FBI surveillance: "The FBI agents are familiar in every laboratory in the land. They are seeking information from me every week, on the thoughts and opinions of my friends, my students." Crippled with polio as a child, which made him a candidate for the spy codenamed RELAY and SERB, he achieved considerable academic prominence at the Massachusetts Institute of Technology and later as professor of physics at Cornell University, where he now lives.[16] He has campaigned ceaselessly for international controls on atomic weapons and regrets having trusted President Truman over the decision to drop the bombs on Japan. "For the first couple or three years we were working out of fear. We felt we were way behind the Germans. I was personally sure they would drop a bomb on London. I used to keep a short-wave radio set on the London frequency, not to listen to the program but to make sure London was still there... I was all for making a suitable warning, dropping leaflets over Japan, but the military ridiculed that. We felt a heavy weight of responsibility. We knew it was going to be a major historical event that would forever change the nature of warfare, but we each did our own thing and hoped that the leadership would know what to do. That was a mistake."*

Morrison has campaigned relentlessly for arms controls, and was one of the first to know that "the race for the bomb" was demonstrably a fraud in 1944, his own research having proved there was no prospect of a Nazi atomic weapon. But did Morrison do more than simply protest? One of his friends, the President of the Federation of American Scientists, Jeremy J. Stone, believed that there was a strong similarity between Morrison's complaint that the Manhattan Project scientists had been tricked into building a bomb, and the views of the atomic spy described by Pavel Sudoplatov and Vladimir Chikov, especially when he reportedly spoke of having been cheated by the American military establishment. Stone "knew

* Interview with Dr. Morrison in the *Boston Globe*, June 24, 1981.

only one atomic scientist whom I could hear, in my mind's ear, expressing himself in that way" and consulted Hans Bethe, Colonel John Lansdale, and Robert Serber about approaching Morrison and inviting him to confess, perhaps with the inducement of official immunity from prosecution offered by the U.S. Department of Justice. This suggestion proved impractical, and when Stone finally wrote to Morrison in September 1996 detailing the circumstantial case he had constructed against him, Morrison emphatically denied the charges. Accordingly, when Stone returned to the subject in his 1999 autobiography, *Every Man Should Try*, he concealed Morrison's identity with semi-transparent references to a "Scientist X."[17] Stone described how he had called on Morrison but did not confront him with his suspicion but had shared "some of the facts [he] had learned about World War II espionage." As Stone "read and shared this information he became visibly frightened" and thought he had been warned off by Morrison's wife who said in an aside, 'Nothing good will come of this.'"

Evidence of the NKVD's willingness to approach CPUSA members associated with the Manhattan Project can be seen in the VENONA traffic relating to Norman F. Ramsey, a senior scientist who worked at Los Alamos between October 1943 and February 1946. On May 4, 1944, Stepan Apresyan advised Moscow that Bernard Schuster had made a special journey to Chicago to take over Ramsey's cultivation from another prominent CPUSA figure, Rosslyn Childs, who was married to Jack Childs and before the war had worked for the Comintern in Moscow, ostensibly as a secretary:

> In reply to No. 950, the object of ECHO's [Bernard Schuster] trips is as follows: OLSEN [Jack Childs] is district leader of the FRATERNAL [Communist Party] in Chicago. OLSEN's wife, who has been meeting RAMSAY, is also an active COMPATRIOT [Communist] and met RAMSAY on the instructions of the organization. At our suggestion ECHO can get a letter from OLSEN with which one or other of our people will meet RAMSAY and thereafter will be able to strike up an acquaintance. Advise your consent to these measures.

By September 18, 1944, it appears from the end of a lengthy *apologia* from Apresyan that the recruitment had been completed:

> Your No. 4161. Your instructions concerning delays on our part in answering telegrams have been taken into account. The delays [1 group unrecovered] regular information about the work [1 group unrecovered] on KhU [Economic Directorate] were due to:
>
> 1. The impossibility of ANTON's [Leonid Kvasnikov] [4 groups unrecovered] the PLANT [Consulate General] in view of surveillance on the PLANT and at times on ANTON himself.
> 2. At the beginning of the year the lack of time at moments of visiting the PLANT owing to the absence of the Master of the OFFICE [*rezident*].
> 3. The great pressure of work for the FACTORY [Amtorg].
>
> Despite the holding up of information at various moments of the work it cannot be said that there has been no information at all. In 1943 the information was regular. In 1944 also, but see letters 1, 5, and parts of others; all the questions put to us could not be answered as your letter no. 5 was received a few days before our letter no. 7 went off and letter no. 6 has not yet been received. We will try not to hold up answers to letters.
>
> By telegrams: Your number 2962 could not be carried out because of surveillance on TWAIN [Semyon Semyonov]. [1 group unrecovered] BERG, who was in liaison with SMART, was without liaison with us; this was evident from the [1 group unrecovered] on the occasion of handing over TWAIN's liaison. There has been a report on SEAMAN's absence (see also our number 701). Your no. 3554. The money was received by MAKSIM [Vasili Zubilin]. ANTON has nothing to do with this matter. Your telegram no. 3338. Refer to our numbers 550 and 711. [28 groups unrecoverable] and passing on your directive was entrusted to ECHO [Bernard Schuster] The task was passed on through X [Joseph Katz]. The task is being protracted by reason of the subsequent absence from TYRE [New York] of X on a trip to the West, ECHO on leave, at present PHLOX [Roz Childs] is absent, has left with her husband for RAMSAY's area. ECHO cannot meet PHLOX until her return in only about three weeks' time.

On December 5, 1944, Leonid Kvasnikov was providing Moscow with a further explanation about Ramsey:

> Your No. 5673. DICK [Bernard Schuster] is directly in touch with PHLOX's [Roz Childs's] husband and not with PHLOX herself. The intention of sending the husband to see RAMSAY is explained by the possibility of avoiding a superfluous stage for transmitting instructions.

The VENONA texts leave little doubt about the overlap between the CPUSA underground cells and the NKVD's spy rings. ENORMOZ was considered such a high priority that Moscow had authorized two radical departures from its usual methodology: the separation between GRU and NKVD operations, and the insulation of the Party from espionage. In reality, as has been seen, the NKVD regarded local Communist organizations, and the CPUSA in particular, as useful pools of talent in which it was expedient either to recruit or at least to check on a candidate's ideological reliability. Although Earl Browder tried to distance himself from illicit activity, he was often drawn in, and he certainly knew a great deal about the underground *apparat*. Indeed, both his sister and his common-law wife, Kitty Harris, had acted as illegals overseas. Only very gradually, and much too late, did the NKVD come to realize the extent to which the CPUSA had been infiltrated by the FBI. Indeed, by the end of the House Un-American Activities Committee hearings, it was often joked that the only CPUSA members who paid their dues on time were FBI informants working on government expenses, and the FBI suspected that several CPUSA branches were supported entirely by its own nominees. Curiously, seven years after the 1944 VENONA cables had been transmitted, Jack Childs and his brother Morris were recruited as FBI informants in an operation codenamed SOLO, and subsequently operated for three decades, supplying exceptionally important information from the very heart of the CPUSA. However, the FBI handlers who supervised the operation were part of an effort, codenamed TOPLEV, to recruit top-level CPUSA members, and never realized that Jack and Roz Childs had participated in the NKVD's wartime spy ring.[18]

Once VENONA had demonstrated that the importance given to ENORMOZ had ensured that almost every CPUSA member connected with Manhattan had been the subject of an unambiguous recruitment pitch, the FBI became increasingly skeptical of those known Party members who subsequently denied ever having been approached. Into this category fell David Hawkins, who had been a member of the San Francisco, Palo Alto, and Berkeley branches of the CPUSA between 1938 and March 1943, before his arrival at Los Alamos as an administrator in May 1943, accompanied by his wife Frances who was to work for Charlotte Serber in the library as a bookbinder. A philosopher by training and a Marxist, Hawkins had achieved his doctorate in 1940 and had written the first draft of the Manhattan Project's official history, for which he had required access to classified data. After the war he had taught at the University of Colorado, and at the time of his testimony to the Senate Internal Security Subcommittee in May 1953 he had been teaching at Harvard. When asked whether Philip Morrison or Leonard Pockman had been Communists, he had refused to answer, invoking the Fifth Amendment against self-incrimination. As regards his own membership of the CPUSA, Hawkins testified that he had left the Party "gradually" because he "wanted to live in the fuller sense of the word among my colleagues and students."

According to the FBI's investigation of both Hawkinses, Frances had moved her CPUSA membership from Berkeley to San Francisco, and was closely associated with Frances Bransten, Grigori Kheifets's mistress. The FBI recorded Steve Nelson and Bernadette Doyle attempting to trace the Hawkinses, and also noted that Frances's brother, Jack C. Pockman, and her sister-in-law, Kathryn Pockman, a journalist for *People's World*, were also CPUSA members, and had visited when the couple were at Los Alamos. Frances's other brother, Leonard Pockman, was also a CPUSA activist, being the Dues Secretary at the Party's New Era branch in San Francisco.

It was VENONA, more than any other single intelligence source, that demonstrated the extent to which the Manhattan Project had been penetrated by the Soviets, but the most frustrating aspect was the continuing doubt about the precise identities of the traitors. Opinion at the time prevailing in leftist scientific circles perpetuated the dangerous proposition that atomic knowledge should be shared internationally, so there were more than a few physicists willing to convey the secrets of the bomb to Moscow. Of those referred to in the texts, only Ted Hall and Melita Norwood have openly declared their role or attempted to justify their actions. Before his death in 1999, Ted Hall, speaking at his retirement in Cambridge, acknowledged that in his youth he acted in a way that, with the benefit of hindsight, he would not have, and although he accepted his identification as MLAD, he only obliquely publicly admitted his espionage, although evidently he did confide in his wife and daughter.

With admissions from Ted Hall. John Chapin, Klaus Fuchs, Allan Nunn May, Melita Norwood, David and Ruth Greenglass, Lona and Morris Cohen, together with compelling evidence against the Rosenbergs, Clarence Hiskey, Al Sarant, Joel Barr, Harry Gold, and others, it is not surprising that the FBI was encouraged to look further in its search for those responsible for helping the Soviet Union acquire the secrets of nuclear weaponry.

Chapter X

Nobel Espionage

A Communist is a person who is more loyal to Russia than to the United States.

Colonel John Lansdale

The FBI's dragnet for spies inside the Manhattan Project was to encompass some of the most famous names of nuclear physics, including some Nobel Prize laureates. Philip Morrison, Enrico Fermi, Hans Bethe, and Robert Serber were among those who acquired large FBI dossiers as J. Edgar Hoover's Special Agents developed leads from surveillance reports, telephone and mail intercepts, informants, and summaries of VENONA texts.

The evidence against Hans Bethe is particularly startling, because of how it was originally acquired, and the way in which it overlapped with Philip Morrison. Trained at the University of Munich, Bethe was appointed chief of the Theoretical Division at Los Alamos and was a key figure in the development of the atom bomb. Yet, according to Jerome Tartakow, both Bethe and Morrison had been members of Julius Rosenberg's network. Tartakow was a CPUSA member and convicted car thief, an armed robber who was befriended in prison by Julius Rosenberg, and acted as a discreet conduit for him to Eugene Dennis, the CPUSA General-Secretary serving a prison sentence for contempt of Congress. Surprisingly, the spy had started confiding in Tartakow, so the petty criminal approached the FBI in December 1950 with the offer of acting as an informant. His subsequent reports over the first half of 1951 were to prove breathtaking, for Rosenberg apparently had no hesitation in sharing the most compromising information with the younger man, referring indirectly to Joel Barr as having headed one of his networks and being safely in Europe, and mentioning that Al Sarant and William Perl also had been members of his organization. All three names, of course, were well known to the FBI, and VENONA texts had served to implicate them. A CPUSA member, Sarant had been interviewed in July 1950, having appeared in a VENONA cable sent on May 5, 1944, under the codename HUGHES. Sarant had acknowledged his friendship with the Rosenbergs and had named Joel Barr as the person who had introduced them. Barr, of course, had also been compromised by VENONA and was the spy codenamed METER. During the course of the interrogation, Sarant had named Bethe as the person who had sponsored his entry into Cornell in September 1946, having been introduced to the professor by his father-in-law, Victor Ross. Sarant had married his stepdaughter Louise earlier in the year, and clearly Ross had attempted to help Sarant leave his job at Bell in New York and move upstate to Ithaca.

The problem for the FBI was that both Sarant and Barr had fled the country, but Tartakow had mentioned a curious link between Sarant and Bethe. Allegedly, Rosenberg had mentioned Sarant's wealthy father, and had claimed that Sarant knew both Bethe and Morrison well at Cornell University. This coincided with a statement made in prison by David Greenglass in July 1951, to Special Agent John Harrington, about a meeting he had held with Harry Gold on June 4, 1944. According to Greenglass, he had recommended Bethe as a candidate for recruitment because an SED colleague, William Spindel, had identified Bethe as a Communist. Supposedly, Bethe's name had been passed on a list of recommended prospects to Gold, then Rosenberg, and finally to Anatoli Yatskov, but there was no direct evidence that the Soviets had acted on the tip.

While Sarant had claimed to have met Bethe in July 1946, the FBI traced a draft board letter, dated a month earlier, in which Sarant had disclosed to his board that he was to take up a research fellowship with Hans Bethe at Cornell later the same year. With Sarant's consent, the FBI had searched his home and come up with a couple of items that appeared to contradict his version of his ostensibly casual relationship with Bethe, who was his next-door neighbor, and to link him to Morrison and William Perl. One document was a receipt for an airline ticket in Morrison's name, which Sarant was unable to explain was doing in his possession. Another was a baby book registering a gift from Hans and Rose Bethe upon the birth of their child. There was also a personal letter from William Perl, a spy who appeared in the VENONA traffic as GNOME and YAKOV.

Hans Bethe was interviewed by Special Agent William Tower in Seattle in July 1950 and acknowledged his friendship with Victor Ross, a lawyer who had done some unpaid work for him, whom he described as holding views "very close to the Communist Party line."[1] He also recalled a meeting with Ross and Al Sarant in his office in May 1946 (whereas Sarant had remembered two months later) but claimed that he had not sponsored Sarant for a post at Cornell, and in fact had told him he was not sufficiently qualified for postgraduate work in the Physics Department, acknowledging it to be "strange" that, despite being rebuffed, Sarant nevertheless had moved up to Ithaca. "Bethe denies close relationship with Sarant, stating has not talked to Sarant for even one hour during entire time he has known him,"[2] reported the FBI. He expressed surprise that Sarant had subsequently applied for, and obtained, a job as an electrical engineer at the Cornell Physics Laboratory in November 1946, but denied that he would have had any access to classified information. During Tower's interview with Bethe, he asked whether the physicist had been in contact with an impressive list of Soviet spies, and seemed to obtain an acknowledgment that he may have been a target of Soviet espionage:

> BETHE denies ever knowing or contacting JULIUS ROSENBERG, WILLIAM PERL, JOEL BARR, MAX ELITCHER, MORTON SOBELL or HARRY GOLD. Denies that any approach in any manner ever made to him of any person to furnish information to an apparent espionage agent. Possibility that BETHE may have been target of Russian espionage and given to SARANT as an assignment in espionage ring presented to BETHE, and he stated that SARANT did not pursue the development of his friendship and BETHE never got the impression that SARANT wanted technical data nor did SARANT ask for such. BETHE states his impression of SARANT is that SARANT is "leftist in his ideology."[3]

The FBI was obviously suspicious of Bethe and found it hard to accept that the physicist had engaged in violent political disagreements with his friend Victor Ross, and was able to characterize Al Sarant as a left-winger if he had only spoken to him briefly. As for Morrison, it was equally odd that Tartakow should have offered his name, along with Bethe's, in connection with Perl and Sarant, as members of Rosenberg's organization. The FBI investigated the possibility that Sarant had some covert relationship with Bethe and Morrison, and in July 1950 undertook a handwriting analysis of Bethe and Morrison to see if they had been responsible for some cryptic postcards found at Sarant's home in New York.

Philip Morrison remained the attention of FBI interest for many years, and as late as July 1954 an informant in Tampa, who before the war had been a member of the CPUSA branch in Alameda County, California, identified the scientist as a probable Communist. The unnamed source claimed to have known Ernest Lawrence, John Backus, James Farley, and Robert Oppenheimer at Berkeley, but was reported by Special Agent Randall McGough as being convinced that only Morrison had been a Communist. In fact, Morrison himself had confirmed to a hearing of the Senate Internal Security Subcommittee in May 1953 that he had been a CPUSA member in 1942, at the time Professor Eugene Wigner had invited him to join the Manhattan Project, and that "atomic security officers and his superiors had known of his Communist background."[4]

In Robert Serber's case, the scrutiny of the Personnel Security Board in August 1948 into his "character, associations and loyalty" proved to be an uncomfortable experience. He was cross-examined about his friendships with Frank Oppenheimer, Haakon Chevalier, David Bohm, and May Ellen Washburn, who had been Robert Oppenheimer's landlady in Berkeley before the war, and asked if he knew that Charlotte's father and brother were members of the CPUSA in Philadelphia. At one point Serber, who had called Ernest Lawrence as a character witness, was asked what he would do if he was approached and asked to obtain classified information from the professor. To the Board's obvious dismay, he replied that he would try and stall for time and then report the matter to Lawrence. Clearly, this was the wrong answer, and he quickly corrected himself, prompted by Lawrence's audible gasp, by asserting that he regarded Lawrence as the "proper authority" for dealing with such incidents. Despite this episode, Serber's security clearance was confirmed, although Charlotte had already lost hers.

These final manifestations of the CINRAD investigation demonstrated the extent of the FBI's knowledge about the CPUSA's organization in California, and established the political and social relationships that linked the Serbers to such well-known Communist activists as Martha Goldberg and Jane Castellanos, not to mention their friendships with Robert Davis and Philip Morrison. However, the appointment of Robert Serber as a Los Alamos security officer, with responsibility as the personnel manager for the SEDs assigned to the Technical Area, quite obviously was fraught with risk. After the war, as guest lecturer at the University of Colorado's Philosophy Department, he continued to espouse radical politics, and in February 1950 announced that, "It is now within the range of technical possibility to destroy all life with the Hydrogen bomb, so it is not a weapon significant to the conduct of war."[5]

Chapter XI

The Canadian Connection

If all the top scientists working on the Atomic Energy Program voluntarily furnished information about themselves and their associates, the Commission would probably have to deny clearances to all.

Dr. Carson Mark

The defection of Igor Gouzenko in Ottawa in September 1945 prompted a Royal Commission and a massive RCMP, MI5, and FBI investigation into the dozens of leads offered by the information contained in the code clerk's collection of purloined GRU documents. While the material shed little light on the NKVD operations supervised by the local *rezident*, Vitali Pavlov, who had arrived in August 1942, the papers removed from Colonel Nikolai Zabotin's GRU *rezidentura* were to prove quite devastating. In the subsequent Special Commission of Inquiry, set up by Stalin under the chairmanship of Grigori Malenkov and consisting of Lavrenti

Beria, Georgi Abakumov, General Kuznetsov, Vsevolod Merkulov, and Beria's assistant Stepan S. Mamulov, Zabotin was found culpable and both he and his wife were arrested and imprisoned in the Gulag, and not released until after Stalin's death.

Gouzenko's collection of 109 papers demonstrated that Zabotin, codenamed GRANT, had relied heavily on two principal sub-agents, Fred Rose, the former Party organizer in Quebec and a Member of Parliament for Montreal since his election in August 1943, and Sam Carr, a longtime Communist Party activist, using a diplomat, Sergei Kudriavtsev, codenamed LION, as their case officer. Originally from the Ukraine, and named Schmil Kogan, Carr had emigrated to Canada in 1924 at the age of eighteen and then, five years later, had attended the Lenin School in Moscow. By 1937 he had been appointed organizing secretary of the Canadian Communist Party, which was later to become the Labour Progressive Party.

Zabotin was also a key figure in ENORMOZ, and had cultivated several sources with access to atomic research in Canada. Those implicated by Gouzenko were a Canadian army officer, Captain D. Gordon Lunan, codenamed BACK, who was in touch with a spy codenamed BADEAU, a member of the National Research Council with access to "secret work" undertaken on "nuclear physics (the bombardment of radioactive substances to produce energy)." BADEAU assured Lunan that this research "is more hush-hush than radar and is being carried on at the University of Montreal and at McMaster University at Hamilton."[1] BADEAU was identified as Philip Durnford Smith, a member of the National Research Council, apparently run by a member of Zabotin's *rezidentura*, Major Vasili Rogov. Among Gouzenko's papers was a request to Rogov to ask BADEAU to obtain a sample of Uranium-235 and to acquire more information about a "radium-producing plant" recently purchased by the Canadian government.[2]

Zabotin's other GRU scientific sources were Israel Halperin, codenamed BACON, then attached to the Directorate of Artillery; Professor Raymond Boyer of McGill University; Edward Mazerall, a radar expert codenamed BAGLEY; and a rather reluctant Allan Nunn May, codenamed ALEK, who had been transferred to Canada and was bullied by the GRU into continuing the cooperation he had given previously in England. As Zabotin reported after a meeting held in August 1945:

> The facts communicated by ALEK are as follows:
>
> 1. Test of the atomic bomb has been conducted in New Mexico. The bomb dropped on Japan was made from Uranium-235. The magnetic separating plant in Clinton is known to be producing 400 grams of Uranium-235 a day… It is planned to publish the research done in this field but minus the technical details. The Americans have already published a book on this.
> 2. Alek handed us a slide with 162 micrograms of uranium oxide on a thin film.[3]

Nunn May's report and the sample were carried personally by the GRU's Colonel Motinov to Moscow, where the GRU Chief General Kuznetsov met him at the airport. Motinov watched as Kuznetsov took the container over to a black limousine parked on the tarmac, in which Beria himself had been waiting. For years afterwards Motinov felt the effects of his exposure to radiation and required regular blood transfusions.

Nunn May's usefulness extended to giving advice on other potential recruits, one of them being Norman Veall, a youthful English physicist who had served in the RAF's Meteorological Service, and had been tutored at Cambridge by May. Veall had been a YCL member and was outspoken in his political allegiance, which led May to warn the GRU against using him as a source.

The strategy adopted for dealing with Gouzenko's revelations was unusual, with a Royal Commission empanelled to investigate the evidence of wholesale Soviet espionage. The relatively inexperienced RCMP, with an Intelligence Branch headed by Superintendent Charles Rivett-Carnac and consisting of a staff of less than two dozen, was at a tremendous disadvantage in the initial stages of the investigation as it had minimal experience of Soviet espionage, and help was slow to arrive. Through a stroke of bad luck, the local MI5 liaison officer, Cyril Mills, was en route to England when Gouzenko defected, so SIS representative in Washington DC,

Peter Dwyer, flew up to Canada, accompanied by Jean-Paul Evans from British Security Coordination in New York. The RCMP Commissioner, Stuart Wood, selected two trusted subordinates, Inspectors Cliff Harvison from Winnipeg and M. F. E. Anthony from Vancouver, to supervise the operation, assisted by Sergeant John Leopold who, as an RCMP trooper, had gone undercover in Regina in 1921, masquerading as an immigrant named Jack Esselwein, to penetrate the communist movement for seven years. Later, MI5's expert on communism, (Sir) Roger Hollis, briefly interviewed Gouzenko, but came away unimpressed. While the defector had much to say, his real value lay in the documents he had stolen from the embassy, and one in particular attracted MI5's attention because it identified ALEK as Dr. Allan Nunn May. Placed under surveillance in London, MI5 mounted an operation codenamed PRIMROSE to catch May passing secrets to his contact. One of Gouzenko's cables had revealed his rendezvous arrangements in London for the evenings of October 7, 17, or 27, and an elaborate scheme was prepared to trap the physicist. Burt and his assistant Reg Spooner established an observation post in a room overlooking Great Russell Street, and even deployed an authentic Russian agent, "Klop" Ustinov, outside the British Museum as had been arranged, but the attempt failed because May never turned up. Instead, May was arrested on March 4, 1946, by Detective Inspector William Whitehead of Special Branch, pleaded guilty to all charges at a brief trial on May 1 and was imprisoned for ten years.

The RCMP's initial ten suspects were placed under surveillance and then arrested simultaneously early on the morning of February 15, 1946, and held *incommunicado* at the RCMP's training barracks at Rockcliffe by Inspector John Leopold for interrogation. Gordon Lunan, who only a month earlier had been transferred to the Canadian High Commission in London, was recalled to Ottawa, and arrested upon his arrival at Dorval Airport the following day. Everyone implicated by Gouzenko was caught, with the single exception of Sam Carr who had fled to the United States and gone into hiding. The preliminary interrogations of those based in Montreal, which was of greatest concern because of the fear of an atomic spy ring, were conducted by Cliff Harvison, a future commissioner who later admitted that "the Gouzenko documents disclosed an espionage apparatus that went far beyond our knowledge or suspicion."[4]

The two members of the Royal Commission interviewed all the suspects and pieced together the various links between the different parts of the GRU network concentrating on scientific intelligence. The principal recruiter appeared to be Fred Rose who talent-spotted for Colonel Rogov by supervising a "current affairs discussion group" and then left the management of individual agents to him. This certainly had happened in Lunan's case, and he had acted as an intermediary between Rogov and his main scientific sources, Halperin, Smith, and Mazerall. Originally Scottish, and from a relatively prosperous background in Yorkshire, Lunan had attended Mill Hill, a public school in London, before working as a copywriter in an advertising agency. In 1938 he had emigrated to Canada and, influenced by the poor treatment he believed his father had received from his employers, had attended Communist Party meetings until it was declared an illegal organization in 1940. Lunan had been commissioned into a Canadian Army signals unit in April 1943 but the following year had been posted to the Wartime Information Service and appointed editor of a military journal, *Canadian Affairs*. Although Lunan had no direct access to classified data, his sub-agents certainly did, and it was not until August 1945 that, as he recalled later, he realized the "shattering significance" of "the casual theoretical explanations of atomic properties with Halperin, and Rogov's interest in the uranium isotope U-235."

Lunan had known all three of his contacts through membership in Rose's study group, which had met in his apartment in Ottawa, and he later confirmed that Smith and Mazerall had been entirely cooperative. "My impression of both was that they were ready to supply information, but only at their own discretion."[5] As for Professor Halperin, a Queen's University mathematician working for the Canadian Army's Directorate of Artillery, Lunan described him as one of "three gifted people orbiting in the upper reaches of contemporary scientific knowledge but down to earth on social and humanitarian issues." When first pitched by Lunan, who "approached him more frankly than the others," he was "anxious to be of help" and was considered by Lunan to be "enthusiastic and politically experienced." However, his initially optimistic opinion that Halperin "is definitely keen and will be helpful," as he wrote to Rogov on March 28, 1945, proved unfounded, and documents purloined by Gouzenko, dated July 5, 1945, showed that he was "unwilling to take any risk in obtaining material which he is convinced is already obtainable."

> He is himself curious about the Chalk River plant and the manufacture of uranium. He claims that there is a great deal of talk and speculation on the subject, but that nothing is known outside of the small and carefully guarded group completely in the know. He emphasized that he himself is as remote from this type of information as I am myself.[6]

Evidently Halperin had been pressed to supply atomic information, but his access had been limited to improving existing ordnance, and in perfecting proximity fuses for artillery shells. "He only gives oral information, but this does not answer our demands," complained Rogov in a handwritten memorandum removed from his briefcase by Gouzenko. "It has become very difficult to work with him, especially after my request for Ur-235. He said that as far as he knows, it is absolutely impossible to obtain it."

> I asked him what is taken into consideration in the construction of the very large plant (Chalk River, near Petawawa, Ontario), in the general opinion the principle of production of which is based on the physical properties of the nucleus; with regard to his expression of opinion that it is impossible to get Uran 235, he replied that he does not know. He believed that the project is still in the experimental stage.[7]

Under cross-examination by the Royal Commission, Halperin proved uncooperative, refused to answer any questions and sacked his lawyer. Although he was completely compromised by the content of seven separate documents removed from the *referentura*,

Lunan refused to give evidence against him (an offense for which he was later imprisoned) and he was freed.

Whereas Halperin proved unhelpful, both Smith and Mazerall gave lengthy replies to the questions posed by the Commission. A mathematician and physicist, Smith had specialized in radioactivity; his work for the National Research Council's microwave section was highly classified and involved some collaboration with MIT. An expert on naval radar, he had been reluctant to help Lunan until he had independently checked on his credentials, and, once satisfied, became an enthusiastic member of the spy ring, actually "the most active," according to the Royal Commission, supplying dozens of top secret documents about naval radar. However, his information was so technical that Lunan was obliged to arrange direct meetings with Rogov, who later reported that BADEAU "asks for permission to change to work on uranium. There is a possibility either by being invited or by applying himself, but he warned that they are very careful in the selection of workers and that they are under strict supervision."[8]

An electrical engineer who had previously worked for Canadian Westinghouse at Hamilton, Ontario, Ned Mazerall had joined the National Research Council in 1943, and had been recruited by Lunan over lunch at the Chateau Laurier in Ottawa. Thereafter he supplied Lunan with classified documents on radio and radar topics, which he passed to Rogov to be photographed at the embassy overnight before returning them the following day. However, because he lived outside Ottawa and was married to a music teacher who disapproved of her husband meeting Communists, Mazerall was somewhat constricted, even though he had promised Lunan in July 1945 "to participate to the furthest of his ability."[9] Mazerall had been an active member of several of Fred Rose's "study groups," one of which had met regularly to discuss Marxist philosophy in the apartment of a Bank of Canada statistician, Agatha Chapman, another detainee who was interrogated by the Royal Commission. Other attendees included Durnford Smith, J. Scott Benning and David Shugar, a Polish-born expert on Asdic employed by the Canadian Naval Staff. Once again, a pattern emerged of left-wing scientists with knowledge of classified military projects gathering at the home of a political activist and then being pitched to supply secrets. In Shugar's case, he was codenamed PROMETHEUS and put in touch with Colonel Rogov by Sam Carr, whereas Benning, a senior member of the Department of Munitions and Supply, was codenamed FOSTER and had been run successively by Major Sokolov, Sergei Koudriavtsev, and the TASS correspondent Zheveinov.

According to Gouzenko, one of Zabotin's best sources of atomic information was Raymond Boyer, codenamed THE PROFESSOR, of the Explosives Division of the National Research Council. Boyer was an expert on RDX on who undertaken post-graduate chemistry at Harvard, Vienna, and Paris, but had not been employed formally until he volunteered his services to the University of Toronto in July 1940. A wealthy man, he had never joined the Party but had made numerous financial contributions, kept a mimeograph machine in the basement of his home in Ottawa and an entire clandestine printing press at his country house for the benefit of "Section 13," an underground Party branch with membership reserved for professionals and scientists. An undated telegram drafted by Colonel Motinov for Zabotin, removed from the *rezidentura* files by Gouzenko, indicated Boyer's area of interest:

> THE PROFESSOR has advised that the Director of the National Chemical research Committee Stacey told him about the new plant under construction: Pilot Plant at Grand Mere, in the Province of Quebec. This plant will produce "Uranium." The engineering personnel are being obtained from McGill University and are already moving into the district of the new plant. As a result of experiments carried out with Uranium it has been found that Uranium may be used for filling bombs, which is already being done in a practical way. The Americans have undertaken wide research work, having invested 660 million dollars in this business.[10]

The information in this message was slightly garbled, in that the Grand Mere manufacturing facility at Shawinigan Falls was actually opened by the St. Maurice Chemical Company in July 1941 to produce RDX, not uranium. Evidently, Fred Rose, with whom Boyer admitted having discussed the matter, had confused RDX and uranium when he had relayed the information to Motinov.

After his release from prison, Lunan recalled that his network of scientists "saw scientific knowledge as international, inching ahead incrementally by the contributions of scientists around the globe."

> Among scientists of the period the possibility of an atom bomb was an open secret. The basic physics was well known and had been developed mostly by non-American scientists. As early as 1943 Associated Press reported from Stockholm that the Danish scientist Dr. Niels Bohr had arrived in London with data for a new invention for an atomic explosive weapon. The Germans, everybody assumed, were among the leading workers in the field. And even the Russians, who had yet to demonstrate to a skeptical world their leadership in space technology, were known to have their Peter Kapitsa and Abraham Yoffes, old hands at juggling atoms. Halperin gave me the impression that he thought that the secrecy surrounding much scientific work to be a bureaucratic smokescreen.[11]

Just a few of Gouzenko's collection of 109 papers concerned the NKVD *rezident*, Vitali Pavlov, who operated in isolation from the GRU, but there was sufficient material to link him to Squadron-Leader Fred Poland, a British-born intelligence officer who acted as secretary to the security subcommittee of the Canadian JIC.

Gouzenko's revelations turned out to provide exceptionally valuable leads for the FBI, for much of the espionage conducted in Canada had been connected to the Manhattan Project research in the U.S. For example, an American scientist named by the Royal Commission as an NKVD source, Dr. Arthur G. Steinberg, was doing research for the U.S. Navy in Washington DC at the time of the arrests. He had arrived in Montreal to teach genetics in 1940 but returned to the U.S. in June 1944. Later he was to work at the Fels Institute, Antioch College, Yellow Springs, Ohio, as an associate professor of genetics. He and his wife Edith were close to Rose, Boyer and Freda Linton, a Communist who worked in the International Bureau of Labor, based on the campus of McGill University. She had been born Freda Lipchitz, of Polish parentage in Montreal, and previously had worked in Ottawa at the Canadian National Film Board as secretary to the chairman, John Grierson. As soon as the RCMP made its arrests, Freda Linton disappeared.

According to Gouzenko, Steinberg was codenamed BERGER, and one of Zabotin's notebooks contained an incriminating entry against his name:

> DEBOUZ [Fred Rose] is to tie up with BERGER and depending on the circumstances is to make a proposal about work for us or for the CORPORATION [Communist Party]. Contact in Washington with DEBOUZ's person. To work out arrangements for a meeting and to telegraph. To give out 600 dollars. If DEBOUZ should be unable to go to USA then there should be a letter from DEBOUZ to BERGER containing a request to assist the person delivering the letter to BERGER.[12]

Under cross-examination by the Commissioners, Gouzenko explained that this memorandum suggested that Fred Rose should contact Arthur Steinberg in Washington DC, and if he was unable to do so in person, arrangements should be made for someone else to do so. He recalled having seen telegrams in which Freda Linton had been Steinberg's principal contact, and had noted that the GRU had taken him over.

Under interrogation by the RCMP, Lunan proved entirely co-operative, and Harvison described him as "burdened with a martyr complex, with an urge toward self-destruction in the fight for some lost cause." Boyer, in contrast, was "utterly incapable of evasion or lying" and "gave direct and complete answers to questions and rounded out these answers by writing a lengthy review of his recruitment, training, motivation, and acts of treason," thereby enabling the RCMP to fill many of the gaps in their knowledge.

Similarly, the FBI was prompted to embark on lengthy investigations into other members of the Manhattan Project associated with the GRU spies, among them the physicist J. Carson Mark, a Canadian by birth who had received his doctorate at the University of Toronto and subsequently worked at the University of

Manitoba in Winnipeg and at Brown University in Rhode Island. In May 1943 he joined the National Research Council in Montreal, where he was active in the Canadian Association of Scientific Workers, and reportedly was close to Norman Veall and Raymond Boyer. Two years later, in May 1945, he was transferred to Los Alamos, where he became close to Robert Davis, who was his neighbor, and took a leading part in the controversial Association of Los Alamos Scientists.

Robert Davis was the D Division group leader and CPUSA member who reintroduced Mark to Robert Marshak, another espionage suspect investigated by the FBI, whom Mark had known years earlier in Canada. Later chairman of the Federation of American Scientists, Marshak was a leader in the Theoretical Physics Division at Los Alamos and had strong family links to Russia. Although he had been born in New York, his parents, Harry and Rose, were Russian immigrants, and his uncle and both aunts were prominent CPUSA members. His parents and his sister Ruth were affiliated with the National Council for American-Soviet Friendship, his aunt Edith was active in Russian War Relief and his first cousin Marsha Schulman had been a YCL member, together with her husband Bernard who resigned from the CPUSA, according to the FBI "in order to do more effective work on the outside."

Mark's referee at Los Alamos was Victor Weisskopf of MIT, who himself held radical views, and had advocated the destruction of America's atomic weapons to appease the Soviets, and a ban placed on all further manufacture of them. The FBI had become concerned about Mark when, in March 1948, he approached Ralph Smith, his division leader at Los Alamos for advice about a request he had received from Robert Davis, who reported that he had been summoned to appear before the HUAC to testify that Lomanitz had recruited him into the CPUSA. Apparently, Mark's job had given him access to AEC personnel files, and FBI security reports on Davis, a fact duly noted in his own top secret security dossier, which included surveillance reports and mail intercepts referring to his friendship with other espionage suspects, such as David Hawkins, Philip Morrison, Robert Davis, and Frank Oppenheimer.

In September 1948, in the aftermath of Gouzenko's defection and the publication of the Canadian Royal Commission report, Mark wrote a curious letter to the Los Alamos Director, Dr. Norris Bradbury:

> I can correctly be reported as having had a close and sympathetic association with Allan Nunn May and Raymond Boyer, each of whom figure rather prominently in the Canadian Royal Commission Report on spy cases. This association began in August 1944 and extended up until the time in April 1945 when I left Montreal to proceed to Los Alamos, and in fact I spent my last evening in Montreal in the company of Boyer and two or three others. Throughout this period I was one of a group of about ten persons, including May and Boyer, which met weekly at Boyer's home, first to form and later to serve as the Executive Committee of the Canadian Association of Scientific Workers. In addition, May frequently attended the meetings of a small study group of the association which met every week or so at my home. In the sober language of the Royal Commission, the CAScW has been described as Communist-infiltrated. I maintained my membership in the organization for about fifteen months after coming to Los Alamos. I admit that this association could be described in a better light and my own recollection of it is not attended by any feelings of guilt or regret. It could, I believe, also be represented in a worse light.

Mark's letter was written, as the author acknowledged, because he believed the information would emerge during the routine background checks conducted for his security clearance. The fact that clearances were only granted when the AEC was satisfied there was no danger involved clearly preoccupied him, and at a meeting of the council of the Federation of American Scientists, held in New York in January 1949, he argued that the law should be changed so clearances were only withheld when there was evidence of danger.

The Canadian connection, or the Montreal branch of ENORMOZ, was to inflict colossal damage on both the NKVD and the GRU. Quite apart from adding a further dimension to the west's knowledge of Soviet espionage, hitherto only glimpsed through intermittent FBI surveillance reports, interrogation of Ovakimyan's contacts and the single 1944 anonymous letter denouncing Zubilin in Washington DC, it was to act as a template for VENONA. From the Soviet perspective, the disaster led to the withdrawal of the entire *rezidenturas* in Ottawa, with Nikolai Zabotin slipping away unannounced to Moscow from New York on the *Aleksandr Suvorov* in December 1944. Networks across the globe were to be "put on ice" and even the most crucial operations suspended indefinitely while the Center attempted to limit the damage and assess precisely who had been compromised, relying on inside information from Kim Philby who, fortuitously, had access to some of the intelligence from Ottawa.

For those directly implicated by Gouzenko, the penalties were grim. Fred Rose's defense counsel, dispatched from England, was the Labour Member of Parliament D. N. Pritt QC, himself a long-time GRU asset who previously had been engaged as a barrister to defend Soviet espionage suspects. Despite Pritt's intervention, Rose was convicted and served a six-year prison sentence in the notorious St. Vincent de Paul Penitentiary and returned to his native Poland in 1953, later to be joined by his wife and daughter and never to be readmitted to Canada. Gordon Lunan was imprisoned for both contempt and breaches of the Official Secrets Act and spent five years at Kingston Penitentiary, where he was eventually joined by Sam Carr, who was apprehended in New York by the FBI in 1949 and sentenced to six years. After his release he remained in Canada, where he died in 1989. Smith received five years, Mazerall four, Willsher three and Boyer two. Of those that kept silent, Halperin, Shugar, Chapman and Poland were acquitted, and charges were withdrawn against Freda Linton.

Conclusion

Justified American anxieties about the security of nuclear secrets led to a temporary ban on the sharing of classified information, as required by the 1946 McMahon Act, but although it is clear that the first detected leakages were traced to British sources—Allan Nunn May, Klaus Fuchs, Bruno Pontecorvo, Donald Maclean, and John Cairncross—it must now be acknowledged that the sheer scale of hostile penetration of the Manhattan Project, at virtually every level, was quite comprehensive.

While admiring the professionalism with which the NKVD and GRU generally conducted their operations, in an era when scarcely the British nor the Americans had even begun to grasp the gigantic nature of the Kremlin's reliance on espionage, it must also be conceded that eventually the FBI did rise to the challenge, although the NKVD's extraordinary overlap between atomic secrets and industrial espionage was probably never appreciated. While the British and Americans draw a clear distinction between proprietary secrets of a commercial nature, classified material and atomic information as separate categories, the Soviets hardly discriminated among them and were content to exploit whatever opportunities arose, in whichever field. This blurring at the margins led to the unconscionable breach of security procedures which allowed Abe Brothman to incriminate Harry Gold, and the links in the chains were followed up by the FBI with enthusiasm, as can be seen from a congratulatory memorandum from Al Belmont addressed to Mickey Ladd in February 1951:

> As a result of the investigation of the Emil Julius Klaus Fuchs' case we have identified and arrested eight persons connected with Soviet Espionage: namely, Harry Gold, Alfred Dean Slack, David Greenglass, Julius and Ethel Rosenberg, Morton Sobell, Abraham Brothman and Miriam Moscowitz. Brothman and Moscowitz were charged with obstruction of justice and the others with espionage or conspiracy to commit espionage.
>
> In addition, seven persons have been identified as Soviet Agents and prosecution is pending or the investigation is continuing: Thomas L. Black, William Perl, Michael and Ann Sidorovich, Alfred Sarant, Joel Barr and Vivian Glassman. Due to the ramifications of the case, numerous other persons are still under investigation as a result of which additional prosecutions may ensue. We have not included in the above Semen Semenov, Anatole Yakovlev and other Russian officials who were identified during the investigation, but have left the country.
>
> In all more than 45 individual cases were opened, based on this investigation, and countless interviews have been conducted.

The single document in the FBI's archives in the J. Edgar Hoover Building that illustrates the point is the memorandum from Lish Whitson, dated September 26, 1949, proposing the imminent disclosure of three names to Dick Thistlethwaite, MI5's long-serving Security Liaison Office in Washington DC. Whitson was intending to share the knowledge, acquired only hours earlier by Arlington Hall, that Klaus Fuchs, Theodore Heilig, and Art Weber had been identified as REST, HEILIG, and GOOSE, respectively, being two cover names appearing in the VENONA traffic. The date itself is significant, not entirely because it was not until December 21, 1949, that the Security Service despatched its interrogator, Jim Skardon, to interview Fuchs at Harwell, but that just two days earlier, on

September 23, the White House and 10 Downing Street simultaneously had issued a statement announcing that the Soviets were known to have conducted their first nuclear test. Suddenly, the balance of power in the world shifted, and the politics of deterrence took on an entirely new meaning. The question then unanswered was, "How had Stalin acquired the atomic bomb so quickly, in the face of assurances from Allied experts that no Russian test was possible until at least 1951?"

The answer, as we have seen, lay in ENORMOZ, and over the coming years MI5 and the FBI were to be engaged in a lengthy forensic exercise to determine the scale of the damage. In their search for Fuchs's collaborators, dossiers were opened on ninety-nine scientists employed at Los Alamos, and the most detailed inquiries were conducted into their loyalties. Some of the investigations turned up questionable associations, dubious friendships, curious political affiliations and memberships of highly suspect organizations and several well-known Communist fronts. Today, some of the files read strangely, with Edward Teller being mistaken for a Communist of the same name who in 1941, according to the FBI's field office in Albany, had been teaching Political Economy, Marxism and Leninism at the Communist Workers School, on 13th Street in New York. When confronted by FBI Special Agents from El Paso in January 1949, Teller was able to persuade them that he had been working at Columbia University at the relevant time. Actually, it would have been hard to find a less likely Marxist that Edward Teller, whose strident anti-Sovietism, advocacy of the hydrogen bomb, and criticism of Robert Oppenheimer's views almost ostracized him from his colleagues.

The Anglo-American investigation into ENORMOZ demonstrates two contrasting approaches to the conduct of counterespionage operations on either side of the Atlantic. The Security Service always appeared reluctant to pursue leads, having inherited a distaste for meddling in politics, and hypersensitive about accusations of Gestapo tactics. The pursuit of Klaus Fuchs was quite leisurely, compared to the resources devoted by the (admittedly much larger) FBI, which reached a strength of 15,000 by the end of the war and preferred to reduce the risk of collusion by interviewing suspects simultaneously in different locations across the country. The plodding approach of the former policeman Sir Percy Sillitoe, not to mention his principal but ineffectual interrogator, the ex-detective Jim Skardon, is thrown into sharp relief by the enthusiasm with which his American counterpart supervised the FOOCASE. It was Skardon who allowed Ursula Kuczynsky and Len Beurton to slip through his fingers, and took weeks to pin down Fuchs.

Certainly the FBI had the advantage of exploiting poor Soviet tradecraft, Rosenberg's apartment at 65 Morton Street being a good example. David Greenglass reported that Julius ran a second apartment in Greenwich Village, and the lease of Apartment 61, which had been packed with photographic equipment, turned out to be in Al Sarant's name. Michael Sidorovich visited there, Vivian Glassman paid the rent there for a period, and William Perl stayed for a week in June or July 1949, at a time when a visiting electrical repairman reported finding seven men asleep in sleeping bags on the floor. Furthermore, Max and Helene Elitcher had recalled parties there attended by Rosenberg's other CCNY classmates, among them Joel Barr and the Sobells. The apartment was a common denominator, and certainly was not operated as a safe house under the iron discipline of the NKVD's rules of *konspiratsia*, but this poor tradecraft was not evidence, as the postwar Soviet apologists on the American left attempted to purvey it, of innocence. All except the most hardened defenders of Rosenberg's circle now concede, following the release of the VENONA texts, that Stalin used willing accomplices in the west to pull off the greatest theft in history. While the KGB enjoyed referring to the era of prewar illegals as the organization's "golden time," the success of ENORMOZ surpasses anything the celebrated illegals ever accomplished, and was not to be repeated. As Oleg Kalugin has pointed out, in 1943 eighteen Soviet intelligence officers in the United States ran some two hundred individual sources. Forty years later, two hundred KGB and GRU men managed barely eighteen spies in America.

Appendixes

Appendix 1

Soviet Intelligence Personnel Engaged in Atomic Espionage

NAME	ALIAS	CODENAME	*REZIDENTURA*
Abbiate, Roland	Pravdin	SERGEI	New York
Adams, Artur		ACHILLES	GRU Illegal
Angelov, Pavel N.			Ottawa
Apresyan, Stepan Z.		MAY	New York San Francisco
Aptekar, Nikolai		SERGEI	London
Barkovsky, Vladimir B.		JERRY	London
Chernyak, Yakov			Ottawa
Chugunov, Konstantin			New York
Dorogov, Vasili G.	Dolgov	EGON	Washington DC
Eitingon, Leonid A.		TOM	Los Angeles
Fedosimov, Pavel I.		STEPAN	New York
Feklisov, Aleksandr	Fomin	CALISTRATUS	New York
Fisher, William G.	Goldfus	VIK	New York
Gorsky, Anatoli V.	Gromov	VADIM	London Washington DC
Harris, Kitty	Dreyfus	ADA	Los Angeles
Ivanov, Piotr			San Francisco
Kamenev, Ivan			New York
Kasparov, Grigori P.		GIFT	San Francisco
Khiefets, Grigori M.		CHARON	San Francisco
Kremer, Semyon		BARCh	London
Kudriavtsev, Sergei		LION	Ottawa
Kukin, Konstantin M.			London
Kurnakov, Sergei N.		CAVALRYMAN BECK	New York
Kvasnikov, Leonid R.		ANTON	New York
Melkishev, Pavel	Mikhailov	MOLIERE	New York
Motinov, Col.			Ottawa
Orlov, Andrei R		WOLF	San Francisco
Panchenko, Gavril			New York

Pastelnyak, Pavel	Klarin	LUKA	New York
Pravdina, Olga B.		MARGARET	New York
Raev, Aleksandr		LIGHT	New York
Rogov, Maj. Vasili M.			Ottawa
Sarytchev, Filipp			New York
Semyonov, Semyon M.		TWAIN	New York
		SMART	New York
Sokolov, Yuri S.,		CLAUDE	New York
Sokolov, Major			Ottawa
Vasilevsky, Lev	Tarasov	YURI	New York
			Mexico City
Yatskov, Anatoli A	Yakovlev	ALEKSEI	New York
Yerzin, Pavel D.			London
Zabotin, Nikolai		GRANT	Ottawa
Zubilin, Vasili M.	Zarubin	MAKSIM	New York
			Washington DC
Zubilina, Elizaveta	Zarubina		New York

Appendix 2

Espionage Suspects in the Manhattan Project

NAME	CODENAME	CONCLUSION
Barr, Joel	METER/SCOUT	Went Abroad, 1948
Bethe, Hans		Unresolved
Bohm, David		Moved abroad
Cairncross, John	LISZT	Confessed 1963
Chapin, John H.		FBI witness
Chevalier, Haakon		Returned to France
Cohen, Lona	LESLEY	Imprisoned 1961
Cohen, Morris	VOLUNTEER	Imprisoned 1961
Connison, Emil		Not Charged
Davis, Robert R.		FBI witness
Eltenton, George C.		Returned to England
Fermi, Enrico	BUSINESS DEBT	Unresolved
Franey, Joseph J.		FBI double agent
Franklin, Zelmond	CHAP	Not Charged
Friedman, Max		Pleaded Fifth
Fuchs, Klaus	REST/CHARLES	Imprisoned 1950
Glasser, Vivian		Unresolved
Gold, Harry	GOOSE	Imprisoned 1951
Greenglass, David	CALIBER	Imprisoned 1951
Greenglass, Ruth	WASP	Not Charged
Gurney, Ronald W.		Unresolved
Hall, Theodore	YOUNG	Exposed 1998
Hawkins, David		Unresolved
Heilig, Theodore		Indicted for fraud
Hiskey, Clarence	RAMSEY	Indicted
Kamen, Martin		Clearance Lifted
Katz, Joseph	INFORMER/X	Moved abroad
Lawrence, Ernest	HURON/ERNEST	Unresolved
Lomanitz, Giovanni R.		Pleaded Fifth
Manning, Edward T.		FBI witness
Morrison, Philip		Unresolved

Nelson, Steve		Imprisoned 1952
Norwood, Melita	TINA	Exposed 1999
Nunn May, Allan	ALEK	Imprisoned 1946
Peierls, Eugenia		Unresolved
Peierls, Rudolf		Clearance lifted
Perl, William	GNOME/YAKOV	Defected 1950
Pontecorvo, Bruno	QUANTUM	Defected 1950
Rosenberg, Ethel		Executed 1953
Rosenberg, Julius	ANTENNA/LIBERAL	Executed 1953
Sarant, Alfred	HUGHES	Defected 1950
Sidorovich, Ann	SQUIRRELL	Not Charged
Sidorovich, Michael	LENS	Arrested
Slack, Alfred	AL	Imprisoned 1950
Sobell, Helen		Not Charged
Sobell, Morton	STONE	Imprisoned 1951
Steinberg, Arthur G.		Unresolved
Veall, Norman		Not Charged
Weber, Arthur P.	FBI witness	
Weinberg, Joseph W.		Pleaded Fifth

Appendix 3

Unidentified Soviet Spies

CODENAME	REZIDENTURA	SOURCE
ERIC	London	Vladimir Barkovsky
ERIE	New York	VENONA
KELLY	London	Vladimir Barkovsky
MAR	New York	Vasili Mitrokhin
MOOR	London	Vladimir Barkovsky
NILE	New York	VENONA
PEARL	New York	Aleksandr Feklisov*
SERB/RELAY	New York	VENONA
SOLID	New York	VENONA
VOLOK	New York	VENONA
VULTURE	New York	Aleksandr Feklisov*

* KhVAT and PEARL are, by acknowledgment of Feklisov, invented codenames, and therefore likely to be duplicates of other known agents.

Appendix 4

Operation ENORMOZ

CASE OFFICERS	AGENTS
	NEW YORK
Rezidents	
Gaik Ovakimyan	Al Slack
Pavel Pastelnyak	Emil Connison
Vasili Zubilin	Steve Nelson
Stepan Apresyan	Klaus Fuchs
Roland Abbiate	Josef Berger
Ivan Kamenev	Harry Gold
Pavel Fedosimov	VOGEL/PERS
	SMART
Semyon Semyonov	Al Slack
	RELAY
	PERS
Andrei Schevchenko	Joseph Franey
Anatoli Yatskov	Harry Gold
Aleksandr Feklisov	Julius Rosenberg
	SAN FRANCISCO
Grigori Kheifets	Martin Kamen
Grigori Kasparov	Martin Kamen
Stepan Apresyan	
Piotr Ivanov	George Eltenton
	OTTAWA
Vitali Pavlov	
Nikolai Zabotin	Freda Linton
Pavel N. Angelov	Allan Nunn May
Sergei Kudriavtsev	Fred Rose
Colonel Motinov	Raymond Boyer

Vasili Rogov	Philip Durnford Smith
Major Sokolov	J. Scott Benning
Captain Zheveinov	J. Scott Benning

SEATTLE

Vladimir Orlov	ERNEST

WASHINGTON DC

Vasili Zubilin	
Anatoli Gorsky	HOMER

LONDON

Anatoli Gorsky	John Cairncross
Konstantin Kukin	Klaus Fuchs
Vladimir Barkovsky	ERIC
Aleksandr Feklisov	Klaus Fuchs
Ivan Sklyarov	J. B. S. Haldane
Pavel Yerzin	

Glossary of NKVD Covernames in VENONA texts

BABYLON	San Francisco
Camp 1	Oak Ridge, Tennessee
Camp 2	Los Alamos
CARLSBAD	Santa Fe, New Mexico
CARTHAGE	Washington DC
COMPATRIOT	Communist Party member
ENORMOZ	Atomic weapons program
FACTORY	Amtorg
FUNICULAR	Atomic bomb
GREENS	Hostile counterintelligence agency
GYMNAST	Young Communist League member
HUT	FBI
PLANT	Soviet Consulate-General
PROBATIONERS	Agents
RESERVATION	Argonne Laboratory
SOLT	G-2 Military Intelligence
TYRE	New York

NOTES

PREFACE

1. *VENONA: Soviet Espionage and the American Response 1939–1957*, edited by Robert Louis Benson and Michael Warner (NSA, 1996), pp. 16–26.
2. *Special Tasks* by Pavel Sudoplatov (Little, Brown, 1994).
3. Ibid., p. 172.
4. Vladimir Chikov and Gary Kern, *Comment Staline a volé la bombe atomique aux Américains—Dossier KGB No. 13676* (Editions Robert Laffont, 1996).
5. *Bombshell* (Time Books, 1997).

Chapter I

THE FRISCH-PEIERLS MEMORANDUM

1. September 25, 1941.
2. *The Big Bomb Hunt.*, unpublished TV interview with Barkovsky, April 1993.
3. *The Enigma Spy* (Century, 1997).
4. *The Big Bomb Hunt.*
5. Ibid.
6. *The Second World War*, Vol. IV, pp. 339–340.

Chapter II

ANGLO-AMERICAN COOPERATION

1. Robert Serber, *Peace and War*, p. 66.
2. Arthur Compton, *Memoirs.*
3. Vannevar Bush, November 27, 1952.
4. Rudolf Peierls, *Bird of Passage* (Princeton University Press, 1986), p. 179.
5. FBI file 65-58805–9.

Chapter III

BERIA'S XY SOLUTION

1. *The Big Bomb Hunt.*
2. Ibid.
3. Ibid.
4. Ibid.
5. *Sonya's Report* (Chatto & Windus, 1991), p. 259.
6. *The Big Bomb Hunt.*

7. Ibid.
8. Gold identified Filipp Sarytchev, but Aleksandr Feklisov named his contact as Ivan Kamenev (*The Man Behind The Rosenbergs* [Enigma Books, 2001], p. 251).
9. *The Big Bomb Hunt*, TV interview with Kvasnikov.
10. *This is My Story* (McGraw-Hill, 1947).
11. Feklisov identified various agents, including KhVAT ("Vulture") but he invented their codenames to conceal their true identities. Among them were DAYVIN and ZHEMCHUG ("Pearl").
12. Depending upon the context, VEKSEL has a negative meaning, referring to the suicides caused when the gambling debts of aristocrats were discounted and bought by third parties. Accordingly, there is an old-fashioned, pejorative meaning.

Chapter IV

PENETRATING LOS ALAMOS

1. The proposition that Moe Berg was part of a plot to either abduct or assassinate Heisenberg has been repeated in several books but there is no evidence to support it.
2. See *Alsos* by Samuel A. Goudsmit (Oxford University Press, 1947).
3. Ibid., p. 142.
4. Ibid., p. ix.
5. R. V. Jones *Reflections on Intelligence* (Heinemann, 1989), p. 284.
6. *The Big Bomb Hunt*, TV interview.
7. Jones, op.cit., p. 284.
8. Kvasnikov, *The Big Bomb Hunt*, TV interview.

Chapter V

THE XY *REZIDENTURA*

1. Artur Adams to General Ilyichev, 1944.
2. Ismail Akhmedov, *In and Out of Stalin's GRU* (Arms and Armour Press, 1984), p. 132.
3. Boris Morros in *My Ten Years as a Counterspy* (The Viking Press, 1959), p. 35.
4. Ibid., p. 86.

Chapter VI

THEODORE HALL AND KLAUS FUCHS

1. In Russian the word for artificial leg (*protez*), is applied to any artificial limb or organ. As the polio epidemic that swept through the United States and

England was avoided in the Soviet Union by widespread innoculation, childhood polio was quite rare, and there are no separate words for leg-brace or caliper. Accordingly, the correct translation of *protez* in the relevant VENONA text may be a caliper and not an artificial leg.

2. *Bombshell*, p. 288.
3. *Bird of Passage*, p. 225.

Chapter VII
The Rosenberg Network

1. *Special Tasks*, p. 191.
2. Michael J. Burd was found by the FBI to have Anglicized his names from Moishe Weisburd and Morris Weisburd.

Chapter VIII
The PERS Mystery

1. Peirels, *Bird of Passage*, p. 163.
2. *The Big Bomb*, TV interview with Yatskov.
3. Akhmedov, *In And Out of Stalin's GRU*, p. 143.

Chapter IX
Oppenheimer and Soviet Espionage

1. Report on Atomic Espionage, September 28, 1948.
2. Ibid.
3. A former FBI Special Agent Jacob Spolansky, long based in the Chicago Field Office to work on Communists, gave an account of Steve Nelson's career in *The Communist Trail in America.* He disguised Kitty Oppenheimer's identity, referring to her merely as "the widow of a volunteer in the International Brigade" who "married one of the leading physicists engaged in the development of the atomic bomb" (p. 157). According to his account, Nelson "offered to pay her for information, but she indignantly refused. When neither bribes nor threats produced any result" he left her alone and concentrated on Lomanitz.
4. Sudoplatov, *Special Tasks*, p. 189.
5. Ibid., p. 194.
6. Walter Krivitsky in *I Was Stalin's Agent* (The Right Book Club, 1940), pp. 272–273.
7. Igor Damaskin in *Kitty Harris: The Spy with Seventeen Names* (St Ermin's Press, 2001), p. 204.
8. Sudoplatov, *Special Tasks*, p. 195.

9. *Laughter in Leningrad* by Dorothea Eltenton (published privately, 1998).
10. *Oppenheimer: The Story of a Friendship* (George Braziller, 1965).
11. Ibid.
12. Sudoplatov, *Special Tasks*, p. 192.
13. *My World Line* by George Gamow (The Viking Press, 1970).
14. Sudoplatov, *Special Tasks*, p. 192. There may be some additional evidence of the existence of a wartime illegal in Los Alamos. When Morris and Lona Cohen were made Heroes of Russia by Boris Yeltsin in 1998, the same decoration was given to an unnamed GRU illegal who was described in the citation as having worked at Los Alamos.
15. Sudoplatov, *Special Tasks*, p. 182.
16. See above, Chapter VII, footnote 1.
17. *Every Man Should Try* (Public Affairs, 1999).
18. The TOPLEV project, intended to cultivate old Communists, succeeded in the recruitment of one other senior CPUSA official. However, according to former Assistant Director Ray Wannall, none of the FBI Special Agents engaged on the program had been indoctrinated into VENONA, so neither of SOLO's handlers knew he and his wife had been NKVD agents. Roz Childs accompanied her husband on five missions to Moscow, and he died in 1967. The fact that the FBI Field Office ran the SOLO case, on the authority of successive presidents and attorneys general, gave rise to the suspicion within the CIA that their rivals had been duped. For further details of the case (but not of VENONA), see *Operation Solo* by John Barron (Regnery, 1996).

Chapter X

Nobel Espionage

1. FBI file 65-3114
2. Ibid.
3. FBI File 65-3114
4. Personnel Security Board Report on Robert Serber.
5. Robert Serber, University of Colorado.

Chapter XI

The Canadian Connection

1. Report of the Royal Commission (1946), p. 440.
2. Ibid., p. 142.
3. Ibid., p. 384.
4. *The Horsemen* by C. W. Harvison (McClelland & Stewart, 1967), p. 149.

5. *The Making of a Spy: A Political Odyssey* by Gordon Lunan (Robert Davies Publishing, 1995), p. 145.
6. Report of the Royal Commission, p. 142.
7. Ibid., p. 144.
8. Ibid., p. 448.
9. Ibid., p. 145.
10. Ibid., p. 448.
11. Lunan, p. 145.
12. Report of the Royal Commission, p. 120.

Bibliography

Albright, Joseph, and Kunstel, Marcia, *Bombshell* (Times Books, 1997)

Alperovitz, Gar, *The Decision to Use the Bomb* (Vintage Books, 1996)

Alvarez, Luis, *Adventure of a Physicist* (Bantam, 1987)

Amrine, Michael, *The Great Decision* (G. P. Putnam's Sons, 1959)

Bar-Zohar, Michel, *The Hunt for Germans Scientists 1944–60* (Arthur Barker, 1967)

Barron, John, *Operation SOLO* (Regnery, 1996)

Baxter, James Phinney, *Scientists Against Time* (Little, Brown, 1952)

Benson, Robert Louis, and Warner, Michael, *Venona: Soviet Espionage and the American Response 1939–1957* (National Security Agency, 1996)

Bernikow, Louise, *Abel* (Trident Press, 1970)

Bernstein, Jeremy, *Hitler's Uranium Club* (AIP Press, 1996)

Blumberg, Stanley, *Edward Teller* (Charles Scribner's Sons, 1990)

Bohm, David, *Unfolding Meaning* (Routledge & Kegan Paul, 1985)

Bothwell, Robert, and Granatstein, J. L., *The Gouzenko Transcripts* (Deneau Publishers, 1982)

Bradley, David, *No Place To Hide* (Little, Brown, 1948)

Braunbek, Werner, *The Drama of the Atom* (Oliver & Boyd, 1958)

Brown, Andrew, *The Neutron and the Bomb* (Oxford University Press, 1997)

Burchard, John, *Q.E.D.* (Chapman & Hall, 1948)

Cairncross, John (MOLIERE), *The Enigma Spy* (Random House, 1999)

Carmichael, Virginia, *Framing History: The Rosenberg Story and the Cold War* (University of Minnesota Press, 1993)

Cathcart, Brian, *The Test of Greatness* (John Murray, 1994)

Chevalier, Haakon, *Oppenheimer: The Story of a Friendship* (George Braziller, 1965)

Chikov, Vladimir, *How Soviet Intelligence Split the American Bomb* (Novoye Vremya, 1991)

Childs, Herbert, *An American Genius* (E. P. Dutton, 1968)

Clark, Ronald, *The Birth of the Bomb* (Horizon Press, 1961)

——, *JBS: The Life and Work of J. B. S. Haldane* (Quality Book Club, 1968)

Curtis, Charles, *The Oppenheimer Case* (Simon & Schuster, 1955)

Dan, Jerry, *Ultimate Deception* (Rare Books & Berry, 2003)

Dippel, John, *Two Against Hitler* (Praeger, 1992)

Dobson, Dennis, *The Rosenberg Letters* (1953)

Eltenton, Dorothea, *Laughter in Leningrad* (privately, 1998)

Engebretson, George, *A Man of Vision: The Story of Paul Pinsky* (Hawaii Insurance Consultants Ltd, 1997)

Evans, Medford, *The Secret War for the A-Bomb* (Henry Regnery, 1953)

Feklisov, Alexander, *The Man Behind the Rosenbergs* (Enigma Books, 2001)

Fermi, Laura, *Atoms in the Family* (University of Chicago Press, 1954)

Fineberg, S. Andhil, *The Rosenberg Case: Fact and Fiction* (Oceana, 1953)

Frank, Charles, *Operation Epsilon: The Farm Hall Transcripts* (IOP Publishing, 1993)

Frisch, Otto, *What Little I Remember* (Cambridge University Press, 1979)

Gamow, George, *My World Line* (Viking, 1970)

Garber, Marjorie (ed.), *Secret Agents* (Routledge, 1995)

Goldschmidt, Bertrand, *Atomic Rivals* (Rutgers University Press, 1990)

Goodchild, Peter, *J. Robert Oppenheimer, Shatterer of Worlds* (Houghton Mifflin, 1981)

Goudsmit, Samuel, *Alsos* (Henry Schuman, 1947)

Gowring, Margaret, *Britain and Atomic Energy 1939–1945* (Macmillan, 1964)

Groves, Leslie, *Now It Can Be Told* (Harper & Brothers, 1962)

Haynes, John Earl, and Klehr, Harvey, *Venona: Decoding Soviet Espionage in America* (Yale University Press, 1999)

Henshall, Philip, *The Nuclear Axis* (Sutton Publishing, 2000)

Herken, Gregg, *Brotherhood of the Bomb* (Henry Holt & Co., 2002)

Hirsch, Richard, *The Soviet Spies* (Nicholas Kaye, 1947)

Holloway, David, *Stalin and the Bomb* (Yale University Press, 1994)

Horowitz, David, *Radical Son* (Simon & Schuster, 1959)

Hyde, H. Montgomery, *The Atom Bomb Spies* (Hamish Hamilton, 1980)

Irving, David, *The German Atomic Bomb* (Simon & Schuster, 1967)

Jones, R. V. *Reflections on Intelligence* (Heinemann, 1989)

Jordan, George Racey, *From Major Jordan's Diaries* (Harcourt Brace, 1952)

Josephson, Paul R., *Red Atom* (W. H. Freeman & Co., 2000)

Kendall, James, *At Home Among The Atoms* (Bell & Sons, 1939)

Kessler, Lauren, *Clever Girl* (HarperCollins, 2003)

Klehr, Harvey, and Haynes, John, *The Secret World of American Communism* (Yale University Press, 1995)

——, *The Soviet World of American Communism* (Yale University Press, 1998)

Knight, Amy, *Beria: Stalin's First Lieutenant* (Princeton University Press, 1994)

Kurzman, Dan, *Day of the Bomb* (McGraw-Hill, 1986)

Lamont, Lansing, *Day of Trinity* (Atheneum, 1965)

Lamphere, Robert, and Schachtman, Tom, *The FBI-KGB War* (Mercer University Press, 1995)
Lawren, William, *The General and the Bomb* (Dodd, Mead & Co, 1988)
Lunan, Gordon, *The Making of a Spy: A Political Odyssey* (Robert Davies Publishing, 1995)
MacPherson, Malcolm, *Time Bomb* (E. P. Dutton, 1986)
Melzer, Richard, *Breakdown* (Sunstone Press, 2000)
Modin, Yuri, *My Five Cambridge Friends* (Headline, 1994)
Moorehead, Alan, *The Traitors* (Harper & Row, 1952)
Morgan, Ted, *A Covert Life* (Random House, 1999)
Moss, Norman, *Klaus Fuchs* (Grafton Books, 1987)
Newman, Bernard, *The Red Spider Web* (Latimer House, 1947)
Nizer, Louis, *The Implosion Conspiracy* (Doubleday, 1973)
Norris, Robert, *Racing for the Bomb* (Steerforth Press, 1992)
Peat, F. David, *Infinite Potential* (Helix Books, 1997)
Peierls, Rudolf, *Bird of Passage* (Princeton University Press, 1985)
Petrie, Ishbel, *Not a Bowl of Cherries* (Pentland Press, 1997)
Philipson, Ilene, *Ethel Rosenberg: Beyond the Myths* (Franklin Watts, 1988)
Pilat, Oliver, *The Atom Spies* (G. P. Putnam's Sons, 1952)
Polenberg, Richard (ed.), *In the Matter of J. Robert Oppenheimer* (Cornell University Press, 2002)
Potter, Robert, *Conquest of the Atom* (Collins, 1947)
Powers, Thomas, *Heisenberg's War* (Jonathan Cape, 1991)
Purcell, John, *The Best-Kept Secret* (Vanguard Press, 1963)
Radosh, Ronald, and Milton, Joyce, *The Rosenberg File* (Holt, Rinehart & Winston, 1983)
Reuben, William A., *The Atom Spy Hoax* (Action Books, 1955)
Rhodes, Richard, *Dark Sun* (Simon & Schuster, 1995)
——, *The Making of the Atomic Bomb* (Simon & Schuster, 1968)
Roberts, Sam, *The Brother* (Random House, 2001)
Romerstein, Herbert, and Breindel, Eric, *The Venona Secrets* (Regnery, 2000)
Root, Jonathan, *The Betrayers* (Coward-McCann, 1963)
Rossi, Bruno, *Moments in the Life of a Scientist* (Cambridge University Press, 1990)
Royal Commission of Canada, *Report on Espionage* (Edmond Cloutier, 1946)
Sakharov, Andrei, *Memoirs* (Alfred Knopf, 1990)
Sawatsky, John, *Gouzenko: The Untold Story* (Macmillan, 1984)
Schneir, Walter and Miriam, *Invitation to an Inquest* (W. H. Allen, 1966)
Schweber, S. S., *In The Shadow of the Bomb* (Princeton, 2000)

Seaborg, Glenn, *The Plutonium Story* (Bartelle Press, 1994)
Serber, Robert, *Peace and War* (Columbia University Press, 1998)
——, *The Los Alamos Primer* (University of California Press, 1992)
Sharlitt, Joseph, *Fatal Error* (Charles Scribner's Sons, 1983)
Sharp, Malcolm, *Was Justice Done?* (Monthly Review Press, 1956)
Shils, Edward, *The Torment of Secrecy* (The Free Press, 1956)
Smyth, Henry D., *Atomic Energy for Military Purposes* (Princeton University Press, 1947)
Sobell, Morton, *On Doing Time* (Charles Scribner's Sons, 1974)
Stern, Philip, *The Oppenheimer Case* (Harper & Row, 1969)
Stone, Jeremy J., *Every Man Should Try* (Public Affairs, 1999)
Sudoplatov, Pavel, *Special Tasks* (Little, Brown, 1994)
Toledano, Ralph de, *The Greatest Plot in History* (Arlington House, 1963)
Udall, Stewart, *The Myths of August* (Pantheon, 1994)
Weale, Adrian, *Science and the Swastika* (Macmillan, 2001)
Weinstein, Allen, and Vassiliev, Alexander, *The Haunted Wood* (Random House, 1999)
West, Rebecca, *The New Meaning of Treason* (Viking, 1964)
White, John Baker, *The Soviet Spy System* (Falcon Press, 1948)
Williams, Robert Chadwell, *Klaus Fuchs: Atom Spy* (Harvard University Press, 1987)
Wilson, Thomas W., *The Great Weapons Heresy* (Houghton Mifflin, 1970)
Zimmerman, David, *Top Secret Exchange* (Alan Sutton, 1996)

Index